CORIOLIS

14455 North Hayden Road, Suite 220 • Scottsdale, Arizona 85260

Dear Reader:

CoriolisOpen™ Press was founded to create a very elite group of books: the ones you keep closest to your machine. Sure, everyone would like to have the Library of Congress at arm's reach, but in the real world, you have to choose the books you rely on every day *very* carefully.

To win a place for our books on that coveted shelf beside your PC, we guarantee several important qualities in every book we publish. These qualities are:

- *Technical accuracy*—It's no good if it doesn't work. Every CoriolisOpen™ Press book is reviewed by technical experts in the topic field, and is sent through several editing and proofreading passes in order to create the piece of work you now hold in your hands.

- *Innovative editorial design*—We've put years of research and refinement into the ways we present information in our books. Our books' editorial approach is uniquely designed to reflect the way people learn new technologies and search for solutions to technology problems.

- *Practical focus*—We put only pertinent information into our books and avoid any fluff. Every fact included between these two covers must serve the mission of the book as a whole.

- *Accessibility*—The information in a book is worthless unless you can find it quickly when you need it. We put a lot of effort into our indexes, and heavily cross-reference our chapters, to make it easy for you to move right to the information you need.

Here at The Coriolis Group we have been publishing and packaging books, technical journals, and training materials since 1989. We're programmers and authors ourselves, and we take an ongoing active role in defining what we publish and how we publish it. We have put a lot of thought into our books; please write to us at **ctp@coriolis.com** and let us know what you think. We hope that you're happy with the book in your hands, and that in the future, when you reach for software development and networking information, you'll turn to one of our books first.

Keith Weiskamp
President and CEO

Jeff Duntemann
VP and Editorial Director

Look For These Other Books From The Coriolis Group:

*Under the Radar: How Red Hat Changed
The Software Business — And Took Microsoft By Surprise*

Perl Black Book

Perl Core Language Little Black Book

Linux Core Kernel Commentary

Linux IP Stacks Commentary

Linux Administration Black Book

Linux System Administration White Papers

Linux Programming White Papers

Linux Internet Server Visual Black Book

Setting Up a Linux Server Visual Black Book

Linux Server Advanced Edition Visual Black Book

Linux Install and Configuration Little Black Book

Apache Server for Windows Little Black Book

Apache Server Commentary

Samba Black Book

GIMP: The Official Handbook

Open Source Development With CVS

Karl Fogel

President, CEO
Keith Weiskamp

Publisher
Steve Sayre

Acquisitions Editor
Stephanie Wall

Marketing Specialist
Tracy Schofield

Project Editor
Toni Zuccarini

Production Coordinator
Jon Gabriel

Cover Design
Jesse Dunn

Layout Design
April Nielsen

Open Source Development With CVS

The Coriolis Group, LLC
14455 North Hayden Road
Suite 220
Scottsdale, Arizona 85260

480/483-0192
FAX 480/483-0193
http://www.coriolis.com

Library of Congress Card Number: 99-048722

Printed in the United States of America
10 9 8 7 6 5 4 3 2 1

This book is dedicated with love to my parents,
Frances and Henry, for everything. Literally.

About The Author

Karl Fogel was born in 1971, and managed to make it all the way through the 1980s personal computer and BBS craze without learning a thing about computers, networks, or email. In this state of technological ignorance—which he has been trying ever since to regain—he headed off to Oberlin College/Conservatory of Music in 1991 to study the piano, but ended up with a degree in Chinese and an accidental education in computer programming.

In 1994 and early 1995 he worked at the University of Illinois writing a gene sequence editor, then co-founded Cyclic Software with Jim Blandy, to provide maintenance and commercial support for CVS. They passed Cyclic (along with the CVS maintainership) to Jim Kingdon in 1996, and Karl headed to southwest China to teach English and Unix/C programming for a year. He now lives in Chicago, working as a programmer and coping with his chronic sinophilia by dreaming of the trip to China he'll take using the royalties from this book.

Acknowledgments

You don't realize, until you try to write a book yourself, why the acknowledgements always go on for so long. I mean, by the time the author's done thanking everyone, you wonder if there's going to be any room left for the book itself.

But now I know why.

Ben Collins Sussman remained the steadfast friend he has been these past thirteen years, despite the fact that I pretty much dropped out of existence for six months while working on this; he also read many of the chapters in draft form, and his intelligent criticisms have made it a better book. Jim Blandy was likewise a forgiving friend, and in turn I forgive him for introducing me to CVS all those years ago; it's okay, Jim, you couldn't possibly have known what you were getting me into! He also gets a big hug for patiently explaining over the phone how CVS's "watch" features work, at a time when we both had deadlines looming. Noel Cragg gave patient friendship and moral support at crucial times—thanks!

Brian Fitzpatrick, friend and manager in that order, took time out from an all-consuming job to read chapter drafts and offer many helpful comments; I can't thank him enough. And our mutual employer, onShore, Inc. (a.k.a. "The Mother Ship") was more tolerant of my erratic schedule than I had any right to ask (thank you, Stel and Za, Eric, and Adam!). It was a big favor and I can't really pay it back, but...dear reader, if you need a fancy Web site or custom programming, be sure to visit http://www.onshore.com. To Lefty, friend and coworker who probably bore the brunt of my absence from work: You know I appreciate it, and I'll have all the iron filings cleaned up by Monday, I promise.

Karen, thanks for advice, friendship, encouragement, draft-reading, and just being yourself. I wish you and David were back from Poland already...but I guess you will be by the time this is printed. Matt Braithwaite, thanks for support and for answering the BSD acronym question. Chris Larkosh gets credit for creating the wonderfully intimidating phrase "parallel ideation." Kennis and Rachel, thank you for your very early encouragement, it meant a lot! To Siu Yuin, thanks for friendship and good idea-bouncing (especially about the profit motive as a force for getting things done). To Noel Taylor, thanks for everything, pal, not least Golosa. And Yong Qing, thank you for reminding me to have a life even when I thought I didn't have time!

Richard Stallman's vision and uncompromising will are responsible for much of the free software movement's success today. He gets plenty of recognition, but not half the recognition he deserves. Thanks, RMS, don't ever change.

Stephanie Wall at Coriolis had a contagious enthusiasm for this book, which was very reassuring to a first-time author, and her flexibility during the many chapter rearrangements is appreciated as well. Most important, she and all the Powers That Be at Coriolis were willing to take a risk by releasing a significant portion of this book under the GNU General Public License; I hope they never regret that decision.

Toni Zuccarini cheerfully and ably performed a difficult task as project editor, managing an inexperienced author and a new, untried technical process, never showing any sign of the headache it must have caused her. To Colleen Brosnan, copy editor, thank you for doing such a thorough job, and for putting up with a computer programmer who was a stubborn but idiosyncratic English professor in a past life. Jon Gabriel and April Nielsen coaxed order out of chaos as production coordinator and layout designer; and thank you, Jody Winkler, for a most handsome cover design.

Tim Pierce, the technical reviewer, infallibly caught errors ranging from simple typos to downright misunderstandings of CVS's behavior...and now I'm going to get all the credit. Sorry, Tim; at least you and I know the truth!

Finally, the biggest "Thank you!" is for my parents, who were a small battalion of support and good advice from the very beginning, and who provided respite in the form of relaxing meals at home—or at strategically located Chinese restaurants—when I needed it most.

Contents At A Glance

Table Of Contents

Introduction

If you're like most programmers, you don't make your living from free software (though it would be nice if you could, wouldn't it?). But chances are you've at least used some free software, and perhaps contributed code or documentation to free projects. In that case, you'll have noticed a couple of things about the free software explosion of the last few years:

♦ A culture and a shared set of values are springing up. Among these: Software has maintainers but not "owners," the line between developers and users is deliberately left undrawn, bugs are publicized instead of denied, and information hoarding of any kind is frowned on.

♦ Many free projects, and especially those with large, distributed development teams, store their source code in a revision control system called CVS.

The second phenomenon is closely related to the first. CVS is flourishing precisely because it supports, and even encourages, the open, evolutionary development methods favored by free software. It allows anyone on the Internet immediate access to the latest version of the source code, it facilitates the creation of the "patch files" so necessary for contributing bug fixes and new features to a project, and it allows active developers to hack away at the same code base without worrying about stepping on each others' toes. Truly, if CVS did not exist, we would have to invent it.

This book has two goals, therefore—one social, the other technical. The social goal is to document this new culture and provide concrete advice for people managing or participating in Open Source projects. The technical goal is to tell you everything you need to know to use CVS, with an eye toward using it on Open Source projects.

As to the first goal: The operative word here is "advice." It would be presumptuous of me to make authoritative pronouncements on a subject so young and unsettled. Remember all those Web page design books that came out when the World Wide Web was barely a year old? Hindsight now shows many of their suggestions to be questionable or just plain wrong. Anxious to avoid the same pitfall, I will try to stick to what I know from personal experience to be true about Open Source practices. When my personal opinions do break into view, as will happen frequently, please do not take them as proven fact.

And as for CVS, note that although it will be taught in the context of Open Source projects, you will learn CVS well enough to use it anywhere. It's not just for managing program source code; people also use it to version—yes, that's a verb now—Web sites, text documents, configuration files, and so on. (You'll also learn how to judge, without resorting to time-consuming experiments, whether CVS is the right tool for a given situation.)

Accordingly, the book is arranged loosely into alternating chapters, some about Open Source development, some about CVS. As it progresses, and you become increasingly familiar with both topics and the strong links between them, this division will become less and less strict. It is assumed that you know something about programming or working with online documents, but previous familiarity with CVS is not required. At least a passing familiarity with Unix will prove handy, because the CVS examples are given in a Unix environment. But if you're a quick study you can get by without previous Unix experience.

A Word About Terminology

Is it "Open Source" or "free software"? This is an old—by Internet standards anyway—and rancorous debate. It has the defining characteristic of a linguistic dispute, namely, that people spend a lot of time arguing about whether there's anything to argue about. In my mind, the two terms are essentially synonymous, and I will use them interchangeably in this book. See Richard Stallman's essay "Why 'Free Software' is better than 'Open Source'" at **http://www.gnu.org/philosophy/open-source-or-free.html** for a well-written presentation of the case that the terms are *not* interchangeable.

The "free" in free software refers, of course, not to price but to liberty—the freedom to modify and redistribute the source code as one wishes. It is this freedom, not the software's low cost, that has been the key to free software's success. It is unfortunate, then, that English does not have separate words for these two largely separate concepts. I hope it is not reflective of our values that our language associates low prices with liberty.

Conventions Used In This Book

Throughout the book there will be command-line examples interspersed with explanatory text. The primary example user's name is jrandom, and she works on a machine named floss.red-bean.com, so the command prompt looks like this:

```
floss$
```

with output (if any) shown in the same font immediately below the prompt:

```
floss$ whoami
jrandom
floss$
```

Occasionally, the command itself is so long that it occupies two or more lines of a standard Unix terminal. In that case, a backslash at the end of a line indicates that the next line is to be considered a continuation, although it will be indented by the length of the prompt for readability. For example:

```
floss$ cvs diff -c -r prerelease-beta-2_09-19990315 -r \
       postrelease-3_0-19990325 fudgewinkle.c
```

(And by the end of the book, you'll know what that command means!)

Sometimes I'll need to show commands run from other locations (when demonstrating concurrent development by two different people, for example). In those cases, the other user's name is qsmith, and he works on a machine named paste:

```
paste$ whoami
qsmith
paste$
```

All commands take place in a Unix (Bourne Shell) environment unless otherwise specified. If you have even a basic familiarity with Unix, you won't encounter anything unusual in this book. However, you may notice that the **ls** command sometimes behaves a little oddly:

```
floss$ ls
foo.txt    bar.c    myproj/
```

The trailing "/" in **myproj/** is not part of the name, it just indicates that myproj is a directory. The reason the slash is displayed is that, in jrandom's environment, the **ls** command is aliased to run **ls -CF**; that is, to show files arranged in columns and displaying their type ("/" for directories, "*" for executable files, "@" for symbolic links, and so on).

I decided to keep this format for many of the examples, because it's often very helpful to be able to distinguish files from directories when reading the output. So even if you don't see the **-CF** options passed to the **ls** command, the output may behave as though they're there.

Practicing What We Preach

The CVS-specific chapters of this book (2, 4, 6, 8, 9, and 10) are copyrighted under the GNU General Public License, and can be browsed or downloaded from **http://cvsbook.red-bean.com**. If you find bugs in either the online or the treeware version, please report them to **bug-cvsbook@red-bean.com**.

Chapter 1

Why Open Source Development And CVS Go Together

What Is Free Software (And Why Should You Care)?

Most people do not buy software. By that, I don't mean that so-called "software piracy" is the most common way to obtain software (although it may well be, come to think of it). Even if everyone in the world piously refused to copy illegally, and even if all software manufacturers priced their products reasonably, very little real software would be bought and sold.

That's because what's available in software stores is not software. If you write free software, you already know that. If not, some explanation is necessary. Most commercial programs are shipped already half-broken—not that they don't work as advertised, but their potential for future maintenance and development has been drastically curtailed because they withhold their source code. For all practical purposes, if you don't have the source code to a program, you are powerless to change its behavior, even though it may be filled with bugs. To change the behavior of the software, you have to change the executable; to change the executable, you must be able to edit the source. Your only choice is not attractive—you have to wait for the next version to be released and hope the manufacturer has fixed the bugs.

Commercial software companies understandably treat their source code as their most treasured secret because it gives the company exclusive control over the behavior of its product. If the source code were available to everyone, someone could modify the program, fix bugs, and add features without concern for a marketing strategy or sales plan. Competitors could surreptitiously copy sections of the code to use in their own executables. Another, perhaps even more common, reason for source code confidentiality is that open code would be subject to peer review, and competitors could publicly point out inefficiencies and poor coding practices.

Thus, commercial software producers have no good reasons to publish their source code and several good reasons why they shouldn't. From a user's point of view, however, there are some disadvantages to this arrangement. For instance, the user is forced to depend on only one supplier for any changes or repairs to the program. Furthermore, if that supplier, for some reason, ceases to support the product line, the user's investment of time and mental effort in learning the program is suddenly a waste. Once unsupported, no program can last long. Operating systems, computer hardware, and interoperability standards will continue to evolve, while the unmaintained program remains frozen in time. Eventually it either becomes too obsolete to run, or it no longer is able to communicate with the newer software and hardware.

Like any other kind of company, software companies can go out of business, or stop providing satisfactory support for their customers. But the customers must often decide to continue using the product anyway, even if reluctantly, because the costs of switching to another product are too high (plus, there's no guarantee that a new vendor would be any more responsive to their needs in the long run). Thus, all users are presented with the possibility of being dissatisfied with their programs and simply unable to do anything about it.

It doesn't have to be like this—and, for an increasing number of people, it isn't. An alternative system has appeared, in which source code is publicly distributed, sharing is encouraged (for both source and executable), and—most importantly—users are invited to repair and improve the code. The movement's strength does not depend on all users being programmers; it is enough that some users understand the art of modifying source code, and that the others know how to find them. The collective concerns of a globeful of committed users turns out to be a powerful force—powerful enough to keep the software not only alive but flourishing.

Today, many of the Internet's underlying services (including email routers, Web servers, and the basic address-lookup system) are running on software maintained under this cooperative system. One reason is that such software has been found to be more reliable and more attuned to the needs of its users than anything offered commercially. Another reason, I suspect, is that too many people have now had the experience of choosing a proprietary product that is poorly maintained and fails to address their needs. When the code is open to modification and redistribution by virtually anyone, there's a high probability that someone, somewhere, will fix the major bugs and add useful features. Everyone benefits when that happens because improvements to a program tend to find their way to every user's computer; bad modifications generally do not.

How It All Started

This system did not somehow emerge spontaneously from the chaos of the Internet, although an argument could be made that it was bound to happen eventually. In any case, the process was greatly accelerated by the stubbornness of one man, Richard Stallman. Informal code sharing had been around for a long time, but until Stallman gave the phenomenon a name and made a cause of it, the participants were generally not aware of the political consequences of their actions.

In the 1970s, Stallman worked at the Massachusetts Institute of Technology's Artificial Intelligence Lab. The Lab was, in his own words (see his essay at **www.gnu.org/gnu/thegnuproject.html**), a "software-sharing community," an environment in which changes to program source code were shared as naturally as the air in the room. If you improved the system, you were expected to share your modifications with anyone else running a similar system, so all could benefit. Indeed, the phrase "your modifications" is itself misleading; the work was "yours" in an associative sense, but not in a possessive sense. You lost nothing by sharing your work and often benefited further when someone else improved on your improvements.

This ideal community disintegrated around Stallman in about 1980. A computer company hired away many of the AI Lab programmers by paying them big money to do essentially the same work, but under an exclusive license. That company's business model was the same as that of most software shops today: Write a really good program (in this case, an operating system), keep the source code under lock and key so no one else can benefit from it, and then charge a fee for each copy of the system in use. A "copy," of course, meant a binary copy. People outside the company could run the system, but they weren't allowed to see or modify the source code from which the executables were produced.

From the point of view of the former AI Lab programmers, the change may have appeared fairly minor. They still were able to share code with each other, because most of them went to work for the same company. However, they weren't able to share their code with anyone outside that company nor, for legal reasons, were they free to incorporate others' code into their products.

For Stallman, however, the prospect of hoarding code was intolerable. He'd had a taste of what a sharing community could be. Instead of accepting the supposedly inevitable and letting his community disappear, he decided to re-create it in a less vulnerable form. He started a nonprofit organization called the Free Software Foundation and began to implement a complete, free, Unix-compatible operating system, which he called GNU ("GNU's Not Unix!"). Even more importantly, he designed a copyright license whose terms ensured the perpetual redistribution of his software's source code. Instead of trying to reserve exclusive copying rights to the author or owner of the code, the General Public License (or GPL, see Appendix B) prevented anyone from claiming exclusive rights to the work. If you had a copy of the covered work, you were free to pass it around to others, but you could not require that they refrain from giving out copies. The rights had to be copied along with the code. These rights extended to modified versions of the work, so that once a work was covered by the GPL, no one could make a few changes and then resell it under a more restrictive license.

Stallman's idea caught on, and other people began releasing programs under the GPL, and occasionally inventing their own similar licenses. In the meantime, the Internet was enabling programmers across the globe to have access to each other's code, if they chose to cooperate. Thus, the new software-sharing community came to include virtually anyone who wanted to join and had a Net connection, regardless of their physical location.

At this point—about 1990—probably only a few people shared Stallman's confidence that public ownership of code was how all software ought to be. Even some regular contributors to the GNU project were not necessarily in favor of *all* software being free, pleased though they may have been with what the GNU project had accomplished so far. Before long, though, the movement (if it could be called that yet) received a tremendous psychological boost from the appearance of some completely free operating systems. In Finland, Linus Torvalds had reimplemented an entire Unix kernel (called *Linux*) and published his source code under the GPL; combined with the Unix utilities already available from the GNU project, this became a usable distribution of Unix. Not long afterwards came the release of 386BSD, based on the Berkeley Software Distribution version of Unix, whose development had actually started before Linux. These were soon followed by the confusingly named NetBSD, FreeBSD, and, more recently, OpenBSD.

The appearance of entirely free operating systems was a real boon for the movement—and not just in technical terms. It proved that free code could result in quality software (in many situations, the free systems performed better and crashed less often than their commercial competitors). Because the vast majority of applications that ran on these systems were also free, there was a dramatic increase in the free software user base, and therefore in the number of developers contributing their talents to free software.

The Two Types Of Development

As more users removed commercial operating systems from their computers and installed free ones, the rest of the world (by which I mean nonprogrammers) began to notice that something unexpected was happening. With his usual timeliness, Eric Raymond published a paper, "The Cathedral and the Bazaar" (**www.tuxedo.org/~esr/writings/cathedral-bazaar/**), which partly explained why free software was often so technically successful. The paper contrasted two styles of software development. The first, "cathedral-style," is tightly organized, centrally planned, and is essentially one creative act from start to finish. (Actually, I rather doubt that real cathedrals are built this way, but that's a topic for another time.) Most commercial software is written cathedral-style, with a guru heading up a team and deciding what features will go into each release.

The other style resembles, in Raymond's memorable phrase, "a great babbling bazaar of differing agendas and approaches (aptly symbolized by the Linux archive sites, which would take submissions from *anyone*) out of which a coherent and stable system could seemingly emerge only by a succession of miracles." But emerge it did, and Raymond hit on the key reason for the recurrence of the miracle: "Given enough eyeballs, all bugs are shallow." The trouble with the cathedral style is that it fails to enlist the software's most natural ally—the users. A small (or even medium-sized) team of developers quickly becomes overwhelmed with the influx of bug reports and feature requests and must spend a fair amount of time simply prioritizing and figuring out what to do next. Even after they know what they want to do, there's no telling how long it will take to track down a particular bug and come up with a maintainable solution. The result is that part of the development team spends too much time solving these issues and is unavailable for other work.

Furthermore, commercial development teams often operate under constraints (budgets, deadlines, and marketing strategies) unrelated to the technical problems of the software. Even the decision to continue maintaining a certain program is often based on business factors having little to do with the software's intrinsic quality and potential.

The users, on the other hand, just want good code. They want a useful program, they want the bugs fixed, and they want appropriate features added and inappropriate ones kept out. In retrospect, the solution seems obvious: Why not give the users the freedom to make all this happen themselves? Even though the vast majority of users are not programmers and cannot contribute to actually changing the code, those few who can will end up benefiting everyone.

What Does CVS Have To Do With It?

As with any popular movement that experiences sudden growth, the free software movement soon discovered that it had logistical problems. It was no longer enough for a free software author merely to place her code on a public Internet server and wait for people to download it. What if people did download it and then sent in hundreds of bug fixes and code contributions? For a popular program, no single author could be expected to organize and integrate all this feedback and still have time to write original code. In a closed-source, centrally directed software company, the number of developers is relatively small and well-paid, and the tasks are divided up in advance. However, the Open Source author is often an unpaid volunteer who has no idea where the next useful snippet of code will come from or what that snippet will do. If she's lucky, she may have an organized core group of codevelopers who can help fix bugs and review incoming contributions to ensure that they meet the project's standards. This type of group probably has a high turnover rate, though, as its members are likely also volunteers.

A geographically distributed volunteer organization obviously cannot afford to spend weeks or months training its members to work together, only to lose this investment whenever a member leaves the group and is replaced by a newcomer. A base set of conventions for contributing to shared projects was needed, so that newcomers could fit in easily. Also needed was an automated system for accepting contributions and keeping everyone up-to-date with changes to the code. These needs were not, of course, unique to free software, but they were particularly pressing there because volunteer projects are less able to devote resources to management and are more likely to seek automated solutions that don't take a long time to learn.

The groundwork for such a system had already been laid. The standard Unix **diff** program knew how to concisely reveal the differences between two files: If you "take the diff" (as we say in the vernacular) between a file before a given modification and the same file afterward, the resulting diff—that is, the output of the **diff** program—consists of only the modification and omits those parts of the file that remained the same. A trained eye can look at a diff and know approximately what happened to the file; more importantly, a trained program can look at a diff and tell *exactly* what happened. Therefore, **diff** was soon augmented, to no one's surprise, by **patch**. Written by Larry Wall and released as free software, **patch** was to **diff** as integrals are to derivatives. If you take the difference between file A and file B (remember that B is often just A after some modifications) and feed it to **patch** along with one of the files, **patch** can reconstruct the other file. (One result of this was that diffs soon came to be called "patches" instead, and that's how I'll usually refer to them in the rest of this book.)

If this seems of dubious utility to you, put yourself in the position of the software developer who needs to accept code contributions from outside sources. A contribution, in practical terms, consists of a set of changes to various files in the project. The maintainer wants to know exactly what those changes are—what files were modified and how. Assuming the changes pass muster, he or she wants to put them into the code with a minimum of fuss. The ideal way to accomplish this is to receive a series of patches that can be inspected by eye, and then automatically incorporated into the current sources via the **patch** program. (In real life, of course, the maintainer's sources may have other changes by that time, but **patch** is smart enough to perform fuzzy matching, so it usually does the right thing even if the files are no longer exactly the same as the ones used to produce the patch.)

With **diff** and **patch**, there was a convenient, standard way to submit contributions, but soon a further need was recognized. Sometimes, a submission was incorporated into the sources that had to be removed later because it contained flaws. Of course, by that time, it was hard to figure out who applied what patch when. Even if the change could be tracked down, manually undoing the effect of a patch long after the fact is a tedious and error-prone process. The solution was a system for keeping track of a project's history—one that allowed the retrieval of previous versions for comparison with the present version. Again, this problem was not limited to free software projects—it was shared by the commercial world, and various systems had been written to solve it. Most free software projects, as well as quite a few commercial ones, chose Walter Tichy's Revision Control System (RCS), which is free and also relatively portable.

RCS did the job, but in hindsight, it lacked several important features. For one thing, it dealt with projects in a file-centric way; it had no concept that the various files comprising a project were related, even though they might all be in the same directory tree. It also used the "lock-modify-unlock" style of development, in which a developer wishing to work on a file first "locked" it so no one else could make changes to it, then did her work, and then unlocked the file. If you tried to lock a file already locked by someone else, you either had to wait until they were done or "steal" the lock. In effect, it was necessary to negotiate with other developers before working on the same files, even if you would be working in different areas of code (and, predictably, people sometimes forgot to unlock files when they were finished). Finally, RCS was not network-aware. Developers had to work on the same machine where RCS's per-file historical data was kept or resort to clumsy handwritten scripts to transfer data between their working machines and the RCS server.

Thus was born the latest (although surely not the last) in this progression of tools: CVS, which stands for "Concurrent Versions System." CVS addresses each of the aforementioned problems in RCS. In fact, it started out as a collection of scripts written by Dick Grune in 1986 that were designed to make RCS a bit easier, and were posted to the Usenet newsgroup **comp.sources.unix**. In 1989, Brian Berliner rewrote CVS in the C programming language, and Jeff Polk later added some key features.

CVS actually continued to use the original RCS format for storing historical data and initially even depended on the RCS utilities to parse that format, but it added some extra abilities. For one thing, CVS was directory-aware and had a mechanism for giving a group of directories a name by which they could be retrieved. This enabled it to treat a project as a single entity, which is how people think of projects. CVS also didn't require that files be locked and unlocked. Instead, developers could hack away at the code simultaneously and, one by one, register their changes into the repository (the place where the project's master sources and change history are kept). CVS took care of the mechanics of recording all these changes, merging simultaneous edits to the same file when necessary, and notifying developers of any conflicts.

Finally, in the early 1990s, Jim Kingdon (then at Cygnus Solutions, now at Cyclic Software) made CVS network-aware. Developers could now access a project's code from anywhere on the Internet. This opened code bases to anyone whose interest was sparked, and because CVS intelligently merged changes to the same files, developers rarely had to worry about the logistics of having multiple people working on the same set of sources. In a sense, CVS did for code what banks do for money: Most of us have been freed from worrying about the logistics of protecting our money, accessing it in faraway places, recording our major transactions, sorting out concurrent accesses, or accidentally spending more than we have. The bank automatically takes care of the first four and notifies us with an alarm when we've done the last.

The CVS way of doing things—networked access to sources, simultaneous development, and intelligent automated merging of changes—has proven attractive to closed-source projects as well as free ones. At present, it is used frequently in both worlds; however, it has really become dominant among the free projects. A central thesis of this book is that CVS became the free software world's first choice for revision control because there's a close match (watch out, I almost said "synergy") between the way CVS encourages a project to be run and the way free projects actually do run. To see this, we need to look a bit more closely at the Open Source process.

Principles Of Open Source Development And How CVS Helps

The first principle (a major shift if one is accustomed to proprietary software development) is that the source code be made accessible to the entire world. Instantly, a question arises: When should the source code be made available, and how often? At first, it would seem that the most recently released version would suffice, but if others are to find and fix bugs, they'll need access to the latest development sources, the same files being worked on by the maintainers. It's terribly discouraging to a potential contributor to spend days tracking down and fixing a bug, only to discover on submitting the patch that the bug has already been found and fixed. As any programmer knows, a release is just a snapshot of a development tree at a particular moment. It may be an unusually well-tested snapshot, but from the code's point of view, the released version is not qualitatively different from a snapshot taken at any other time. As far as contributing authors are concerned, a free software project is in a state of continuous release.

Unfortunately, traditional methods of software distribution weren't designed for continuous, incremental updates. They were designed around the idea that a release is a monumental event, deserving of special treatment. In the Grand Event way of doing things, the release was packaged into a static collection of files, detached from the project's past history and future changes, and distributed to users, who would stay with that release until the next one was ready, sometimes months or years later. Naturally, the development sources did not remain static during that time. All of the changes that were to go into the next release would start slowly accumulating in the developer's copy of the sources, so that by the time the new release neared, the code was already in a substantially different state from the previous release. Thus, even if full source code were included in every release, it still wouldn't have helped much. Users would soon be working with out-of-date files and have no convenient way to check the state of the master sources accessed by the maintainer and core developers.

For a while, this situation was handled with workarounds—partial solutions that were not terribly convenient but could at least be tolerated. Snapshots of the development sources were made available online on a regular basis, and any users who wanted to keep up with the project's state could retrieve those sources and install them. For those who did this regularly, the process could be partially automated by scripts that retrieved and installed each "development release" nightly. However, this was still an unsatisfactory way to receive changes. If even one line of code in one file changed, and everything else stayed the same, the interim release would still have to be retrieved in its entirety.

The answer (you knew this was coming) is CVS. In addition to giving active developers a convenient way to enter their changes into the master repository, CVS also supports anonymous, read-only access to the repository. This means that anyone can keep a development tree on their local machine, and when they want to start working on a particular area of code, they simply run one command to make sure the tree is up-to-date. Then, after checking to make sure that the problem they're trying to solve hasn't already been fixed in the batch of changes just received, they begin work. Finally, when the changes are ready, CVS automates the process of producing a patch, which is then sent to the maintainers for inspection and possible incorporation into the master source tree.

The point here is not that CVS makes something possible that had previously been impossible; retrieving up-to-date sources and producing patches had all been theoretically possible before. The difference is that CVS makes it *convenient*. In a system that relies largely on volunteer energy, convenience is not merely a luxury—it is often the factor that determines whether someone will contribute to your project or turn their attention to something with fewer obstacles to participation. Projects are competing for volunteer attention on their merits, and those merits include not only the quality of the software itself but also the ease with which potential developers are given access to the source and the readiness with which good contributions are accepted by the maintainers. CVS's great advantage is that it reduces the overhead involved in running a volunteer-friendly project by giving the general public easy access to the sources and by offering features designed specifically to aid the generation of patches to the sources.

The percentage of free software projects that keep their master sources in CVS is impressive by itself. Even more impressive is that some of those projects are among the largest (in terms of number of contributors) and most successful (in terms of installed base) on the Internet. They include the Apache WWW server, the GNOME free desktop environment, FreeBSD, NetBSD, OpenBSD, the PostgreSQL database, the XEmacs text editor, and many more. In later chapters, we'll examine in detail how projects use CVS to manage their sources and aid their volunteers.

What Makes It All Tick?

Until now, I've focused on the advantages of free software for users. However, developers still face an interesting choice when they consider free software. As long as copyright law exists in its current form, it will probably always be more lucrative for a programmer to work on proprietary code—the profits can be enormous (even after illegal sharing is taken into account) when each running copy of a popular program is paid for individually. If you want to get rich, your course is clear: Write a useful piece of closed-source software, get it noticed, and wait for Microsoft to make an offer for your company.

Yet somehow, free software projects still manage to find programmers. There are probably as many different explanations for this as there are people writing free code. Nevertheless, if you spend enough time watching mailing lists and developer discussion groups, a few core reasons become apparent: necessity, community, glory, and money, not necessarily in that order and certainly not mutually exclusive.

The first reason, necessity (the need to "scratch an itch"), is hypothesized by Eric Raymond to be the chief reason why most free software projects get started at all. If you just want a problem solved, once and forever, and you aren't looking to bring in any revenue from the code (aside from the time you'll save by using it), then it makes a lot of sense to release your program under a free license. If you're lucky, your solution will turn out to be useful to other people, and they'll help you maintain it. Call it the Kropotkin Factor—sometimes, cooperation is simply the most winning strategy.

My favorite reason, though, is actually the second: community. The sheer pleasure of working in partnership with a group of committed developers is a strong motivation in itself. The fact that little or no money is involved merely attests to the strength of the group's desire to make the program work, and the presence of collaborators also confirms that the work is valuable outside one's own narrow situation. The educational value of working with a group of experienced programmers should not be discounted either; I've certainly learned more about programming from reading freely available code, following online discussions about the code, and asking questions, than from any book or classroom. Many active free software developers would probably say the same. Most seem quite conscious that they are participating in a kind of informal, peer-to-peer university and will happily explain things to a newcomer, as long as they feel the newcomer shows promise of contributing to the code base eventually.

Meanwhile, in the back of everyone's mind (well, okay, not *yours* or *mine*, of course!), is glory—the fame that comes from occupying a prominent position on the developer team of a widely used free program. Most programmers with even a peripheral involvement in free software are likely to recognize the names Linus Torvalds and Alan Cox (for work on the Linux kernel), Brian Behlendorf (of the Apache Web Server team), and Larry Wall (inventor of, among other things, the popular Perl programming language). Raw self-aggrandizement may not be the most attractive motive, but properly harnessed, it can bring about a lot of useful code. Happily, in the free software culture, glory is achieved by sharing the benefits of one's work, rather than restricting them. Note that there is often no official (that is, legal) recognition of what constitutes a "prominent position" in a group of developers. People acquire influence by writing good code, finding and fixing bugs, and consistently contributing constructively in public forums. Such an unregulated system may seem open to exploitation, but in practice, attempts to steal credit don't succeed—too many people are too close to the code to be fooled by any false claims. A developer's influence in the community is directly proportional to the frequency and usefulness of her contributions, and usually everyone involved knows this.

One side effect of this is an uncommon scrupulousness about giving credit where credit is due. You've probably noticed that I'm being careful to mention developers' names when talking about specific pieces of software. Giving credit by name is a common practice in the free software world, and it makes sense. Because the work is often done for little or no pay, the possibility that contributions will be recognized and reputations correspondingly enhanced makes it attractive. Fortunately, another side effect of using CVS (or any version control system) is that the precise extent of every developer's modifications is recorded in the change history, which can be retrieved and examined by anyone at any time.

Finally, there is money. People have begun to find ways to get paid to work on free software. In many cases, the wages are considerably more than a bare living, and even if not quite as lucrative as, say, stock options at a proprietary software company, the pleasure of seeing one's code widely distributed is often enough to compensate for a little income foregone.

One way for people to make money is to sell services centered around a particular code base. The software may be free, but expertise is still in limited supply. A common strategy is to specialize in knowing everything there is to know about a particular free tool or suite of tools and offer technical support, customizations, and training. Often, the company also contributes to the maintenance of the program (and no wonder, as it's in its interest to ensure that the code remains healthy and free of bitrot). More recently, companies have begun to specialize in packaging particular distributions of free software and trading on the "brand name" they earn through making reliable bundles. Oddly enough, this actually seems to work. Red Hat Software has been profitably selling Linux distributions on CD-ROM for several years, despite the fact that anyone is free to copy its CDs and resell them or even just download the software directly from Red Hat. Apparently, the reliability of its distribution is important enough to consumers that people will pay a little more for the extra reassurance of getting it on CD-ROM directly from Red Hat instead of from a reseller.

Also, hardware companies sometimes devote resources to guaranteeing that popular free applications will run on their machines. If a company formerly offered proprietary software as a sideline to its hardware and service businesses, it may now ship free software that it has tested and perhaps modified to perform better on its hardware. You may think that it would want to keep its modifications secret (were that permitted by the software's license at all), but it turns out to be entirely to the company's advantage to release any changes back into the common distribution. By doing so, the company avoids having to shoulder the entire maintenance burden itself. By releasing the source, it has empowered its users to give feedback on whether the program runs well on the hardware. (The goodwill thus gained among its customers may also be a factor.) Because it isn't in the software business anyway, it's not looking for a direct return on investment in that area.

The arrival of big money into the formerly pure free software world has not been seen universally as a positive development and, in fact, has led to some rather heated debate about the ultimate purpose of free software. To attempt to summarize that debate would be diving into shark-infested waters, indeed; however, it's a significant issue right now, so I'll don shark repellent and do my best. The issue arose because free software has been so technically successful. Stable, bug-free software—whatever its origins—is something any business wants to offer its clients, as long as doing so doesn't conflict with any other goals (such as increasing sales of one's own closed-source software). In the for-profit consulting world, the innate quality of the software, in a purely technical sense, is the only concern. If the best "product" is free software, so be it; if it's something else, use that instead.

The terms of redistribution are not a major factor in the decision to use the software, except in how it affects one's ability to use it. Thus, some people are for free software simply because it leads to better code, which may also imply reduced hassle and higher profits. For others, however, cooperation itself *is* the goal. Richard Stallman is one of the most forceful evangelists for this position (for him, sharing information is a moral crusade), but he is not alone in viewing profit-driven development with distrust.

Although I personally lean toward the "cooperation is the goal" attitude, I also don't think free software is really threatened by the influx of corporate money. For free software, the only truly important currency is developer attention. To the degree that corporate money subsidizes developers who devote time to free software, it helps the software and the community. When that money is used to pay for closed-source software, programmers will still create and maintain free code, and that code will continue to be of high quality. That's simply what many programmers want, and what they do on their own time is up to them. Perhaps occasionally, a company will promote a program as "open source" when it's not and briefly tempt a few developers into wasting their time with non-free code. However, the legal language of the software's license is open for inspection, and no amount of marketing or propaganda can make it mean something it doesn't. Inevitably, developers will realize this and turn their attention to truly free work.

In the end, the appearance of factionalism (of which the disagreement about the role of money is only one example) in the free software movement is probably a sign of strength. It means that people are now secure enough about free software's success that they no longer feel the need to present a unified public front or avoid rocking the boat. From here, it's merely a matter of taking over the world.

Chapter 2
An Overview Of CVS

CVS Basics

This chapter introduces the fundamental concepts of CVS and then provides an in-depth guided tour of everyday CVS usage. After completing it, you'll be at least partway to CVS guru-hood.

If you've never used CVS (or any version control system) before, it's easy to get tripped up by some of its underlying assumptions. What seems to cause the most initial confusion about CVS is that it is used for two apparently unrelated purposes: record keeping and collaboration. It turns out, however, that these two functions are closely connected.

Record keeping became necessary because people wanted to compare a program's current state with how it was at some point in the past. For example, in the normal course of implementing a new feature, a developer may bring the program into a thoroughly broken state, where it will probably remain until the feature is mostly finished. Unfortunately, this is just the time when someone usually calls to report a bug in the last publicly released version. To debug the problem (which may also exist in the current version of the sources), the program has to be brought back to a useable state.

Restoring the state poses no difficulty if the source code history is kept under CVS. The developer can simply say, in effect, "Give me the program as it was three weeks ago," or perhaps "Give me the program as it was at the time of our last public release." If you've never had this kind of convenient access to historical snapshots before, you may be surprised at how quickly you come to depend on it. Personally, I always use revision control on my coding projects now—it's saved me many times.

To understand what this has to do with facilitating collaboration, we'll need to take a closer look at the mechanism that CVS provides to help numerous people work on the same project. But before we do that, let's take a look at a mechanism that CVS *doesn't* provide (or at least, doesn't encourage): file locking. If you've used other version control systems, you may be familiar with the **lock-modify-unlock** development model, wherein a developer first obtains exclusive write access (a *lock*) to the file to be edited, makes the changes, and then releases the lock to allow other developers access to the file. If someone else already has a lock on the file, they have to "release" it before you can lock it and start making changes (or, in some implementations, you may "steal" their lock, but that is often an unpleasant surprise for them and not good practice!).

This system is workable if the developers know each other, know who's planning to do what at any given time, and can communicate with each other quickly if someone cannot work because of access contention. However, if the developer group becomes too large or too spread out, dealing with all the locking issues begins to chip away at coding time; it becomes a constant hassle that can discourage people from getting real work done.

CVS takes a more mellow approach. Rather than requiring that developers coordinate with each other to avoid conflicts, CVS enables developers to edit simultaneously, assumes the burden of integrating all the changes, and keeps track of any conflicts. This process uses the **copy-modify-merge** model, which works as follows:

1. Developer A requests a *working copy* (a directory tree containing the files that make up the project) from CVS. This is also known as "checking out" a working copy, like checking a book out of the library.

2. Developer A edits freely in her working copy. At the same time, other developers may be busy in their own working copies. Because these are all separate copies, there is no interference—it is as though all of the developers have their own copy of the same library book, and they're all at work scribbling comments in the margins or rewriting certain pages independently.

3. Developer A finishes her changes and *commits* them into CVS along with a "log message," which is a comment explaining the nature and purpose of the changes. This is like informing the library of what changes she made to the book and why. The library then incorporates these changes into a "master" copy, where they are recorded for all time.

4. Meanwhile, other developers can have CVS query the library to see if the master copy has changed recently. If it has, CVS automatically updates their working copies. (This part is magical and wonderful, and I hope you appreciate it. Imagine how different the world would be if real books worked this way!)

As far as CVS is concerned, all developers on a project are equal. Deciding when to update or when to commit is largely a matter of personal preference or project policy. One common strategy for coding projects is to always update before commencing work on a major change and to commit only when the changes are complete and tested so that the master copy is always in a "runnable" state.

Perhaps you're wondering what happens when developers A and B, each in their own working copy, make different changes to the same area of text and then both commit their changes? This is called a *conflict*, and CVS notices it as soon as developer B tries to commit changes. Instead of allowing developer B to proceed, CVS announces that it has discovered a conflict and places *conflict markers* (easily recognizable textual flags) at the conflicting location in his copy. That location also shows both sets of changes, arranged for easy comparison. Developer B must sort it all out and commit a new revision with the conflict resolved. Perhaps the two developers will need to talk to each other to settle the issue. CVS only alerts the developers that there is a conflict; it's up to human beings to actually resolve it.

What about the master copy? In official CVS terminology, it is called the project's *repository*. The repository is simply a file tree kept on a central server. Without going into too much detail about its structure (but see Chapter 4), let's look at what the repository must do to meet the requirements of the checkout-commit-update cycle. Consider the following scenario:

1. Two developers, A and B, check out working copies of a project at the same time. The project is at its starting point—no changes have been committed by anyone yet, so all the files are in their original, pristine state.

2. Developer A gets right to work and soon commits her first batch of changes.

3. Meanwhile, developer B watches television.

4. Developer A, hacking away like there's no tomorrow, commits her second batch of changes. Now, the repository's history contains the original files, followed by A's first batch of changes, followed by this set of changes.

5. Meanwhile, developer B plays video games.

6. Suddenly, developer C joins the project and checks out a working copy from the repository. Developer C's copy reflects A's first two sets of changes, because they were already in the repository when C checked out her copy.

7. Developer A, continuing to code as one possessed by spirits, completes and commits her *third* batch of changes.

8. Finally, blissfully unaware of the recent frenzy of activity, developer B decides it's time to start work. He doesn't bother to update his copy; he just commences editing files, some of which may be files that A has worked in. Shortly thereafter, developer B commits his first changes.

At this point, one of two things can happen. If none of the files edited by developer B have been edited by A, the commit succeeds. However, if CVS realizes that some of B's files are out of date with respect to the repository's latest copies, *and* those files have also been changed by B in his working copy, CVS informs B that he must do an update before committing those files.

When developer B runs the update, CVS merges all of A's changes into B's local copies of the files. Some of A's work may conflict with B's uncommitted changes, and some may not. Those parts that don't are simply applied to B's copies without further complication; the conflicting ones must be resolved by B before being committed.

If developer C does an update now, she'll receive several batches of changes from the repository: A's third commit, then B's first, and then possibly B's second commit (if B had to resolve any conflicts).

In order for CVS to serve up changes, in the correct sequence, to developers whose working copies may be out of sync by varying degrees, the repository needs to store all commits since the project's beginning. In practice, the CVS repository stores them all as successive **diff**s. Thus, even for a very old working copy, CVS is able to calculate the difference between the working copy's files and the current state of the repository, and is thereby able to bring the working copy up to date efficiently. This makes it easy for developers to view the project's history at any point and to revive even very old working copies.

Although, strictly speaking, the repository could achieve the same results by other means, in practice, storing **diff**s is a simple, intuitive means of implementing the necessary functionality. The process has the added benefit that, by using **patch** appropriately, CVS can reconstruct any previous state of the file tree and thus bring any working copy from one state to another. It can allow someone to check out the project as it looked at any particular time. It can also show the differences, in **diff** format, between two states of the tree without affecting someone's working copy.

Thus, the very features necessary to give convenient access to a project's history are also useful for providing a decentralized, uncoordinated developer team with the ability to collaborate on the project.

For now, you can ignore the details of setting up a repository, administering user access, and navigating CVS-specific file formats (those will be covered in Chapter 4). For the moment, we'll concentrate on how to make changes in a working copy.

But first, here is a quick review of terms:

- *Revision*—A committed change in the history of a file or set of files. A revision is one "snapshot" in a constantly changing project.

- *Repository*—The master copy where CVS stores a project's full revision history. Each project has exactly one repository.

- *Working copy*—The copy in which you actually make changes to a project. There can be many working copies of a given project; generally each developer has his or her own copy.

- *Check out*—To request a working copy from the repository. Your working copy reflects the state of the project as of the moment you checked it out; when you and other developers make changes, you must use **commit** and **update** to "publish" your changes and view others' changes.

- *Commit*—To send changes from your working copy into the central repository. Also known as *check-in*.

- *Log message*—A comment you attach to a revision when you **commit** it, describing the changes. Others can page through the log messages to get a summary of what's been going on in a project.

◆ *Update*—To bring others' changes from the repository into your working copy and to show if your working copy has any uncommitted changes. Be careful not to confuse this with **commit**; they are complementary operations. Mnemonic: **update** brings your working copy up to date with the repository copy.

◆ *Conflict*—The situation when two developers try to commit changes to the same region of the same file. CVS notices and points out conflicts, but the developers must resolve them.

A Day With CVS

An introduction to fundamental CVS usage is provided in this section, followed by a sample session that covers all of the most typical CVS operations. As the tour progresses, we'll also start to look at how CVS works internally.

Although you don't need to understand every last detail of CVS's implementation to use it, a basic knowledge of how it works is invaluable in choosing the best way to achieve a given result. CVS is more like a bicycle than an automobile, in the sense that its mechanisms are entirely transparent to anyone who cares to look. As with a bicycle, you can just hop on and start riding immediately. However, if you take a few moments to study how the gears work, you'll be able to ride it much more efficiently. (In the case of CVS, I'm not sure whether transparency was a deliberate design decision or an accident, but it does seem to be a property shared by many free programs. Externally visible implementations have the advantage of encouraging the users to become contributing developers by exposing them to the system's inner workings right from the start.)

The tour takes place in a Unix environment. CVS also runs on Windows and Macintosh operating systems, and Tim Endres of Ice Engineering has even written a Java client (see **www.ice.com/java/jcvs/**), which can be run anywhere Java runs. However, I'm going to take a wild guess and assume that the majority of CVS users—present and potential—are most likely working in a Unix command-line environment. If you aren't one of these, the examples in the tour should be easy to translate to other interfaces. Once you understand the concepts, you can sit down at any CVS front end and work with it (trust me, I've done it many times).

The examples in the tour are oriented toward people who will be using CVS to keep track of programming projects. However, CVS operations are applicable to all text documents, not just source code.

The tour also assumes that you already have CVS installed (it's present by default on many of the popular free Unix systems, so you might already have it without knowing it) and that you have access to a repository. Even if you are not set up, you can still benefit from reading the tour. In Chapter 4, you'll learn how to install CVS and set up repositories.

Assuming CVS is installed, you should take a moment to find the online CVS manual. Known familiarly as the "Cederqvist" (after Per Cederqvist, its original author), it comes with the CVS source distribution and is usually the most up-to-date reference available. It's written in Texinfo format and should be available on Unix systems in the "Info" documentation hierarchy. You can read it either with the command line **info** program

```
floss$ info cvs
```

or by pressing Ctrl+H and then typing "i" inside Emacs. If neither of these works for you, consult your local Unix guru (or see Chapter 4 regarding installation issues). You'll definitely want to have the Cederqvist at your fingertips if you're going to be using CVS regularly.

Invoking CVS

CVS is one program, but it can perform many different actions: updating, committing, branching, diffing, and so on. When you invoke CVS, you must specify which action you want to perform. Thus, the format of a CVS invocation is:

```
floss$ cvs command
```

For example, you can use

```
floss$ cvs update
floss$ cvs diff
floss$ cvs commit
```

and so on. (Don't bother to try running any of those particular commands yet, though; they won't do anything until you're in a working copy, which we'll get to shortly.)

Both CVS and the command can take options. Options that affect the behavior of CVS, independently of the command being run, are called *global options*; command-specific options are just called *command options*. Global options always go to the left of the command; command options, to its right. So in

```
floss$ cvs -Q update -p
```

-**Q** is a global option, and -**p** is a command option. (If you're curious, -**Q** means "quietly"— that is, suppress all diagnostic output, and print error messages only if the command absolutely cannot be compiled for some reason; -**p** means to send the results of **update** to standard output instead of to files.)

Accessing A Repository

Before you can do anything, you must tell CVS the location of the repository you'll be accessing. This isn't a concern if you already have a working copy checked out—any working copy knows what repository it came from, so CVS can automatically deduce the repository for a given working copy. However, let's assume you don't have a working copy yet, so you need to tell CVS explicitly where to go. This is done with the **-d** global option (the **-d** stands for "directory," an abbreviation for which there is a historical justification, although **-r** for "repository" might have been better), followed by the path to the repository. For example, assuming the repository is on the local machine in /usr/local/cvs (a fairly standard location):

```
floss$ cvs -d /usr/local/cvs command
```

In many cases, however, the repository is on another machine and must therefore be reached over the network. CVS provides a choice of network access methods; which one you'll use depends mostly on the security needs of the repository machine (hereinafter referred to as "the server"). Setting up the server to allow various remote access methods is covered in Chapter 4; here we'll deal only with the client side.

Fortunately, all the remote access methods share a common invocation syntax. In general, to specify a remote repository as opposed to a local one, you just use a longer repository path. You first name the access method, delimited on each side by colons, followed by the username and the server name (joined with an @ sign), another separator colon, and finally the path to the repository directory on the server.

Let's look at the **pserver** access method, which stands for "password-authenticated server":

```
floss$ cvs -d :pserver:jrandom@cvs.foobar.com:/usr/local/cvs login
(Logging in to jrandom@cvs.foobar.com)
CVS password: (enter your CVS password here)
floss$
```

The long repository path following **-d** told CVS to use the **pserver** access method, with the username **jrandom**, on the server **cvs.foobar.com**, which has a CVS repository in **/usr/local/ cvs**. There's no requirement that the hostname be "cvs.something.com," by the way; that's a common convention, but it could just as easily have been:

```
floss$ cvs -d :pserver:jrandom@fish.foobar.org:/usr/local/cvs command
```

The command actually run was **login**, which verifies that you are authorized to work with this repository. It prompts for a password, then contacts the server to verify the password. Following Unix custom, **cvs login** returns silently if the login succeeds; it shows an error message if it fails (for instance, because the password is incorrect).

You only have to log in once from your local machine to a given CVS server. After a successful login, CVS stores the password in your home directory, in a file called .cvspass. It consults that file every time a repository is contacted via the **pserver** method, so you only have to run **login** the first time you access a given CVS server from a particular client machine. Of course, you can rerun **cvs login** anytime if the password changes.

pserver is currently the only access method requiring an initial login like this; with the others, you can start running regular CVS commands immediately.

Once you've stored the authentication information in your .cvspass file, you can run other CVS commands using the same command-line syntax:

```
floss$ cvs -d :pserver:jrandom@cvs.foobar.com:/usr/local/cvs command
```

Getting **pserver** to work in Windows may require an extra step. Windows doesn't have the Unix concept of a home directory, so CVS doesn't know where to put the .cvspass file. You'll have to specify a location. It's normal to designate the root of the C: drive as the home directory:

```
C:\WINDOWS> set HOME=C:
C:\WINDOWS> cvs -d :pserver:jrandom@cvs.foobar.com:/usr/local/cvs login
(Logging in to jrandom@cvs.foobar.com)
CVS password: (enter password here)
C:\WINDOWS>
```

Any folder in the file system will suffice. You may want to avoid network drives, though, because the contents of your .cvspass file would then be visible to anyone with access to the drive.

In addition to **pserver**, CVS supports the **ext** method (which uses an external connection program, such as rsh or ssh), **kserver** (for the Kerberos security system version 4), and **gserver** (which uses the GSSAPI, or Generic Security Services API, and also handles Kerberos versions 5 and higher). These methods are similar to **pserver**, but each has its own idiosyncrasies.

Of these, the **ext** method is probably the most commonly used. If you can log into the server with rsh or ssh, you can use the **ext** method. You can test it like this:

```
floss$ rsh -l jrandom cvs.foobar.com
Password: enter your login password here
```
Okay, let's assume you successfully logged in and logged out of the server with rsh, so now you're back on the original client machine:

```
floss$ CVS_RSH=rsh; export CVS_RSH
floss$ cvs -d :ext:jrandom@cvs.foobar.com:/usr/local/cvs command
```

The first line sets (in Unix Bourne shell syntax) the **CVS_RSH** environment variable to **rsh**, which tells CVS to use the rsh program to connect. The second line can be any CVS command; you will be prompted for your password so CVS can log into the server.

If you're in C shell rather than in Bourne shell, try this:

```
floss% setenv CVS_RSH rsh
```

and for Windows, try this:

```
C:\WINDOWS> set CVS_RSH=rsh
```

The rest of the tour will use the Bourne syntax; translate for your environment as necessary.

To use ssh (the Secure Shell) instead of rsh, just set the **CVS_RSH** variable appropriately:

```
C:\WINDOWS> CVS_RSH=ssh; export CVS_RSH
```

Don't get thrown by the fact that the variable's name is **CVS_RSH** but you're setting its value to **ssh**. There are historical reasons for this (the catch-all Unix excuse, I know). **CVS_RSH** can point to the name of any program capable of logging you into the remote server, running commands, and receiving their output. After rsh, ssh is probably the most common such program, although there are probably others. Note that this program must not modify its data stream in any way. This disqualifies the Windows NT rsh, because it converts (or attempts to convert) between the DOS and Unix line-ending conventions. You'd have to get some other rsh for Windows or use a different access method.

The **gserver** and **kserver** methods are not used as often as the others and are not covered here. They're quite similar to what we've covered so far; see the Cederqvist for details.

If you only use one repository and don't want to type *-d repos* each time, just set the **CVSROOT** environment variable (which perhaps should have been named **CVSREPOS**, but it's too late to change that now):

```
floss$ CVSROOT=/usr/local/cvs
floss$ export CVSROOT
floss$ echo $CVSROOT
/usr/local/cvs
floss$
```

or maybe

```
floss$ CVSROOT=:pserver:jrandom@cvs.foobar.com:/usr/local/cvs
floss$ export CVSROOT
floss$ echo $CVSROOT
:pserver:jrandom@cvs.foobar.com:/usr/local/cvs
floss$
```

The rest of this tour assumes that you've set **CVSROOT** to point to your repository, so the examples will not show the -**d** option. If you need to access many different repositories, you should not set **CVSROOT** and should just use -**d** *repos* when you need to specify the repository.

Starting A New Project

If you're learning CVS in order to work on a project that's already under CVS control (that is, it is kept in a repository somewhere), you'll probably want to skip down to the next section, "Checking Out A Working Copy." On the other hand, if you want to take existing source code and put it into CVS, this is the section for you. Note that it still assumes you have access to an existing repository; see Chapter 4 if you need to set up a repository first.

Putting a new project into a CVS repository is known as *importing*. The CVS command, as you may have guessed, is

```
floss$ cvs import
```

except that it needs some more options (and needs to be in the right location) to succeed. First, go into the top-level directory of your project tree:

```
floss$ cd myproj
floss$ ls
README.txt   a-subdir/   b-subdir/   hello.c
floss$
```

This project has two files—README.txt and hello.c—in the top level, plus two sub-directories—a-subdir and b-subdir—plus some more files (not shown in the example) inside those subdirectories. When you import a project, CVS imports *everything* in the tree, starting from the current directory and working its way down. Therefore, you should make sure that the only files in the tree are ones you want to be permanent parts of the project. Any old backup files, scratch files, and so on should all be cleaned out.

The general syntax of an **import** command is

```
floss$ cvs import -m "log msg" projname vendortag releasetag
```

The -**m** flag (for *message*) is for specifying a short message describing the import. This will be the first log message for the entire project; every commit thereafter will also have its own log message. These messages are mandatory; if you don't give the -**m** flag, CVS automatically starts up an editor (by consulting the **EDITOR** environment variable) for you to type a log message in. After you save the log message and exit the editor, the **import** then continues.

The next argument is the project's name (we'll use "myproj"). This is the name under which you'll check out the project from the repository. (What actually happens is that a directory of that name gets created in the repository, but more on that in Chapter 4.) The name you choose now does not need to be the same as the name of the current directory, although in most cases it usually is.

The **vendortag** and **releasetag** arguments are a bit of bookkeeping for CVS. Don't worry about them now; it hardly matters what you use. In Chapter 6 you'll learn about the rare circumstances where they're significant. For now, we'll use a username and "start" for those arguments.

We're ready to run **import**:

```
floss$ cvs import -m "initial import into CVS" myproj jrandom start
N myproj/hello.c
N myproj/README.txt
cvs import: Importing /usr/local/cvs/myproj/a-subdir
N myproj/a-subdir/whatever.c
cvs import: Importing /usr/local/cvs/myproj/a-subdir/subsubdir
N myproj/a-subdir/subsubdir/fish.c
cvs import: Importing /usr/local/cvs/myproj/b-subdir
N myproj/b-subdir/random.c

No conflicts created by this import
floss$
```

Congratulations! If you ran that command (or something similar), you've finally done something that affects the repository.

Reading over the output of the **import** command, you'll notice that CVS precedes each filename with a single letter—in this case, "N" for "new file." The use of a single letter on the left to indicate the status of a file is a general pattern in CVS command output. We'll see it later in checkout and update as well.

You might think that, having just imported the project, you can start working in the tree immediately. This is not the case, however. The current directory tree is still not a CVS working copy. It was the source for the **import** command, true, but it wasn't magically changed into a CVS working copy merely by virtue of having been imported. To get a working copy, you need to check one out from the repository.

First, though, you might want to archive the current project tree. The reason is that once the sources are in CVS, you don't want to confuse yourself by accidentally editing copies that aren't in version control (because those changes won't become part of the project's history). You want to do all of your editing in a working copy from now on. However, you also don't want to remove the imported tree entirely, because you haven't yet verified that the repository actually has the files. Of course, you can be 99.999 percent certain that it does because the **import** command returned with no error, but why take chances? Paranoia pays, as every programmer knows. Therefore, do something like this:

```
floss$ ls
README.txt  a-subdir/   b-subdir/   hello.c
floss$ cd ..
floss$ ls
myproj/
floss$ mv myproj was_myproj
floss$ ls
was_myproj/
floss$
```

There. You still have the original files, but they're clearly named as an obsolete version, so they won't be in the way when you get a real working copy. Now you're ready to check out.

Checking Out A Working Copy

The command to check out a project is exactly what you think it is:

```
floss$ cvs checkout myproj
cvs checkout: Updating myproj
U myproj/README.txt
U myproj/hello.c
cvs checkout: Updating myproj/a-subdir
U myproj/a-subdir/whatever.c
cvs checkout: Updating myproj/a-subdir/subsubdir
U myproj/a-subdir/subsubdir/fish.c
cvs checkout: Updating myproj/b-subdir
U myproj/b-subdir/random.c

floss$ ls
myproj/       was_myproj/
floss$ cd myproj
floss$ ls
CVS/          README.txt a-subdir/   b-subdir/   hello.c
floss$
```

Behold—your first working copy! Its contents are exactly the same as what you imported, with the addition of a subdirectory named "CVS." That's where CVS stores version control information. Actually, each directory in the project has a CVS subdirectory:

```
floss$ ls a-subdir
CVS/          subsubdir/  whatever.c
floss$ ls a-subdir/subsubdir/
CVS/    fish.c
floss$ ls b-subdir
CVS/      random.c
```

The fact that CVS keeps its revision information in subdirectories named CVS means that your project can never contain subdirectories of its own named CVS. In practice, I've never heard of this being a problem.

Before editing any files, let's take a peek inside the black box:

```
floss$ cd CVS
floss$ ls
Entries      Repository   Root
floss$ cat Root
/usr/local/cvs
floss$ cat Repository
myproj
floss$
```

Nothing too mysterious there. The Root file points to repository, and the Repository file points to a project inside the repository. If that's a little confusing, let me explain.

There is a longstanding confusion about terminology in CVS. The word "repository" is used to refer to two different things. Sometimes, it means the root directory of a repository (for example, /usr/local/cvs), which can contain many projects; this is what the Root file refers to. But other times, it means one particular project-specific subdirectory *within* a repository root (for example, /usr/local/cvs/myproj, /usr/local/cvs/yourproj, or /usr/local/cvs/fish). The Repository file inside a CVS subdirectory takes the latter meaning.

In this book, "repository" generally means Root (that is, the top-level repository), although it may occasionally be used to mean a project-specific subdirectory. If the intended sense can't be figured out from the context, there will be clarifying text.

Note that the Repository file may sometimes contain an absolute path to the project name instead of a relative path. This can make it slightly redundant with the Root file:

```
floss$ cd CVS
floss$ cat Root
:pserver:jrandom@cvs.foobar.com:/usr/local/cvs
floss$ cat Repository
/usr/local/cvs/myproj
floss$
```

The Entries file stores information about the individual files in the project. Each line deals with one file, and there are only lines for files or subdirectories in the immediate parent directory. Here's the top-level CVS/Entries file in myproj:

```
floss$ cat Entries
/README.txt/1.1.1.1/Sun Apr 18 18:18:22 1999//
/hello.c/1.1.1.1/Sun Apr 18 18:18:22 1999//
D/a-subdir////
D/b-subdir////
```

The format of each line is

```
/filename/revision number/last modification date//
```

and the directory lines are prefixed with "D." (CVS doesn't really keep a change history for directories, so the fields for revision number and datestamp are empty.)

The datestamps record the date and time of the last update (in Universal Time, not local time) of the files in the working copy. That way, CVS can easily tell whether a file has been modified since the last **checkout**, **update**, or **commit**. If the file system timestamp differs from the timestamp in the CVS/Entries file, CVS knows (without even having to consult the repository) that the file was probably modified.

If you take a look at the CVS/* files in one of the subdirectories

```
floss$ cd a-subdir/CVS
floss$ cat Root
/usr/local/cvs
floss$ cat Repository
myproj/a-subdir
floss$ cat Entries
/whatever.c/1.1.1.1/Sun Apr 18 18:18:22 1999//
D/subsubdir////
floss$
```

you can see that the root repository has not changed, but the Repository file spells out the location of this subdirectory of the project, and the Entries file contains different lines.

Immediately after import, the revision number of every file in the project is shown as 1.1.1.1. This initial revision number is a bit of a special case, so we won't examine it in detail just yet; we'll take a closer look at revision numbers after we've committed some changes.

Version Vs. Revision

The internal revision number that CVS keeps for each file is unrelated to the version number of the software product of which the files are part. For example, you may have a project composed of three files, whose internal revision numbers on May 3, 1999, were 1.2, 1.7, and 2.48. On that day, you package up a new release of the software and release it as SlickoSoft Version 3. This is purely a marketing decision and doesn't affect the CVS revisions at all. The CVS revision numbers are invisible to your customers (unless you give them repository access); the only publicly visible number is the "3" in Version 3. You could have called it Version 1729 as far as CVS is concerned—the version number (or "release" number) has nothing to do with CVS's internal change tracking.

To avoid confusion, I'll use the word "revision" to refer exclusively to the internal revision numbers of files under CVS control. I may still call CVS a "version control system," however, because "revision control system" just sounds too awkward.

Making A Change

The project as it stands doesn't do much. Here are the contents of hello.c:

```
floss$ cat hello.c
#include <stdio.h>

void
main ()
{
    printf ("Hello, world!\n");
}
```

Let's make the first change to the project since importing it; we'll add the line

```
printf ("Goodbye, world!\n");
```

right after the **Hello, world!**. Invoke your favorite editor and make the change:

```
floss$ emacs hello.c
  ...
```

This was a fairly simple change, one where you're not likely to forget what you did. But in a larger, more complex project, it's quite possible you may edit a file, be interrupted by something else, and return several days later and be unable to remember exactly what you did, or even to remember if you changed anything at all. Which brings us to our first "CVS Saves Your Life" situation: comparing your working copy against the repository.

Finding Out What You (And Others) Did: **update** And **diff**

Previously, I've talked about updating as a way of bringing changes down from the repository into your working copy—that is, as a way of getting other people's changes. However, **update** is really a bit more complex; it compares the overall state of the working copy with the state of the project in the repository. Even if nothing in the repository has changed since checkout, something in the working copy may have, and **update** will show that, too:

```
floss$ cvs update
cvs update: Updating .
M hello.c
cvs update: Updating a-subdir
cvs update: Updating a-subdir/subsubdir
cvs update: Updating b-subdir
```

The **M** next to **hello.c** means the file has been modified since it was last checked out, and the modifications have not yet been committed to the repository.

Sometimes, merely knowing which files you've edited is all you need. However, if you want a more detailed look at the changes, you can get a full report in **diff** format. The **diff** command compares the possibly modified files in the working copy to their counterparts in the repository and displays any differences:

```
floss$ cvs diff
cvs diff: Diffing .
Index: hello.c
===================================================================
RCS file: /usr/local/cvs/myproj/hello.c,v
retrieving revision 1.1.1.1
diff -r1.1.1.1 hello.c
6a7
>     printf ("Goodbye, world!\n");
cvs diff: Diffing a-subdir
cvs diff: Diffing a-subdir/subsubdir
cvs diff: Diffing b-subdir
```

That's helpful, if a bit obscure, but there's still a lot of cruft in the output. For starters, you can ignore most of the first few lines. They just name the repository file and give the number of the last checked-in revision. These are useful pieces of information under other circumstances (we'll look more closely at them later), but you don't need them when you're just trying to get a sense of what changes have been made in the working copy.

A more serious impediment to reading the **diff** is that CVS is announcing its entry as it goes into each directory during the update. This can be useful during long updates on large projects, as it gives you a sense of how much longer the command will take, but right now it's just getting in the way of reading the **diff**. Let's tell CVS to be quiet about where it's working, with the **-Q** global option:

```
floss$ cvs -Q diff
Index: hello.c
===================================================================
RCS file: /usr/local/cvs/myproj/hello.c,v
retrieving revision 1.1.1.1
diff -r1.1.1.1 hello.c
6a7
>     printf ("Goodbye, world!\n");
```

Better—at least some of the cruft is gone. However, the **diff** is still hard to read. It's telling you that at line 6, a new line was added (that is, what became line 7), whose contents were:

```
printf ("Goodbye, world!\n");
```

The preceding ">" in the **diff** tells you that this line is present in the newer version of the file but not in the older one.

The format could be made even more readable, however. Most people find "context" **diff** format easier to read because it displays a few lines of context on either side of a change. Context **diff**s are generated by passing the **-c** flag to **diff**:

```
floss$ cvs -Q diff -c
Index: hello.c
===================================================================
RCS file: /usr/local/cvs/myproj/hello.c,v
retrieving revision 1.1.1.1
diff -c -r1.1.1.1 hello.c
*** hello.c     1999/04/18 18:18:22     1.1.1.1
--- hello.c     1999/04/19 02:17:07
***************
*** 4,7 ****
---4,8 --
  main ()
  {
    printf ("Hello, world!\n");
+   printf ("Goodbye, world!\n");
  }
```

Now *that's* clarity! Even if you're not used to reading context **diff**s, a glance at the preceding output will probably make it obvious what happened: a new line was added (the **+** in the first column signifies an added line) between the line that prints **Hello, world!** and the final curly brace.

We don't need to be able to read context **diff**s perfectly (that's **patch**'s job), but it's worth taking the time to acquire at least a passing familiarity with the format. The first two lines (after the introductory cruft) are

```
*** hello.c      1999/04/18 18:18:22      1.1.1.1
--- hello.c      1999/04/19 02:17:07
```

and they tell you what is being **diff**ed against what. In this case, revision 1.1.1.1 of hello.c is being compared against a modified version of the same file (thus, there's no revision number for the second line, because only the working copy's changes haven't been committed to the repository yet). The lines of asterisks and dashes identify sections farther down in the **diff**. Later on, a line of asterisks, with a line number range embedded, precedes a section from the original file. Then a line of dashes, with a new and potentially different line number range embedded, precedes a section from the modified file. These sections are organized into contrasting pairs (known as "hunks"), one side from the old file and the other side from the new.

Our **diff** has one hunk:

```
***************
*** 4,7 ****
--- 4,8 --
  main ()
  {
    printf ("Hello, world!\n");
+   printf ("Goodbye, world!\n");
  }
```

The first section of the hunk is empty, meaning that no material was removed from the original file. The second section shows that, in the corresponding place in the new file, one line has been added; it's marked with a "+". (When **diff** quotes excerpts from files, it reserves the first two columns on the left for special codes, such as "+" so the entire excerpt appears to be indented by two spaces. This extra indentation is stripped off when the **diff** is applied, of course.)

The line number ranges show the hunk's coverage, including context lines. In the original file, the hunk was in lines 4 through 7; in the new file, it's lines 4 through 8 (because a line has been added). Note that the **diff** didn't need to show any material from the original file because nothing was removed; it just showed the range and moved on to the second half of the hunk.

Here's another context **diff**, from an actual project of mine:

```
floss$ cvs -Q diff -c
Index: cvs2cl.pl
===================================================================
RCS file: /usr/local/cvs/kfogel/code/cvs2cl/cvs2cl.pl,v
retrieving revision 1.76
diff -c -r1.76 cvs2cl.pl
```

```
*** cvs2cl.pl   1999/04/13 22:29:44    1.76
--- cvs2cl.pl   1999/04/19 05:41:37
***************
*** 212,218 ****
        # can contain uppercase and lowercase letters, digits, '-',
        # and '_'. However, it's not our place to enforce that, so
        # we'll allow anything CVS hands us to be a tag:
!       /^\s([^:]+): ([0=9.]+)$/;
        push (@{$symbolic_names{$2}}, $1);
      }
    }
-- 212,218 --
        # can contain uppercase and lowercase letters, digits, '-',
        # and '_'. However, it's not our place to enforce that, so
        # we'll allow anything CVS hands us to be a tag:
!       /^\s([^:]+): ([\d.]+)$/;
        push (@{$symbolic_names{$2}}, $1);
      }
    }
```

The exclamation point shows that the marked line differs between the old and new files. Since there are no "+" or "-" signs, we know that the total number of lines in the file has remained the same.

Here's one more context diff from the smae project, slightly more complex this time:

```
floss$ cvs -Q diff -c
Index: cvs2cl.pl
===================================================================
RCS file: /usr/local/cvs/kfogel/code/cvs2cl/cvs2cl.pl,v
retrieving revision 1.76
diff -c -r1.76 cvs2cl.pl
*** cvs2cl.pl   1999/04/13 22:29:44    1.76
--- cvs2cl.pl   1999/04/19 05:58:51
***************
*** 207,217 ****
  }
        else    # we're looking at a tag name, so parse & store it
        {
-         # According to the Cederqvist manual, in node "Tags", "Tag
-         # names must start with an uppercase or lowercase letter and
-         # can contain uppercase and lowercase letters, digits, '-',
-         # and '_'. However, it's not our place to enforce that, so
-         # we'll allow anything CVS hands us to be a tag:
          /^\s([^:]+): ([0-9.]+)$/;
          push (@{$symbolic_names{$2}}, $1);
```

```
        }
— 207,212 —
***************
*** 223,228 ****
--- 218,225 --
        if (/^revision (\d\.[0-9.]+)$/) {
          $revision = "$1";
        }
+
+       # This line was added, I admit, solely for the sake of a diff example.

        # If have file name but not time and author, and see date or
        # author, then grab them:
```

This **diff** has two hunks. In the first, five lines were removed (these lines are only shown in the first section of the hunk, and the second section's line count shows that it has five fewer lines). An unbroken line of asterisks forms the boundary between hunks, and in the second hunk we see that two lines have been added: a blank line and a pointless comment. Note how the line numbers compensate for the effect of the previous hunk. In the original file, the second hunk's range of the area was lines 223 through 228; in the new file, because of the deletion that took place in the *first* hunk, the range is in lines 218 through 225.

Congratulations, you are probably now as expert as you'll ever need to be at reading **diff**s.

CVS And Implied Arguments

In each of the CVS commands so far, you may have noticed that no files were specified on the command line. We ran

```
floss$ cvs diff
```

instead of

```
floss$ cvs diff hello.c
```

and

```
floss$ cvs update
```

instead of

```
floss$ cvs update hello.c
```

The principle at work here is that if you don't name any files, CVS acts on all files for which the command could possibly be appropriate. This even includes files in subdirectories beneath the current directory; CVS automatically descends from the current directory through every subdirectory in the tree. For example, if you modified b-subdir/random.c and a-subdir/subsubdir/fish.c, running **update** may result in this:

```
floss$ cvs update
cvs update: Updating .
M hello.c
cvs update: Updating a-subdir
cvs update: Updating a-subdir/subsubdir
M a-subdir/subsubdir/fish.c
cvs update: Updating b-subdir
M b-subdir/random.c
floss$
```

or better yet:

```
floss$ cvs -q update
M hello.c
M a-subdir/subsubdir/fish.c
M b-subdir/random.c
floss$
```

Note

*The **-q** flag is a less emphatic version of **-Q**. Had we used **-Q**, the command would have printed out nothing at all, because the modification notices are considered nonessential informational messages. Using the lowercase **-q** is less strict; it suppresses the messages we probably don't want, while allowing certain, more useful messages to pass through.*

You can also name specific files for the update:

```
floss$ cvs update hello.c b-subdir/random.c
M hello.c
M b-subdir/random.c
floss$
```

and CVS will only examine those files, ignoring all others.

In truth, it's more common to run **update** without restricting it to certain files. In most situations, you'll want to update the entire directory tree at once. Remember, the updates we're doing here only show that some files have been locally modified, because nothing has changed yet in the repository. When other people are working on the project with you, there's always the chance that running **update** will pull some new changes down from the repository and incorporate them into your local files. In that case, you may find it slightly more useful to name which files you want updated.

The same principle can be applied to other CVS commands. For example, with **diff**, you can choose to view the changes one file at a time

```
floss$ cvs diff -c b-subdir/random.c
Index: b-subdir/random.c
===================================================================
RCS file: /usr/local/cvs/myproj/b-subdir/random.c,v
retrieving revision 1.1.1.1
diff -c -r1.1.1.1 random.c
*** b-subdir/random.c    1999/04/18 18:18:22        1.1.1.1
--- b-subdir/random.c    1999/04/19 06:09:48
***************
*** 1 ****
! /* A completely empty C file. */
--- 1,8 --
! /* Print out a random number. */
!
! #include <stdio.h>
!
! void main ()
! {
!   printf ("a random number\n");
! }
```

or see all the changes at once (hang on to your seat, this is going to be a big **diff**):

```
floss$ cvs -Q diff -c
Index: hello.c
===================================================================
RCS file: /usr/local/cvs/myproj/hello.c,v
retrieving revision 1.1.1.1
diff -c -r1.1.1.1 hello.c
*** hello.c    1999/04/18 18:18:22        1.1.1.1
--- hello.c    1999/04/19 02:17:07
***************
*** 4,7 ****
--- 4,8 --
  main ()
  {
    printf ("Hello, world!\n");
+   printf ("Goodbye, world!\n");
  }
Index: a-subdir/subsubdir/fish.c
===================================================================
RCS file: /usr/local/cvs/myproj/a-subdir/subsubdir/fish.c,v
```

```
retrieving revision 1.1.1.1
diff -c -r1.1.1.1 fish.c
*** a-subdir/subsubdir/fish.c    1999/04/18 18:18:22      1.1.1.1
--- a-subdir/subsubdir/fish.c    1999/04/19 06:08:50
***************
*** 1 ****
! /* A completely empty C file. */
--- 1,8 --
! #include <stdio.h>
!
! void main ()
! {
!   while (1) {
!     printf ("fish\n");
!   }
! }
Index: b-subdir/random.c
===================================================================
RCS file: /usr/local/cvs/myproj/b-subdir/random.c,v
retrieving revision 1.1.1.1
diff -c -r1.1.1.1 random.c
*** b-subdir/random.c    1999/04/18 18:18:22      1.1.1.1
--- b-subdir/random.c    1999/04/19 06:09:48
***************
*** 1 ****
! /* A completely empty C file. */
--- 1,8 --
! /* Print out a random number. */
!
! #include <stdio.h>
!
! void main ()
! {
!   printf ("a random number\n");
! }
```

Anyway, as you can see from these **diff**s, this project is clearly ready for prime time. Let's commit the changes to the repository.

Committing

The **commit** command sends modifications to the repository. If you don't name any files, a **commit** will send all changes to the repository; otherwise, you can pass the names of one or more files to be committed (other files would be ignored, in that case).

Here, we **commit** one file by name and two by inference:

```
floss$ cvs commit -m "print goodbye too" hello.c
Checking in hello.c;
/usr/local/cvs/myproj/hello.c,v  <--  hello.c
new revision: 1.2; previous revision: 1.1
done
floss$ cvs commit -m "filled out C code"
cvs commit: Examining .
cvs commit: Examining a-subdir
cvs commit: Examining a-subdir/subsubdir
cvs commit: Examining b-subdir
Checking in a-subdir/subsubdir/fish.c;
/usr/local/cvs/myproj/a-subdir/subsubdir/fish.c,v  <--  fish.c
new revision: 1.2; previous revision: 1.1
done
Checking in b-subdir/random.c;
/usr/local/cvs/myproj/b-subdir/random.c,v  <--  random.c
new revision: 1.2; previous revision: 1.1
done
floss$
```

Take a moment to read over the output carefully. Most of what it says is pretty self-explanatory. One thing you may notice is that revision numbers have been incremented (as expected), but the original revisions are listed as 1.1 instead of 1.1.1.1 as we saw in the Entries file earlier.

There is an explanation for this discrepancy, but it's not very important. It concerns a special meaning that CVS attaches to revision 1.1.1.1. For most purposes, we can just say that files receive a revision number of 1.1 when imported, but the number is displayed—for reasons known only to CVS—as 1.1.1.1 in the Entries file, until the first **commit**.

Revision Numbers

Each file in a project has its own revision number. When a file is committed, the last portion of the revision number is incremented by one. Thus, at any given time, the various files comprising a project may have very different revision numbers. This just means that some files have been changed (committed) more often than others.

(You may be wondering, what's the point of the part to the left of the decimal point, if only the part on the right ever changes? Actually, although CVS never automatically increments the number on the left, that number can be incremented on request by a user. This is a rarely used feature, and we won't cover it in this tour.)

In the example project that we've been using, we just committed changes to three files. Each of those files is now revision 1.2, but the remaining files in the project are still revision

1.1. When you check out a project, you get each file at its highest revision so far. Here is what qsmith would see if he checked out myproj right now and looked at the revision numbers for the top-level directory:

```
paste$ cvs -q -d :pserver:qsmith@cvs.foobar.com:/usr/local/cvs co myproj
U myproj/README.txt
U myproj/hello.c
U myproj/a-subdir/whatever.c
U myproj/a-subdir/subsubdir/fish.c
U myproj/b-subdir/random.c
paste$ cd myproj/CVS
paste$ cat Entries
/README.txt/1.1.1.1/Sun Apr 18 18:18:22 1999//
/hello.c/1.2/Mon Apr 19 06:35:15 1999//
D/a-subdir////
D/b-subdir////
paste$
```

The file hello.c (among others) is now at revision 1.2, while README.txt is still at the initial revision (revision 1.1.1.1, also known as 1.1).

If he adds the line

```
printf ("between hello and goodbye\n");
```

to hello.c and **commit** it, the file's revision number will be incremented once more:

```
paste$ cvs ci -m "added new middle line"
cvs commit: Examining .
cvs commit: Examining a-subdir
cvs commit: Examining a-subdir/subsubdir
cvs commit: Examining b-subdir
Checking in hello.c;
/usr/local/cvs/myproj/hello.c,v  <--  hello.c
new revision: 1.3; previous revision: 1.2
done
paste$
```

Now hello.c is revision 1.3, fish.c and random.c still are revision 1.2, and every other file is revision 1.1.

Note

*Note that the command was given as **cvs ci** instead of **cvs commit**. Most CVS commands have short forms, to make typing easier. For **checkout**, **update**, and **commit**, the abbreviated versions are **co**, **up**, and **ci**, respectively. You can get a list of all of the short forms by running the command **cvs --help-synonyms**.*

You can usually ignore a file's revision number. In most situations, the numbers are just internal bookkeeping that CVS handles automatically. However, being able to find and compare revision numbers is extremely handy when you have to retrieve (or **diff** against) an earlier copy of a file.

Examining the Entries file isn't the only way to discover a revision number. You can also use the **status** command

```
paste$ cvs status hello.c
=================================================================
File: hello.c           Status: Up-to-date

   Working revision:    1.3     Tue Apr 20 02:34:42 1999
   Repository revision: 1.3     /usr/local/cvs/myproj/hello.c,v
   Sticky Tag:          (none)
   Sticky Date:         (none)
   Sticky Options:      (none)
```

which, if invoked without any files being named, shows the status of every file in the project:

```
paste$ cvs status
cvs status: Examining.
=================================================================
File: README.txt        Status: Up-to-date

   Working revision:    1.1.1.1 Sun Apr 18 18:18:22 1999
   Repository revision: 1.1.1.1 /usr/local/cvs/myproj/README.txt,v
   Sticky Tag:          (none)
   Sticky Date:         (none)
   Sticky Options:      (none)


=================================================================
File: hello.c           Status: Up-to-date

   Working revision:    1.3     Tue Apr 20 02:34:42 1999
   Repository revision: 1.3     /usr/local/cvs/myproj/hello.c,v
   Sticky Tag:          (none)
   Sticky Date:         (none)
   Sticky Options:      (none)

cvs status: Examining a-subdir
=================================================================
File: whatever.c        Status: Up-to-date

   Working revision:    1.1.1.1 Sun Apr 18 18:18:22 1999
```

```
Repository revision: 1.1.1.1 /usr/local/cvs/myproj/a-subdir/whatever.c,v
Sticky Tag:          (none)
Sticky Date:         (none)
Sticky Options:      (none)

cvs status: Examining a-subdir/subsubdir
===============================================================================
File: fish.c            Status: Up-to-date

   Working revision:    1.2        Mon Apr 19 06:35:27 1999
   Repository revision: 1.2        /usr/local/cvs/myproj/
                                   a-subdir/subsubdir/fish.c,v
   Sticky Tag:          (none)
   Sticky Date:         (none)
   Sticky Options:      (none)

cvs status: Examining b-subdir
===============================================================================
File: random.c          Status: Up-to-date

   Working revision:    1.2        Mon Apr 19 06:35:27 1999
   Repository revision: 1.2        /usr/local/cvs/myproj/b-subdir/random.c,v
   Sticky Tag:          (none)
   Sticky Date:         (none)
   Sticky Options:      (none)

paste$
```

Just ignore the parts of that output that you don't understand. In fact, that's generally good advice with CVS. Often, the one little bit of information you're looking for will be accompanied by reams of information that you don't care about at all, and maybe don't even understand. This situation is normal. Just pick out what you need, and don't worry about the rest.

In the previous example, the parts we care about are the first three lines (not counting the blank line) of each file's status output. The first line is the most important; it tells you the file's name, and its status in the working copy. All of the files are currently in sync with the repository, so they all say, **Up-to-date**. However, if random.c has been modified but not committed, it might read like this:

```
===============================================================================
File: random.c          Status: Locally Modified

   Working revision:    1.2        Mon Apr 19 06:35:27 1999
   Repository revision: 1.2        /usr/local/cvs/myproj/b-subdir/random.c,v
   Sticky Tag:          (none)
```

```
Sticky Date:        (none)
Sticky Options:     (none)
```

The **Working revision** and **Repository revision** tell you whether the file is out of sync with the repository. Returning to our original working copy (jrandom's copy, which hasn't seen the new change to hello.c yet), we see:

```
floss$ cvs status hello.c
===============================================================
File: hello.c           Status: Needs Patch

    Working revision:    1.2      Mon Apr 19 02:17:07 1999
    Repository revision: 1.3      /usr/local/cvs/myproj/hello.c,v
    Sticky Tag:          (none)
    Sticky Date:         (none)
    Sticky Options:      (none)

floss$
```

This tells us that someone has committed a change to hello.c, bringing the repository copy to revision 1.3, but that this working copy is still on revision 1.2. The line **Status: Needs Patch** means that the next **update** will retrieve those changes from the repository and "patch" them into the working copy's file.

Let's pretend for the moment that we don't know anything about qsmith's change to hello.c, so we don't run **status** or **update**. Instead, we just start editing the file, making a slightly different change at the same location. This brings us to our first conflict.

Detecting And Resolving Conflicts

Detecting a conflict is easy enough. When you run **update**, CVS tells you, in no uncertain terms, that there's a conflict. But first, let's create the conflict. We edit hello.c to insert the line

```
printf ("this change will conflict\n");
```

right where qsmith committed this:

```
printf ("between hello and goodbye\n");
```

At this point, the status of our copy of hello.c is

```
floss$ cvs status hello.c
===============================================================
File: hello.c           Status: Needs Merge
```

```
Working revision:     1.2      Mon Apr 19 02:17:07 1999
Repository revision: 1.3      /usr/local/cvs/myproj/hello.c,v
Sticky Tag:           (none)
Sticky Date:          (none)
Sticky Options:       (none)

floss$
```

meaning that there are changes both in the repository and the working copy, and these changes need to be merged. (CVS isn't aware that the changes will conflict, because we haven't run **update** yet.) When we do the update, we see this:

```
floss$ cvs update hello.c
RCS file: /usr/local/cvs/myproj/hello.c,v
retrieving revision 1.2
retrieving revision 1.3
Merging differences between 1.2 and 1.3 into hello.c
rcsmerge: warning: conflicts during merge
cvs update: conflicts found in hello.c
C hello.c
floss$
```

The last line of output is the giveaway. The **C** in the left margin next to the filename indicates that changes have been merged, but that they conflict. The contents of hello.c now shows both changes:

```
#include <stdio.h>

void
main ()
{
  printf ("Hello, world!\n");
<<<<<<< hello.c
  printf ("this change will conflict\n");
=======
  printf ("between hello and goodbye\n");
>>>>>>> 1.3
  printf ("Goodbye, world!\n");
}
```

Conflicts are always shown delimited by *conflict markers*, in the following format:

```
<<<<<<< (filename)
  the uncommitted changes in the working copy
  blah blah blah
=======
```

```
     the new changes that came from the repository
     blah blah blah
     and so on
>>>>>>> (latest revision number in the repository)
```

The Entries file also shows that the file is in a halfway state at the moment:

```
floss$ cat CVS/Entries
/README.txt/1.1.1.1/Sun Apr 18 18:18:22 1999//
D/a-subdir////
D/b-subdir////
/hello.c/1.3/Result of merge+Tue Apr 20 03:59:09 1999//
floss$
```

The way to resolve the conflict is to edit the file so that it contains whatever text is appropriate, removing the conflict markers in the process, and then to commit. This doesn't necessarily mean choosing one change over another; you could decide neither change is sufficient and rewrite the conflicting section (or indeed the whole file) completely. In this case, we'll adjust in favor of the first change, but with capitalization and punctuation slightly different from qsmith's:

```
floss$ emacs hello.c
  (make the edits...)
floss$ cat hello.c
#include <stdio.h>

void
main ()
{
  printf ("Hello, world!\n");
  printf ("BETWEEN HELLO AND GOODBYE.\n");
  printf ("Goodbye, world!\n");
}
floss$ cvs ci -m "adjusted middle line"
cvs commit: Examining .
cvs commit: Examining a-subdir
cvs commit: Examining a-subdir/subsubdir
cvs commit: Examining b-subdir
Checking in hello.c;
/usr/local/cvs/myproj/hello.c,v  <-  hello.c
new revision: 1.4; previous revision: 1.3
done
floss$
```

Finding Out Who Did What (Browsing Log Messages)

By now, the project has undergone several changes. If you're trying to get an overview of what has happened so far, you don't necessarily want to examine every **diff** in detail. Browsing the log messages would be ideal, and you can accomplish this with the **log** command:

```
floss$ cvs log
(pages upon pages of output omitted)
```

The log output tends to be a bit verbose. Let's look at the log messages for just one file:

```
floss$ cvs log hello.c
RCS file: /usr/local/cvs/myproj/hello.c,v
Working file: hello.c
head: 1.4
branch:
locks: strict
access list:
symbolic names:
        start: 1.1.1.1
        jrandom: 1.1.1
keyword substitution: kv
total revisions: 5;     selected revisions: 5
description:
----------------
revision 1.4
date: 1999/04/20 04:14:37;  author: jrandom;  state: Exp;  lines: +1 -1
adjusted middle line
----------------
revision 1.3
date: 1999/04/20 02:30:05;  author: qsmith;  state: Exp;  lines: +1 -0
added new middle line
----------------
revision 1.2
date: 1999/04/19 06:35:15;  author: jrandom;  state: Exp;  lines: +1 -0
print goodbye too
----------------
revision 1.1
date: 1999/04/18 18:18:22;  author: jrandom;  state: Exp;
branches:  1.1.1;
Initial revision
----------------
revision 1.1.1.1
date: 1999/04/18 18:18:22;  author: jrandom;  state: Exp;  lines: +0 -0
initial import into CVS
================================================================
floss$
```

As usual, there's a lot of information at the top that you can just ignore. The good stuff comes after each line of dashes, in a format that is self-explanatory.

When many files are sent in the same **commit**, they all share the same log message; a fact that can be useful in tracing changes. For example, remember back when we committed fish.c and random.c simultaneously? It was done like this:

```
floss$ cvs commit -m "filled out C code"
Checking in a-subdir/subsubdir/fish.c;
/usr/local/cvs/myproj/a-subdir/subsubdir/fish.c,v  <-  fish.c
new revision: 1.2; previous revision: 1.1
done
Checking in b-subdir/random.c;
/usr/local/cvs/myproj/b-subdir/random.c,v  <-  random.c
new revision: 1.2; previous revision: 1.1
done
floss$
```

The effect of this was to **commit** both files with the same log message: "Filled out C code." (As it happened, both files started at revision 1.1 and went to 1.2, but that's just a coincidence. If random.c had been at revision 1.29, it would have moved to 1.30 with this commit, and its revision 1.30 would have had the same log message as fish.c's revision 1.2.)

When you run **cvs log** on them, you'll see the shared message:

```
floss$ cvs log a-subdir/subsubdir/fish.c b-subdir/random.c

RCS file: /usr/local/cvs/myproj/a-subdir/subsubdir/fish.c,v
Working file: a-subdir/subsubdir/fish.c
head: 1.2
branch:
locks: strict
access list:
symbolic names:
        start: 1.1.1.1
        jrandom: 1.1.1
keyword substitution: kv
total revisions: 3;     selected revisions: 3
description:
---------------
revision 1.2
date: 1999/04/19 06:35:27;  author: jrandom;  state: Exp;  lines: +8 -1
filled out C code
---------------
```

```
revision 1.1
date: 1999/04/18 18:18:22;  author: jrandom;  state: Exp;
branches:  1.1.1;
Initial revision
---------------
revision 1.1.1.1
date: 1999/04/18 18:18:22;  author: jrandom;  state: Exp;  lines: +0 -0
initial import into CVS
=================================================================
RCS file: /usr/local/cvs/myproj/b-subdir/random.c,v
Working file: b-subdir/random.c
head: 1.2
branch:
locks: strict
access list:
symbolic names:
        start: 1.1.1.1
        jrandom: 1.1.1
keyword substitution: kv
total revisions: 3;     selected revisions: 3
description:
---------------
revision 1.2
date: 1999/04/19 06:35:27;  author: jrandom;  state: Exp;  lines: +8 -1
filled out C code
---------------
revision 1.1
date: 1999/04/18 18:18:22;  author: jrandom;  state: Exp;
branches:  1.1.1;
Initial revision
---------------
revision 1.1.1.1
date: 1999/04/18 18:18:22;  author: jrandom;  state: Exp;  lines: +0 -0
initial import into CVS
=================================================================
floss$
```

From this output, you'll know that the two revisions were part of the same **commit** (the fact that the timestamps on the two revisions are the same, or very close, is further evidence).

Browsing log messages is a good way to get a quick overview of what's been going on in a project or to find out what happened to a specific file at a certain time. There are also free tools available to convert raw **cvs log** output to more concise and readable formats (such as GNU ChangeLog style); we won't cover those tools in this tour, but they'll be introduced in Chapter 10.

Examining And Reverting Changes

Suppose that, in the course of browsing the logs, qsmith sees that jrandom made the most recent change to hello.c:

```
revision 1.4
date: 1999/04/20 04:14:37;  author: jrandom;  state: Exp;  lines: +1 -1
adjusted middle line
```

and wonders what jrandom did? In formal terms, the question that qsmith is asking is, "What's the difference between my revision (1.3) of hello.c, and jrandom's revision right after it (1.4)?" The way to find out is with the **diff** command, but this time by comparing two past revisions using the **-r** command option to specify both of them:

```
paste$ cvs diff -c -r 1.3 -r 1.4 hello.c
Index: hello.c
===================================================================
RCS file: /usr/local/cvs/myproj/hello.c,v
retrieving revision 1.3
retrieving revision 1.4
diff -c -r1.3 -r1.4
*** hello.c     1999/04/20 02:30:05     1.3
--- hello.c     1999/04/20 04:14:37     1.4
***************
*** 4,9 ****
  main ()
  {
    printf ("Hello, world!\n");
!   printf ("between hello and goodbye\n");
    printf ("Goodbye, world!\n");
  }
--- 4,9 --
  main ()
  {
    printf ("Hello, world!\n");
!   printf ("BETWEEN HELLO AND GOODBYE.\n");
    printf ("Goodbye, world!\n");
  }
paste$
```

The change is pretty clear, when viewed this way. Because the revision numbers are given in chronological order (usually a good idea), the **diff** shows them in order. If only one revision number is given, CVS uses the revision of the current working copy for the other.

When qsmith sees this change, he instantly decides he likes his way better and resolves to "undo"—that is, to step back by one revision.

However, this doesn't mean that he wants to lose his revision 1.4. Although, in an absolute technical sense, it's probably possible to achieve that effect in CVS, there's almost never any reason to do so. It's much preferable to keep revision 1.4 in the history and make a new revision 1.5 that looks exactly like 1.3. That way the **undo** event itself is part of the file's history.

The only question is, how can you retrieve the contents of revision 1.3 and put them into 1.5?

In this particular case, because the change is a very simple one, qsmith can probably just edit the file by hand to mirror revision 1.3 and then **commit**. However, if the changes are more complex (as they usually are in a real-life project), trying to re-create the old revision manually will be hopelessly error-prone. Therefore, we'll have qsmith use CVS to retrieve and recommit the older revision's contents.

There are two equally good ways to do this: the slow, plodding way and the fast, fancy way. We'll examine the slow, plodding way first.

The Slow Method Of Updating

This method involves passing the **-p** flag to **update**, in conjunction with **-r**. The **-p** option sends the contents of the named revision to standard output. By itself, this isn't terribly helpful; the contents of the file fly by on the display, leaving the working copy unchanged. However, by redirecting the standard output into the file, the file will now hold the contents of the older revision. It's just as though the file had been hand-edited into that state.

First, though, qsmith needs to get up to date with respect to the repository:

```
paste$ cvs update
cvs update: Updating .
U hello.c
cvs update: Updating a-subdir
cvs update: Updating a-subdir/subsubdir
cvs update: Updating b-subdir
paste$ cat hello.c
#include <stdio.h>

void
main ()
{
  printf ("Hello, world!\n");
  printf ("BETWEEN HELLO AND GOODBYE.\n");
  printf ("Goodbye, world!\n");
}
paste$
```

Next, he runs **update -p** to make sure that the revision 1.3 is the one he wants:

```
paste$ cvs update -p -r 1.3 hello.c
=================================================================
Checking out hello.c
RCS:  /usr/local/cvs/myproj/hello.c,v
VERS: 1.3
***************
#include <stdio.h>

void
main ()
{
  printf ("Hello, world!\n");
  printf ("between hello and goodbye\n");
  printf ("Goodbye, world!\n");
}
```

Oops, there are a few lines of cruft at the beginning. They aren't actually being sent to standard output, but rather to standard error, so they're harmless. Nevertheless, they make reading the output more difficult and can be suppressed with **-Q**:

```
paste$ cvs -Q update -p -r 1.3 hello.c
#include <stdio.h>

void
main ()
{
  printf ("Hello, world!\n");
  printf ("between hello and goodbye\n");
  printf ("Goodbye, world!\n");
}
paste$
```

There—that's exactly what qsmith was hoping to retrieve. The next step is to put that content into the working copy's file, using a Unix redirect (that's what the ">" does):

```
paste$ cvs -Q update -p -r 1.3 hello.c > hello.c
paste$ cvs update
cvs update: Updating .
M hello.c
cvs update: Updating a-subdir
cvs update: Updating a-subdir/subsubdir
cvs update: Updating b-subdir
paste$
```

Now when **update** is run, the file is listed as modified, which makes sense because its contents have changed. Specifically, it has the same content as the old revision 1.3 (not that

CVS is aware of its being identical to a previous revision—it just knows the file has been modified). If qsmith wants to make extra sure, he can do a **diff** to check:

```
paste$ cvs -Q diff -c
Index: hello.c
===================================================================
RCS file: /usr/local/cvs/myproj/hello.c,v
retrieving revision 1.4
diff -c -r1.4 hello.c
*** hello.c     1999/04/20 04:14:37     1.4
--- hello.c     1999/04/20 06:02:25
***************
*** 4,9 ****
  main ()
  {
    printf ("Hello, world!\n");
!   printf ("BETWEEN HELLO AND GOODBYE.\n");
    printf ("Goodbye, world!\n");
  }
--- 4,9 --
  main ()
  {
    printf ("Hello, world!\n");
!   printf ("between hello and goodbye\n");
    printf ("Goodbye, world!\n");
  }
paste$
```

Yes, that's exactly what he wanted: a pure reversion—in fact, it is the reverse of the **diff** he previously obtained. Satisfied, he commits:

```
paste$ cvs ci -m "reverted to 1.3 code"
cvs commit: Examining .
cvs commit: Examining a-subdir
cvs commit: Examining a-subdir/subsubdir
cvs commit: Examining b-subdir
Checking in hello.c;
/usr/local/cvs/myproj/hello.c,v  <-  hello.c
new revision: 1.5; previous revision: 1.4
done
paste$
```

The Fast Method Of Updating

The fast, fancy way of updating is to use the **-j** (for "join") flag to the **update** command. This flag is like **-r** in that it takes a revision number, and you can use up to two **-j**'s at once. CVS calculates the difference between the two named revisions and applies that difference as a patch to the file in question (so the order in which you give the revisions is important).

Thus, assuming qsmith's copy is up to date, he can just do this:

```
paste$ cvs update -j 1.4 -j 1.3 hello.c
RCS file: /usr/local/cvs/myproj/hello.c,v
retrieving revision 1.4
retrieving revision 1.3
Merging differences between 1.4 and 1.3 into hello.c
paste$ cvs update
cvs update: Updating .
M hello.c
cvs update: Updating a-subdir
cvs update: Updating a-subdir/subsubdir
cvs update: Updating b-subdir
paste$ cvs ci -m "reverted to 1.3 code" hello.c
Checking in hello.c;
/usr/local/cvs/myproj/hello.c,v  <--  hello.c
new revision: 1.5; previous revision: 1.4
done
paste$
```

When you only need to revert one file, there's not really much difference between the plodding and fast methods. Later in the book, you'll see how the fast method is much better for reverting multiple files at once. In the meantime, use whichever way you're more comfortable with.

Reverting Is Not A Substitute For Communication

In all likelihood, what qsmith did in our example was quite rude. When you're working on a real project with other people and you think that someone has committed a bad change, the first thing you should do is talk to him or her about it. Maybe there's a good reason for the change, or maybe he or she just didn't think things through. Either way, there's no reason to rush and revert. A full record of everything that happens is stored permanently in CVS, so you can always revert to a previous revision after consulting with whoever made the changes.

If you're a project maintainer facing a deadline or you feel you have the right and the need to revert the change unconditionally, then do so—but follow it immediately with an email to the author whose change was reverted, explaining why you did it and what needs to be fixed to recommit the change.

Other Useful CVS Commands

At this point, you should be pretty comfortable with basic CVS operation. I'll abandon the tour narrative and introduce a few more useful commands in summarized form.

Adding Files

Adding a file is a two-step process: First you run the **add** command on it, then **commit**. The file won't actually appear in the repository until **commit** is run:

```
floss$ cvs add newfile.c
cvs add: scheduling file 'newfile.c' for addition
cvs add: use 'cvs commit' to add this file permanently
floss$ cvs ci -m "added newfile.c" newfile.c
RCS file: /usr/local/cvs/myproj/newfile.c,v
done
Checking in newfile.c;
/usr/local/cvs/myproj/newfile.c,v  <- newfile.c
initial revision: 1.1
done
floss$
```

Adding Directories

Unlike adding a file, adding a new directory is done in one step; there's no need to do a **commit** afterwards:

```
floss$ mkdir c-subdir
floss$ cvs add c-subdir
Directory /usr/local/cvs/myproj/c-subdir added to the repository
floss$
```

If you look inside the new directory in the working copy, you'll see that a CVS subdirectory was created automatically by **add**:

```
floss$ ls c-subdir
CVS/
floss$ ls c-subdir/CVS
Entries      Repository   Root
floss$
```

Now you can add files (or new directories) inside it, as with any other working copy directory.

CVS And Binary Files

Until now, I've left unsaid the dirty little secret of CVS, which is that it doesn't handle binary files very well (well, there are other dirty little secrets, but this definitely counts as one of the dirtiest). It's not that CVS doesn't handle binaries at all; it does, just not with any great panache.

All the files we've been working with until now have been plain text files. CVS has some special tricks for text files. For example, when it's working between a Unix repository and a Windows or Macintosh working copy, it converts file line endings appropriately for each platform. For example, Unix convention is to use a linefeed (LF) only, whereas Windows expects a carriage return/linefeed (CRLF) sequence at the end of each line. Thus, the files in a working copy on a Windows machine will have CRLF endings, but a working copy of the same project on a Unix machine will have LF endings (the repository itself is always stored in LF format).

Another trick is that CVS detects special strings, known as *RCS keyword strings*, in text files and replaces them with revision information and other useful things. For example, if your file contains this string

```
$Revision$
```

CVS will expand on each **commit** to include the revision number. For example, it may get expanded to

```
$Revision: 1.3 $
```

CVS will keep that string up to date as the file is developed. (The various keyword strings are documented in Chapters 6 and 10.)

This string expansion is a very useful feature in text files, as it allows you to see the revision number or other information about a file while you're editing it. But what if the file is a JPG image? Or a compiled executable program? In those kinds of files, CVS could do some serious damage if it blundered around expanding any keyword string that it encountered. In a binary, such strings may even appear by coincidence.

Therefore, when you add a binary file, you have to tell CVS to turn off both keyword expansion and line-ending conversion. To do so, use **-kb**:

```
floss$ cvs add -kb filename
floss$ cvs ci -m "added blah" filename
  (etc)
```

Also, in some cases (such as text files that are likely to contain spurious keyword strings), you may wish to disable just the keyword expansion. That's done with **-ko**:

```
floss$ cvs add -ko filename
floss$ cvs ci -m "added blah" filename
  (etc)
```

(In fact, this chapter is one such document, because of the "$Revision$" example shown here.)

Note that you can't meaningfully run **cvs diff** on two revisions of a binary file. **Diff** uses a text-based algorithm that can only report whether two binary files differ, but not how they differ. Future versions of CVS may provide a way to **diff** binary files.

Removing Files

Removing a file is similar to adding one, except there's an extra step: You have to remove the file from the working copy first:

```
floss$ rm newfile.c
floss$ cvs remove newfile.c
cvs remove: scheduling 'newfile.c' for removal
cvs remove: use 'cvs commit' to remove this file permanently
floss$ cvs ci -m "removed newfile.c" newfile.c
Removing newfile.c;
/usr/local/cvs/myproj/newfile.c,v  <-  newfile.c
new revision: delete; previous revision: 1.1
done
floss$
```

Notice how, in the second and third commands, we name newfile.c explicitly even though it doesn't exist in the working copy anymore. Of course, in the **commit**, you don't absolutely need to name the file, as long as you don't mind the **commit** encompassing any other modifications that may have taken place in the working copy.

Removing Directories

As I said before, CVS doesn't really keep directories under version control. Instead, as a kind of cheap substitute, it offers certain odd behaviors that in most cases do the "right thing." One of these odd behaviors is that empty directories can be treated specially. If you want to remove a directory from a project, you first remove all the files in it

```
floss$ cd dir
floss$ rm file1 file2 file3
floss$ cvs remove file1 file2 file3
  (output omitted)
floss$ cvs ci -m "removed all files" file1 file2 file3
  (output omitted)
```

and then run **update** in the directory above it with the **-P** flag:

```
floss$ cd ..
```

```
floss$ cvs update -P
  (output omitted)
```

The **-P** option tells **update** to "prune" any empty directories—that is, to remove them from the working copy. Once that's done, the directory can be said to have been removed; all of its files are gone, and the directory itself is gone (from the working copy, at least, although there is actually still an empty directory in the repository).

An interesting counterpart to this behavior is that when you run a plain **update**, CVS does not automatically bring new directories from the repository into your working copy. There are a couple of different justifications for this, none really worth going into here. The short answer is that from time to time you should run **update** with the **-d** flag, telling it to bring down any new directories from the repository.

Renaming Files And Directories

Renaming a file is equivalent to creating it under the new name and removing it under the old. In Unix, the commands are:

```
floss$ cp oldname newname
floss$ rm oldname
```

Here's the equivalent in CVS:

```
floss$ mv oldname newname
floss$ cvs remove oldname
  (output omitted)
floss$ cvs add newname
  (output omitted)
floss$ cvs ci -m "renamed oldname to newname" oldname newname
  (output omitted)
floss$
```

For files, that's all there is to it. Renaming directories is not done very differently: create the new directory, **cvs add** it, move all the files from the old directory to the new one, **cvs remove** them from the old directory, **cvs add** them in the new one, **cvs commit** so everything takes effect, and then do **cvs update -P** to make the now-empty directory disappear from the working copy. That is to say:

```
floss$ mkdir newdir
floss$ cvs add newdir
floss$ mv olddir/* newdir
mv: newdir/CVS: cannot overwrite directory
floss$ cd olddir
floss$ cvs rm foo.c bar.txt
```

```
floss$ cd ../newdir
floss$ cvs add foo.c bar.txt
floss$ cd ..
floss$ cvs commit -m "moved foo.c and bar.txt from olddir to newdir"
floss$ cvs update -P
```

Note

Note the warning message after the third command. It's telling you that it can't copy olddir's CVS/ subdirectory into newdir because newdir already has a directory of that name. This is fine, because you want olddir to keep its CVS/ subdirectory anyway.

Obviously, moving directories around can get a bit cumbersome. The best policy is to try to come up with a good layout when you initially import your project so you won't have to move directories around very often. Later, you'll learn about a more drastic method of moving directories that involves making the change directly in the repository. However, that method is best saved for emergencies; whenever possible, it's best to handle everything with CVS operations inside working copies.

Avoiding Option Fatigue

Most people tire pretty quickly of typing the same option flags with every command. If you know that you always want to pass the **-Q** global option or you always want to use **-c** with **diff**, why should you have to type it out each time?

There is help, fortunately. CVS looks for a .cvsrc file in your home directory. In that file, you can specify default options to apply to every invocation of CVS. Here's an example .cvsrc:

```
diff -c
update -P
cvs -q
```

If the leftmost word on a line matches a CVS command (in its unabbreviated form), the corresponding options are used for that command every time. For global options, you just use **cvs**. So, for example, every time that user runs **cvs diff**, the **-c** flag is automatically included.

Getting Snapshots (Dates And Tagging)

Let's return to the example of the program that's in a broken state when a bug report comes in. The developer suddenly needs access to the *entire* project as it was at the time of the last release, even though many files may have been changed since then, and each file's revision number differs from the others. It would be far too time-consuming to look over the log messages, figure out what each file's individual revision number was at the time of release, and then run **update** (specifying a revision number with **-r**) on each one of them. In medium- to large-sized projects (tens to hundreds of files), such a process would be too unwieldy to attempt.

CVS, therefore, provides a way to retrieve previous revisions of the files in a project en masse. In fact, it provides two ways: by date, which selects the revisions based on the time that they were committed, and by tag, which retrieves a previously marked "snapshot" of the project.

Which method you use depends on the situation. The date-based retrievals are done by passing **update** the **-D** flag, which is similar to **-r** but takes dates instead of revision numbers:

```
floss$ cvs -q update -D "1999-04-19"
U hello.c
U a-subdir/subsubdir/fish.c
U b-subdir/random.c
floss$
```

With the **-D** option, **update** retrieves the highest revision of each file as of the given date, and it will revert the files in the working copy to prior revisions if necessary.

When you give the date, you can, and often should, include the time. For example, the previous command ended up retrieving revision 1.1 of everything (only three files showed changes, because all of the others are still at revision 1.1 anyway). Here's the status of hello.c to prove it:

```
floss$ cvs -Q status hello.c
===============================================================
File: hello.c              Status: Up-to-date
   Working revision:       1.1.1.1 Sat Apr 24 22:45:03 1999
   Repository revision:    1.1.1.1 /usr/local/cvs/myproj/hello.c,v
   Sticky Date:            99.04.19.05.00.00
floss$
```

But a glance back at the log messages from earlier in this chapter shows that revision 1.2 of hello.c was definitely committed on April 19, 1999. So why did we now get revision 1.1 instead of 1.2?

The problem is that the date "1999-04-19" was interpreted as meaning "the midnight that begins 1999-04-19"—that is, the very first instant on that date. This is probably not what you want. The 1.2 **commit** took place later in the day. By qualifying the date more precisely, we can retrieve revision 1.2:

```
floss$ cvs -q update -D "1999-04-19 23:59:59"
U hello.c
U a-subdir/subsubdir/fish.c
U b-subdir/random.c
floss$ cvs status hello.c
===============================================================
```

```
File: hello.c                    Status: Locally Modified
   Working revision: 1.2         Sat Apr 24 22:45:22 1999
   Repository revision:          1.2     /usr/local/cvs/myproj/hello.c,v
   Sticky Tag:                   (none)
   Sticky Date:                  99.04.20.04.59.59
   Sticky Options:     (none)
floss$
```

We're almost there. If you look closely at the date/time on the **Sticky Date** line, it seems to indicate 4:59:59 A.M., not 11:59 as the command requested (later we'll get to what the "sticky" means). As you may have guessed, the discrepancy is due to the difference between local time and Universal Coordinated Time (also known as "Greenwich mean time"). The repository always stores dates in Universal Time, but CVS on the client side usually assumes the local system time zone. In the case of **-D**, this is rather unfortunate because you're probably most interested in comparing against the repository time and don't care about the local system's idea of time. You can get around this by specifying the GMT zone in the command:

```
floss$ cvs -q update -D "1999-04-19 23:59:59 GMT"
U hello.c
floss$ cvs -q status hello.c
======================================================================
File: hello.c                    Status: Up-to-date
   Working revision: 1.2         Sun Apr 25 22:38:53 1999
   Repository revision:          1.2     /usr/local/cvs/myproj/hello.c,v
   Sticky Tag:                   (none)
   Sticky Date:                  99.04.19.23.59.59
   Sticky Options:     (none)
floss$
```

There—that brought the working copy back to the final commits from April 19 (unless there were any commits during the last minute of the day, which there weren't).

What happens now if you run **update**?

```
floss$ cvs update
cvs update: Updating .
cvs update: Updating a-subdir
cvs update: Updating a-subdir/subsubdir
cvs update: Updating b-subdir
floss$
```

Nothing happens at all. But you know that there are more recent versions of at least three files. Why aren't these included in your working copy?

That's where the "sticky" comes in. Updating ("downdating"?) with the **-D** flag causes the working copy to be restricted permanently to that date or before. In CVS terminology, the working copy has a "sticky date" set. Once a working copy has acquired a sticky property, it stays sticky until told otherwise. Therefore, subsequent updates will not automatically retrieve the most recent revision. Instead, they'll stay restricted to the sticky date. Stickiness can be revealed by running **cvs status** or by directly examining the CVS/Entries file:

```
floss$ cvs -q update -D "1999-04-19 23:59:59 GMT"
U hello.c
floss$ cat CVS/Entries
D/a-subdir////
D/b-subdir////
D/c-subdir////
/README.txt/1.1.1.1/Sun Apr 18 18:18:22 1999//D99.04.19.23.59.59
/hello.c/1.2/Sun Apr 25 23:07:29 1999//D99.04.19.23.59.59
floss$
```

If you were to modify hello.c and then try to **commit**

```
floss$ cvs update
M hello.c
floss$ cvs ci -m "trying to change the past"
cvs commit: cannot commit with sticky date for file 'hello.c'
cvs [commit aborted]: correct above errors first!
floss$
```

CVS would not permit the **commit** to happen because that would be like allowing you to go back and change the past. CVS is all about record keeping and, therefore, will not allow you to do that.

This does not mean CVS is unaware of all the revisions that have been committed since that date, however. You can still compare the sticky-dated working copy against other revisions, including future ones:

```
floss$ cvs -q diff -c -r 1.5 hello.c
Index: hello.c
===================================================================
RCS file: /usr/local/cvs/myproj/hello.c,v
retrieving revision 1.5
diff -c -r1.5 hello.c
*** hello.c    1999/04/24 22:09:27      1.5
--- hello.c    1999/04/25 00:08:44
***************
*** 3,9 ****
  void
  main ()
  {
```

```
    printf ("Hello, world!\n");
-   printf ("between hello and goodbye\n");
    printf ("Goodbye, world!\n");
  }
--- 3,9 --
  void
  main ()
  {
+   /* this line was added to a downdated working copy */
    printf ("Hello, world!\n");
    printf ("Goodbye, world!\n");
  }
```

This **diff** reveals that, as of April 19, 1999, the **between hello and goodbye** line had not yet been added. It also shows the modification that we made to the working copy (adding the comment shown in the preceding code snippet).

You can remove a sticky date (or any sticky property) by updating with the **-A** flag (**-A** stands for "reset," don't ask me why), which brings the working copy back to the most recent revisions:

```
floss$ cvs -q update -A
U hello.c
floss$ cvs status hello.c
===============================================================
File: hello.c                   Status: Up-to-date
    Working revision:  1.5      Sun Apr 25 22:50:27 1999
    Repository revision:        1.5     /usr/local/cvs/myproj/hello.c,v
    Sticky Tag:                 (none)
    Sticky Date:                (none)
    Sticky Options:     (none)
floss$
```

Acceptable Date Formats

CVS accepts a wide range of syntaxes to specify dates. You'll never go wrong if you use ISO 8601 format (that is, the International Standards Organization standard #8601, see also **www.saqqara.demon.co.uk/datefmt.htm**), which is the format used in the preceding examples. You can also use Internet email dates as described in RFC 822 and RFC 1123 (see **www.rfc-editor.org/rfc/**). Finally, you can use certain unambiguous English constructs to specify dates relative to the current date.

You will probably never need all of the formats available, but here are some more examples to give you an idea of what CVS accepts:

```
floss$ cvs update -D "19 Apr 1999"
floss$ cvs update -D "19 Apr 1999 20:05"
```

```
floss$ cvs update -D "19/04/1999"
floss$ cvs update -D "3 days ago"
floss$ cvs update -D "5 years ago"
floss$ cvs update -D "19 Apr 1999 23:59:59 GMT"
floss$ cvs update -D "19 Apr"
```

The double quotes around the dates are there to ensure that the Unix shell treats the date as one argument even if it contains spaces. The quotes will do no harm if the date doesn't contain spaces, so it's probably best to always use them.

Marking A Moment In Time *(Tags)*

Retrieving by date is useful when the mere passage of time is your main concern. But more often what you really want to do is retrieve the project as it was at the time of a specific event—perhaps a public release, a known stable point in the software's development, or the addition or removal of some major feature.

Trying to remember the date when that event took place or deducing the date from log messages would be a tedious process. Presumably, the event, because it was important, was marked as such in the formal revision history. The method CVS offers for making such marks is known as *tagging*.

Tags differs from commits in that they don't record any particular textual change to files, but rather a change in the developers' attitude *about* the files. A tag gives a label to the collection of revisions represented by one developer's working copy (usually, that working copy is completely up to date so the tag name is attached to the "latest and greatest" revisions in the repository).

Setting a tag is as simple as this:

```
floss$ cvs -q tag Release-1999_05_01
T README.txt
T hello.c
T a-subdir/whatever.c
T a-subdir/subsubdir/fish.c
T b-subdir/random.c
floss$
```

That command associates the symbolic name "Release-1999_05_01" with the snapshot represented by this working copy. Defined formally, *snapshot* means a set of files and associated revision numbers from the project. Those revision numbers do not have to be the same from file to file and, in fact, usually aren't. For example, assuming that **tag** was done on the same myproj directory that we've been using throughout this chapter and that the working copy was completely up to date, the symbolic name "Release-1999_05_01" will be attached to hello.c at revision 1.5, to fish.c at revision 1.2, to random.c at revision 1.2, and to everything else at revision 1.1.

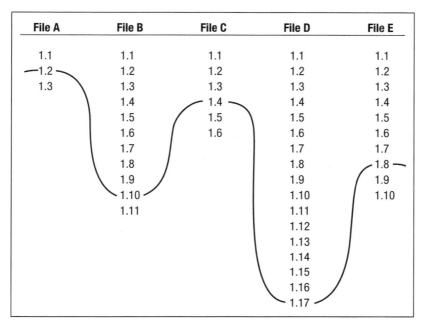

Figure 2.1
How a tag might stand in relation to a project's revision history.

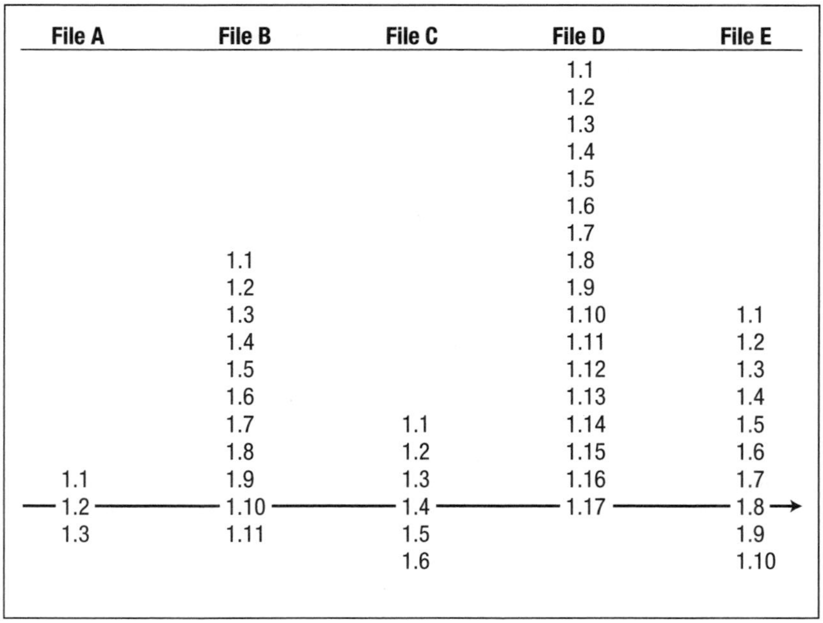

File A	File B	File C	File D	File E
			1.1	
			1.2	
			1.3	
			1.4	
			1.5	
			1.6	
			1.7	
	1.1		1.8	
	1.2		1.9	
	1.3		1.10	1.1
	1.4		1.11	1.2
	1.5		1.12	1.3
	1.6		1.13	1.4
	1.7	1.1	1.14	1.5
	1.8	1.2	1.15	1.6
1.1	1.9	1.3	1.16	1.7
1.2 —	1.10 —	1.4 —	1.17 —	1.8 →
1.3	1.11	1.5		1.9
		1.6		1.10

Figure 2.2
The tag is a "straight sight" through a revision history.

It may help to visualize a tag as a path or string linking various revisions of files in the project. In Figure 2.1, an imaginary string passes through the tagged revision number of each file in a project.

If you pull the string taut and sight directly along it, you'll see a particular moment in the project's history—namely, the moment that the tag was set (Figure 2.2).

As you continue to edit files and commit changes, the tag will not move along with the increasing revision numbers. It stays fixed, "stickily," at the revision number of each file at the time the tag was made.

Given their importance as descriptors, it's a bit unfortunate that log messages can't be included with tags or that the tags themselves can't be full paragraphs of prose. In the preceding example, the tag is fairly obviously stating that the project was in a releasable state as of a certain date. However, sometimes you may want to make snapshots of a more complex state, which can result in ungainly tag names such as:

```
floss$ cvs tag testing-release-3_pre-19990525-public-release
```

As a general rule, you should try to keep tags as terse as possible while still including all necessary information about the event that you're trying to record. When in doubt, err on the side of being overly descriptive—you'll be glad later when you're able to tell from some verbose tag name exactly what circumstance was recorded.

You've probably noticed that no periods or spaces were used in the tag names. CVS is rather strict about what constitutes a valid tag name. The rules are that it must start with a letter and contain letters, digits, hyphens ("-"), and underscores ("_"). No spaces, periods, colons, commas, or any other symbols may be used.

To retrieve a snapshot by tag name, the tag name is used just like a revision number. There are two ways to retrieve snapshots: You can check out a new working copy with a certain tag, or you can switch an existing working copy over to a tag. Both result in a working copy whose files are at the revisions specified by the tag.

Most of the time, what you're trying to do is take a look at the project as it was at the time of the snapshot. You may not necessarily want to do this in your main working copy, where you presumably have uncommitted changes and other useful states built up, so let's assume you just want to check out a separate working copy with the tag. Here's how (but make sure to invoke this somewhere other than in your existing working copy or its parent directory!):

```
floss$ cvs checkout -r Release-1999_05_01 myproj
cvs checkout: Updating myproj
U myproj/README.txt
U myproj/hello.c
cvs checkout: Updating myproj/a-subdir
U myproj/a-subdir/whatever.c
```

```
cvs checkout: Updating myproj/a-subdir/subsubdir
U myproj/a-subdir/subsubdir/fish.c
cvs checkout: Updating myproj/b-subdir
U myproj/b-subdir/random.c
cvs checkout: Updating myproj/c-subdir
```

We've seen the **-r** option before in the **update** command, where it preceded a revision number. In many ways a tag is just like a revision number because, for any file, a given tag corresponds to exactly one revision number (it's illegal, and generally impossible, to have two tags of the same name in the same project). In fact, anywhere you can use a revision number as part of a CVS command, you can use a tag name instead (as long as the tag has been set previously). If you want to **diff** a file's current state against its state at the time of the last release, you can do this:

```
floss$ cvs diff -c -r Release-1999_05_01 hello.c
```

And if you want to revert it temporarily to that revision, you can do this:

```
floss$ cvs update -r Release-1999_05_01 hello.c
```

The interchangeability of tags and revision numbers explains some of the strict rules about valid tag names. Imagine if periods were legal in tag names; you could have a tag named "1.3" attached to an actual revision number of "1.47." If you then issued the command

```
floss$ cvs update -r 1.3 hello.c
```

how would CVS know whether you were referring to the tag named "1.3," or the much earlier revision 1.3 of hello.c? Thus, restrictions are placed on tag names so that they can always be easily distinguished from revision numbers. A revision number has a period; a tag name doesn't. (There are reasons for the other restrictions, too, mostly having to do with making tag names easy for CVS to parse.)

As you've probably guessed by this point, the second method of retrieving a snapshot—that is, switching an existing working directory over to the tagged revisions—is also done by updating:

```
floss$ cvs update -r Release-1999_05_01
cvs update: Updating .
cvs update: Updating a-subdir
cvs update: Updating a-subdir/subsubdir
cvs update: Updating b-subdir
cvs update: Updating c-subdir
floss$
```

The preceding command is just like the one we used to revert hello.c to Release-1999_05_01, except that the filename is omitted because we want to revert the entire project over. (You can, if you want, revert just one subtree of the project to the tag by invoking the preceding command in that subtree instead of from the top level, although you hardly ever would want to do that.)

Note that no files appear to have changed when we updated. The working copy was completely up to date when we tagged, and no changes had been committed since the tagging.

However, this does not mean that nothing changed at all. The working copy now knows that it's at a tagged revision. When you make a change and try to **commit** it (let's assume we modified hello.c):

```
floss$ cvs -q update
M hello.c
floss$ cvs -q ci -m "trying to commit from a working copy on a tag"
cvs commit: sticky tag 'Release-1999_05_01' for file 'hello.c' is not a branch
cvs [commit aborted]: correct above errors first!
floss$
```

CVS does not permit the commit to happen. (Don't worry about the exact meaning of that error message yet—we'll cover branches next in this chapter.) It doesn't matter whether the working copy got to be on a tag via a **checkout** or an **update**. Once it is on a tag, CVS views the working copy as a static snapshot of a moment in history, and CVS won't let you change history, at least not easily. If you run **cvs status** or look at the CVS/Entries files, you'll see that there is a sticky tag set on each file. Here's the top level Entries file, for example:

```
floss$ cat CVS/Entries
D/a-subdir////
D/b-subdir////
D/c-subdir////
/README.txt/1.1.1.1/Sun Apr 18 18:18:22 1999//TRelease-1999_05_01
/hello.c/1.5/Tue Apr 20 07:24:10 1999//TRelease-1999_05_01
floss$
```

Tags, like other sticky properties, are removed with the **-A** flag to **update**:

```
floss$ cvs -q update -A
M hello.c
floss$
```

The modification to hello.c did not go away, however; CVS is still aware that the file changed with respect to the repository:

```
floss$ cvs -q diff -c hello.c
Index: hello.c
===================================================================
RCS file: /usr/local/cvs/myproj/hello.c,v
retrieving revision 1.5
diff -c -r1.5 hello.c
*** hello.c    1999/04/20 06:12:56      1.5
--- hello.c    1999/05/04 20:09:17
***************
*** 6,9 ****
--- 6,10 --
    printf ("Hello, world!\n");
    printf ("between hello and goodbye\n");
    printf ("Goodbye, world!\n");
+   /* a comment on the last line */
  }
floss$
```

Now that you've reset with **update**, CVS will accept a **commit**:

```
floss$ cvs ci -m "added comment to end of main function"
cvs commit: Examining .
cvs commit: Examining a-subdir
cvs commit: Examining a-subdir/subsubdir
cvs commit: Examining b-subdir
cvs commit: Examining c-subdir
Checking in hello.c;
/usr/local/cvs/myproj/hello.c,v  <- hello.c
new revision: 1.6; previous revision: 1.5
done
floss$
```

The tag "Release-1999_05_01" is still attached to revision 1.5, of course. Compare the file's status before and after a reversion to the tag:

```
floss$ cvs -q status hello.c
===================================================================
File: hello.c                 Status: Up-to-date
   Working revision:  1.6     Tue May  4 20:09:17 1999
   Repository revision:       1.6    /usr/local/cvs/myproj/hello.c,v
   Sticky Tag:                (none)
   Sticky Date:               (none)
   Sticky Options:            (none)
floss$ cvs -q update -r Release-1999_05_01
U hello.c
floss$ cvs -q status hello.c
===================================================================
```

```
File: hello.c                 Status: Up-to-date
   Working revision:   1.5    Tue May  4 20:21:12 1999
   Repository revision:       1.5     /usr/local/cvs/myproj/hello.c,v
   Sticky Tag:                Release-1999_05_01 (revision: 1.5)
   Sticky Date:               (none)
   Sticky Options:            (none)
floss$
```

Now, having just told you that CVS doesn't let you change history, I'll show you how to change history.

Branches

We've been viewing CVS as a kind of intelligent, coordinating library. However, it can also be thought of as a time machine (thanks to Jim Blandy for the analogy). So far, we've only seen how you can examine the past with CVS, without affecting anything. Like all good time machines, CVS also allows you to go back in time to change the past. What do you get then? Science fiction fans know the answer to that question: an alternate universe, running parallel to ours, but diverging from ours at exactly the point where the past was changed. A CVS *branch* splits a project's development into separate, parallel histories. Changes made on one branch do not affect the other.

Why is this useful?

Let's return for a moment to the scenario of the developer who, in the midst of working on a new version of the program, receives a bug report about an older released version. Assuming the developer fixes the problem, she still needs a way to deliver the fix to the customer. It won't help to just find an old copy of the program somewhere, patch it up without CVS's knowledge, and ship it off. There would be no record of what was done; CVS would be unaware of the fix; and later if something was discovered to be wrong with the patch, no one would have a starting point for reproducing the problem.

It's even more ill-advised to fix the bug in the current, unstable version of the sources and ship that to the customer. Sure, the reported bug may be solved, but the rest of the code is in a half-implemented, untested state. It may run, but it's certainly not ready for prime time.

Because the last released version is thought to be stable, aside from this one bug, the ideal solution is to go back and correct the bug in the old release—that is, to create an alternate universe in which the last public release includes this bug fix.

That's where branches come in. The developer splits off a branch, rooted in the main line of development (the *trunk*) not at its most recent revisions, but back at the point of the last release. Then she checks out a working copy of this branch, makes whatever changes are necessary to fix the bug, and commits them on that branch, so there's a record of the bug fix. Now she can package up an interim release based on the branch and ship it to the customer.

Her change won't have affected the code on the trunk, nor would she want it to without first finding out whether the trunk needs the same bug fix or not. If it does, she can **merge** the branch changes into the trunk. In a **merge**, CVS calculates the changes made on the branch between the point where it diverged from the trunk and the branch's *tip* (its most recent state), then applies those differences to the project at the tip of the trunk. The difference between the branch's root and its tip works out, of course, to be precisely the bug fix.

Another good way to think of a merge is as a special case of updating. The difference is that in a merge, the changes to be incorporated are derived by comparing the branch's root and tip, instead of by comparing the working copy against the repository.

The act of updating is itself similar to receiving patches directly from their authors and applying them by hand. In fact, to do an **update**, CVS calculates the difference (that's "difference" as in the **diff** program) between the working copy and the repository and then applies that **diff** to the working copy just as the **patch** program would. This mirrors the way in which a developer takes changes from the outside world, by manually applying **patch** files sent in by contributors.

Thus, merging the bug fix branch into the trunk is just like accepting some outside contributor's patch to fix the bug. The contributor would have made the patch against the last released version, just as the branch's changes are against that version. If that area of code in the current sources hasn't changed much since the last release, the merge will succeed with no problems. If the code is now substantially different, however, the merge will fail with conflict (that is, the patch will be rejected), and some manual fiddling will be

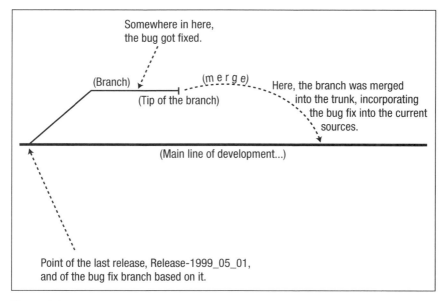

Figure 2.3
Branching and merging.

necessary. Usually this is accomplished by reading the conflicting area, making the necessary changes by hand, and committing. Figure 2.3 shows a picture of what happens in a branch and merge.

We'll now walk through the steps necessary to make this picture happen. Remember that it's not really time that's flowing from left to right in the diagram, but rather the revision history. The branch will not have been made at the time of the release, but is created later, rooted back at the release's revisions.

In our case, let's assume the files in the project have gone through many revisions since they were tagged as "Release-1999_05_01," and perhaps files have been added as well. When the bug report regarding the old release comes in, the first thing we'll want to do is create a branch rooted at the old release, which we conveniently tagged "Release-1999_05_01."

One way to do this is to first check out a working copy based on that tag, then create the branch by re-tagging with the **-b** (branch) option:

```
floss$ cd ..
floss$ ls
myproj/
floss$ cvs -q checkout -d myproj_old_release -r Release-1999_05_01 myproj
U myproj_old_release/README.txt
U myproj_old_release/hello.c
U myproj_old_release/a-subdir/whatever.c
U myproj_old_release/a-subdir/subsubdir/fish.c
U myproj_old_release/b-subdir/random.c
floss$ ls
myproj/      myproj_old_release/
floss$ cd myproj_old_release
floss$ ls
CVS/      README.txt  a-subdir/   b-subdir/   hello.c
floss$ cvs -q tag -b Release-1999_05_01-bugfixes
T README.txt
T hello.c
T a-subdir/whatever.c
T a-subdir/subsubdir/fish.c
T b-subdir/random.c
floss$
```

Take a good look at that last command. It may seem somewhat arbitrary that **tag** is used to create branches, but there's actually a reason for it: The tag name will serve as a label by which the branch can be retrieved later. Branch tags do not look any different from non-branch tags, and are subject to the same naming restrictions. Some people like to always include the word *branch* in the tag name itself (for example, "Release-1999_05_01-bugfix-branch"), so they can distinguish branch tags from other kinds of tags. You may want to do this if you find yourself often retrieving the wrong tag.

(And while we're at it, note the **-d myproj_old_release** option to **checkout** in the first CVS command. This tells **checkout** to put the working copy in a directory called myproj_ old_release, so we won't confuse it with the current version in myproj. Be careful not to confuse this use of **-d** with the global option of the same name, or with the **-d** option to **update**.)

Of course, merely running the **tag** command does not switch this working copy over to the branch. Tagging never affects the working copy; it just records some extra information in the repository to allow you to retrieve that working copy's revisions later on (as a static piece of history or as a branch, as the case may be).

Retrieval can be done one of two ways (you're probably getting used to this motif by now!). You can check out a new working copy on the branch

```
floss$ pwd
/home/whatever
floss$ cvs co -d myproj_branch -r Release-1999_05_01-bugfixes myproj
```

or switch an existing working copy over to it:

```
floss$ pwd
/home/whatever/myproj
floss$ cvs update -r Release-1999_05_01-bugfixes
```

The end result is the same (well, the name of the new working copy's top-level directory may be different, but that's not important for CVS's purposes). If your current working copy has uncommitted changes, you'll probably want to use **checkout** instead of **update** to access the branch. Otherwise, CVS attempts to merge your changes into the working copy as it switches it over to the branch. In that case, you might get conflicts, and even if you didn't, you'd still have an impure branch. It won't truly reflect the state of the program as of the designated tag, because some files in the working copy will contain modifications made by you.

Anyway, let's assume that by one method or another you get a working copy on the desired branch:

```
floss$ cvs -q status hello.c
===============================================================
File: hello.c                 Status: Up-to-date
    Working revision:   1.5    Tue Apr 20 06:12:56 1999
    Repository revision:        1.5    /usr/local/cvs/myproj/hello.c,v
    Sticky Tag:                 Release-1999_05_01-bugfixes
(branch: 1.5.2)
    Sticky Date:                (none)
    Sticky Options:             (none)
floss$ cvs -q status b-subdir/random.c
===============================================================
```

```
File: random.c                    Status: Up-to-date
   Working revision:   1.2        Mon Apr 19 06:35:27 1999
   Repository revision:           1.2 /usr/local/cvs/myproj/b-subdir/random.c,v
   Sticky Tag:                    Release-1999_05_01-bugfixes (branch: 1.2.2)
   Sticky Date:                   (none)
   Sticky Options:                (none)
floss$
```

(The contents of those **Sticky Tag** lines will be explained shortly.) If you modify hello.c and random.c, and commit

```
floss$ cvs -q update
M hello.c
M b-subdir/random.c
floss$ cvs ci -m "fixed old punctuation bugs"
cvs commit: Examining .
cvs commit: Examining a-subdir
cvs commit: Examining a-subdir/subsubdir
cvs commit: Examining b-subdir
Checking in hello.c;
/usr/local/cvs/myproj/hello.c,v  <- hello.c
new revision: 1.5.2.1; previous revision: 1.5
done
Checking in b-subdir/random.c;
/usr/local/cvs/myproj/b-subdir/random.c,v  <- random.c
new revision: 1.2.2.1; previous revision: 1.2
done
floss$
```

you'll notice that there's something funny going on with the revision numbers:

```
floss$ cvs -q status hello.c b-subdir/random.c
===============================================================
File: hello.c                     Status: Up-to-date
   Working revision:   1.5.2.1 Wed May  5 00:13:58 1999
   Repository revision:           1.5.2.1 /usr/local/cvs/myproj/hello.c,v
   Sticky Tag:                    Release-1999_05_01-bugfixes (branch: 1.5.2)
   Sticky Date:                   (none)
   Sticky Options:                (none)
===============================================================
File: random.c                    Status: Up-to-date
   Working revision:   1.2.2.1 Wed May  5 00:14:25 1999
   Repository revision:           1.2.2.1 /usr/local/cvs/myproj/b-subdir/random.c,v
   Sticky Tag:                    Release-1999_05_01-bugfixes (branch: 1.2.2)
   Sticky Date:                   (none)
   Sticky Options:                (none)
floss$
```

They now have four digits instead of two!

A closer look reveals that each file's revision number is just the branch number (as shown on the **Sticky Tag** line) plus an extra digit on the end.

What you're seeing is a little bit of CVS's inner workings. Although you almost always use a branch to mark a project-wide divergence, CVS actually records the branch on a per-file basis. This project had five files in it at the point of the branch, so five individual branches were made, all with the same tag name: "Release-1999_05_01-bugfixes."

Note

Most people consider this per-file scheme a rather inelegant implementation on CVS's part. It's a bit of the old RCS legacy showing through—RCS didn't know how to group files into projects, and even though CVS does, it still uses code inherited from RCS to handle branches.

Ordinarily, you don't need to be too concerned with how CVS is keeping track of things internally, but in this case, it helps to understand the relationship between branch numbers and revision numbers. Let's look at the hello.c file; everything I'm about to say about hello.c applies to the other files in the branch (with revision/branch numbers adjusted accordingly).

The hello.c file was on revision 1.5 at the point where the branch was rooted. When we created the branch, a new number was tacked onto the end to make a *branch number* (CVS chooses the first unused even, nonzero integer). Thus, the branch number in this case became "1.5.2." The branch number by itself is not a revision number, but it is the *root* (that is, the prefix) of all the revision numbers for hello.c along this branch.

However, when we ran that first CVS status in a branched working copy, hello.c's revision number showed up as only "1.5," not "1.5.2.0" or something similar. This is because the initial revision on a branch is always the same as the trunk revision of the file, where the branch sprouts off. Therefore, CVS shows the trunk revision number in status output, for as long as the file is the same on both branch and trunk.

Once we had committed a new revision, hello.c was no longer the same on both trunk and branch—the branch incarnation of the file had changed, while the trunk remained the same. Accordingly, hello.c was assigned its first branch revision number. We saw this in the status output after the **commit**, where its revision number is clearly "1.5.2.1."

The same story applies to the random.c file. Its revision number at the time of branching was "1.2," so its first branch is "1.2.2," and the first new **commit** of random.c on that branch received the revision number "1.2.2.1."

There is no numeric relationship between 1.5.2.1 and 1.2.2.1—no reason to think that they are part of the same branch event, except that both files are tagged with "Release-1999_05_01-bugfixes," and the tag is attached to branch numbers 1.5.2 and 1.2.2 in the respective files. Therefore, the tag name is your only handle on the branch as a project-wide entity. Although it is perfectly possible to move a file to a branch by using the revision number directly

```
floss$ cvs update -r 1.5.2.1 hello.c
U hello.c
floss$
```

it is almost always ill-advised. You would be mixing the branch revision of one file with non-branch revisions of the others. Who knows what losses may result? It is better to use the branch tag to refer to the branch and do all files at once by not specifying any particular file. That way you don't have to know or care what the actual branch revision number is for any particular file.

It is also possible to have branches that sprout off other branches, to any level of absurdity. A file with a revision number of 1.5.4.37.2.3.12.1 is depicted graphically by Figure 2.4.

Admittedly, it's hard to imagine what circumstances would make such a branching depth necessary, but isn't it nice to know that CVS will go as far as you're willing to take it? Nested branches are created the same way as any other branch: Check out a working copy on branch N, run **cvs tag -b** *branchname* in it, and you'll create branch *N.M* in the repository (where "N" represents the appropriate branch revision number in each file, such as "1.5.2.1," and "M" represents the next available branch at the end of that number, such as "2").

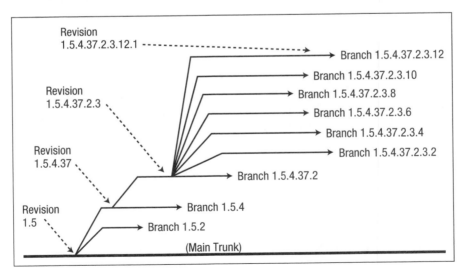

Figure 2.4
A ridiculously high degree of branching.

Merging Changes From Branch To Trunk

Now that the bug fix has been committed on the branch, let's switch the working copy over to the highest trunk revisions and see if the bug fix needs to be done there, too. We'll move the working copy off the branch by using **update -A** (branch tags are like other sticky properties in this respect) and then **diff**ing against the branch we just left:

```
floss$ cvs -q update -A
U hello.c
U b-subdir/random.c
floss$ cvs -q diff -c -r Release-1999_05_01-bugfixes
Index: hello.c
===================================================================
RCS file: /usr/local/cvs/myproj/hello.c,v
retrieving revision 1.5.2.1
retrieving revision 1.6
diff -c -r1.5.2.1 -r1.6
*** hello.c     1999/05/05 00:15:07     1.5.2.1
--- hello.c     1999/05/04 20:19:16     1.6
***************
*** 4,9 ****
  main ()
  {
    printf ("Hello, world!\n");
!   printf ("between hello and good-bye\n");
    printf ("Goodbye, world!\n");
  }
--- 4,10 --
  main ()
  {
    printf ("Hello, world!\n");
!   printf ("between hello and goodbye\n");
    printf ("Goodbye, world!\n");
+   /* a comment on the last line */
  }
Index: b-subdir/random.c
===================================================================
RCS file: /usr/local/cvs/myproj/b-subdir/random.c,v
retrieving revision 1.2.2.1
retrieving revision 1.2
diff -c -r1.2.2.1 -r1.2
*** b-subdir/random.c 1999/05/05 00:15:07     1.2.2.1
--- b-subdir/random.c 1999/04/19 06:35:27     1.2
***************
*** 4,8 ****
```

```
   void main ()
   {
!   printf ("A random number.\n");
   }
--- 4,8 --
   void main ()
   {
!   printf ("a random number\n");
   }
floss$
```

The **diff** shows that **good-bye** is spelled with a hyphen in the branch revision of hello.c, and that the trunk revision of that file has a comment near the end that the branch revision doesn't have. Meanwhile, in random.c, the branch revision has a capital "A" and a period, whereas the trunk doesn't.

To actually merge the branch changes into the current working copy, run **update** with the **-j** flag (the same **j** for "join" that we used to revert a file to an old revision before):

```
floss$ cvs -q update -j Release-1999_05_01-bugfixes
RCS file: /usr/local/cvs/myproj/hello.c,v
retrieving revision 1.5
retrieving revision 1.5.2.1
Merging differences between 1.5 and 1.5.2.1 into hello.c
RCS file: /usr/local/cvs/myproj/b-subdir/random.c,v
retrieving revision 1.2
retrieving revision 1.2.2.1
Merging differences between 1.2 and 1.2.2.1 into random.c
floss$ cvs -q update
M hello.c
M b-subdir/random.c
floss$ cvs -q ci -m "merged from branch Release-1999_05_01-bugfixes"
Checking in hello.c;
/usr/local/cvs/myproj/hello.c,v  <- hello.c
new revision: 1.7; previous revision: 1.6
done
Checking in b-subdir/random.c;
/usr/local/cvs/myproj/b-subdir/random.c,v  <- random.c
new revision: 1.3; previous revision: 1.2
done
floss$
```

This takes the changes from the branch's root to its tip and merges them into the current working copy (which subsequently shows those modifications just as though the files had been hand-edited into that state). The changes are then committed onto the trunk, since nothing in the repository changed when a working copy underwent a merge.

Although no conflicts were encountered in this example, it's quite possible (even probable) that there would be some in a normal merge. If that happens, they need to be resolved like any other conflict, and then committed.

Multiple Merges

Sometimes a branch will continue to be actively developed even after the trunk has undergone a merge from it. For example, this can happen if a second bug in the previous public release is discovered and has to be fixed on the branch. Maybe someone didn't get the joke in random.c, so on the branch, you have to add a line explaining it

```
floss$ pwd
<Body /home/whatever/myproj_branch
floss$ cat b-subdir/random.c
/* Print out a random number. */
#include <stdio.h
void main ()
{
  printf ("A random number.\n");
  printf ("Get the joke?\n");
}
floss$
```

and **commit**. If that bug fix also needs to be merged into the trunk, you might be tempted to try the same **update** command as before in the trunk working copy to "re-merge":

```
floss$ cvs -q update -j Release-1999_05_01-bugfixes
RCS file: /usr/local/cvs/myproj/hello.c,v
retrieving revision 1.5
retrieving revision 1.5.2.1
Merging differences between 1.5 and 1.5.2.1 into hello.c
RCS file: /usr/local/cvs/myproj/b-subdir/random.c,v
retrieving revision 1.2
retrieving revision 1.2.2.2
Merging differences between 1.2 and 1.2.2.2 into random.c
rcsmerge: warning: conflicts during merge
floss$
```

As you can see, that didn't have quite the desired effect—we got a conflict, even though the trunk copy hadn't been modified there and, therefore, no conflict was expected.

The trouble was that the **update** command behaved exactly as described: It tried to take all the changes between the branch's root and tip and merge them into the current working copy. The only problem is, some of those changes had already been merged into this working copy. That's why we got the conflict:

```
floss$ pwd
/home/whatever/myproj
floss$ cat b-subdir/random.c
/* Print out a random number. */
#include <stdio.h
void main ()
{
<<<<<<< random.c
  printf ("A random number.\n");
=======
  printf ("A random number.\n");
  printf ("Get the joke?\n");
 1.2.2.2
}
floss$
```

You could go through resolving all such conflicts by hand—it's usually not hard to tell what you need to do in each file. Nevertheless, it is even better to avoid a conflict in the first place. By passing two **-j** flags instead of one, you'll get only those changes from where you last merged to the tip instead of all of the changes on the branch, from root to tip. The first **-j** gives the starting point on the branch, and the second is just the plain branch name (which implies the tip of the branch).

The question then is, how can you specify the point on the branch from which you last merged? One way is to qualify by using a date along with the branch tag name. CVS provides a special syntax for this:

```
cvs update -j "Release-1999_05_01-bugfixes:2 days ago" \
           -j Release-1999_05_01-bugfixes
floss$ cvs -q update -j "Release-1999_05_01-bugfixes:2 days ago" \
                     -j Release-1999_05_01-bugfixes
RCS file: /usr/local/cvs/myproj/b-subdir/random.c,v
retrieving revision 1.2.2.1
retrieving revision 1.2.2.2
Merging differences between 1.2.2.1 and 1.2.2.2 into random.c
floss$
```

If the branch tag name is followed by a colon and then a date (in any of the usual CVS date syntaxes), CVS will include only changes later than that date. So if you knew that the original bug fix was committed on the branch three days ago, the preceding command would merge the second bug fix only.

A better way, if you plan ahead, is to tag the branch after each bug fix (just a regular tag—we're not starting a new branch here or anything like that). Suppose after fixing the bug in the branch and committing, you do this in the branch's working copy:

```
floss$ cvs -q tag Release-1999_05_01-bugfixes-fix-number-1
T README.txt
T hello.c
T a-subdir/whatever.c
T a-subdir/subsubdir/fish.c
T b-subdir/random.c
floss$
```

Then, when it's time to merge the second change into the trunk, you can use that conveniently placed tag to delimit the earlier revision:

```
floss$ cvs -q update -j
Release-1999_05_01-bugfixes-fix-number-1 -j Release-1999_05_01-bugfixes
RCS file: /usr/local/cvs/myproj/b-subdir/random.c,v
retrieving revision 1.2.2.1
retrieving revision 1.2.2.2
Merging differences between 1.2.2.1 and 1.2.2.2 into random.c
floss$
```

This way, of course, is much better than trying to recall how long ago you made one change versus another, but it only works if you remember to tag the branch every time it is merged to the trunk. The lesson, therefore, is to tag early and tag often! It's better to err on the side of too many tags (as long as they all have descriptive names) than to have too few. In these last examples, for instance, there was no requirement that the new tag on the branch have a name similar to the branch tag itself. Although I named it "Release-1999_05_01-bugfixes-fix-number-1," it could just as easily have been "fix1." However, the former is preferable, because it contains the name of the branch and thus won't ever be confused with a tag on some other branch. (Remember that tag names are unique within files, not within branches. You can't have two tags named "fix1" in the same file, even if they refer to revisions on different branches.)

Creating A Tag Or Branch Without A Working Copy

As stated earlier, tagging affects the repository, not the working copy. That begs the question: Why require a working copy at all when tagging? The only purpose that it serves is to designate which project and which revisions of the various files in the project are being tagged. If you could specify the project and revisions independently of the working copy, no working copy would be necessary.

There is such a way: the **rtag** command (for "repository tag"). It's very similar to **tag**; a couple of examples will explain its usage. Let's go back to the moment when the first bug report came in and we needed to create a branch rooted at the last public release. We checked out a working copy at the release tag and then ran **tag -b** on it:

```
floss$ cvs tag -b Release-1999_05_01-bugfixes
```

This created a branch rooted at "Release-1999_05_01." However, because we know the release tag, we could have used it in an **rtag** command to specify where to root the branch, not even bothering with a working copy:

```
floss$ cvs rtag -b -r Release-1999_05_01 Release-1999_05_01-bugfixes myproj
```

That's all there is to it. That command can be issued from anywhere, inside or outside a working copy. However, your CVSROOT environment variable would have to point to the repository, of course, or you can specify it with the global **-d** option. It works for non-branch tagging, too, but it's less useful that way because you have to specify each file's revision number, one by one. (Or you can refer to it by tag, but then you'd obviously already have a tag there, so why would you want to set a second one on the exact same revisions?)

You now know enough to get around in CVS and probably enough to start working with other people on a project. There are still a few minor features that haven't been introduced, as well as some unmentioned but useful options to features already seen. These will all be presented as appropriate in chapters to come, in scenarios that will demonstrate both how and why to use them. When in doubt, don't hesitate to consult the Cederqvist manual; it is an indispensable resource for serious CVS users.

Chapter 3
The Open Source Process

Failure And Success

If you've been participating in—or even just observing—the free software world for any length of time (especially during the rapid growth spurt of the last few years), you've probably noticed that some projects succeed and others fail. In fact, more projects may fail than succeed. Of course, hardly anyone sends out press releases saying, "The Foo Project Is Officially Declared Dead." Instead, the project home page stops getting updated, announcements of new releases stop appearing on mailing lists, and if you contact the maintainer, she says something like, "Oh yeah, I haven't touched that code in months. Go ahead and see what you can do with it, though." Software, like old soldiers, never dies; it just fades away.

However, all projects begin with the expectation of success and the hope that the software will be immediately adopted by hordes of enthusiastic users, some of whom will contribute bug reports and patches. In most cases, the project finds a kind of comfortable middle ground: A modest number of users grow to depend on the software, they find each other and band together, usually on a mailing list or newsgroup, and stay in close contact with the maintainer or maintainers. Some of them are able to help out with debugging, creating new features, and generally keeping the code healthy. This is what I like to call a "fireside user community"; every program needs one if it is to stay alive. Although software may be temporarily sustained by artificial means (for example, influxes of money, or unusual dedication from a single programmer who is emotionally attached to the code), a program is doomed to extinction unless it has some committed users who depend on it to get things done. Many projects that appear initially promising end up as failures—that is, they don't spread beyond their original authors—because they don't fulfill this basic requirement.

Successful projects tend to have certain organizational qualities in common with each other; the failures have certain structural flaws in common as well. Doubtless every project's fate is also partially determined by its unique circumstances, but the outlines of some general principles of free software development have become clear in the last year or two. In this chapter, I'll try to explain how to run a free software project so it survives.

Did warning bells go off in your head just now?

I hope so. Open Source development is still a very young field; anyone making authoritative pronouncements about it should be regarded with extreme suspicion. Humility, or at least common sense, compels me to issue a few disclaimers up front.

First, remember that free software is still in that wonderfully anarchic, early-evolution stage when a wide variety of ideas and methods proliferate, because the unsuccessful variations have not yet had enough time to fail convincingly. Indeed, the entire field of computer programming is still a bit fresh when measured against older, better-understood crafts such as writing novels or conducting chemistry experiments. No mere human intelligence can compete with an evolutionary process when it comes to distinguishing good practices from bad ones, yet that is what we must try to do in software development, with far too little history to guide us.

Second, keep in mind that "success" means different things for different projects. Sometimes a "failure" at least accomplished an educational purpose, or perhaps it served as a useful stopgap measure until some other, more complete or robust piece of code was developed to replace it.

Most software projects start out with roughly the same goals, though: to solve a particular problem and to acquire users. As in many endeavors, starting off on the wrong foot can seriously reduce the project's chances of meeting either of these goals, so first we'll consider the most fragile stage of every free project's life cycle: the beginning.

Starting A Project

As I said before, if the code doesn't have a user community committed to keeping it alive, it will fade away. But clearly, no program starts out with dedicated users from day one. The code has to be reasonably stable and actually do something before users will even take the time to try it out. How does it get to that stage? This is the chicken-and-egg dilemma faced by every new project and is probably where the majority of fatalities occur.

As it happens, there is already a well-received theory in the free software world about how projects begin. Specifically, it is Eric Raymond's influential paper, "The Cathedral and the Bazaar." If you haven't read it already, it's worth taking a moment to do so—Raymond is a lively writer, and you are unlikely to regret the time spent. You can find it online at **www.tuxedo.org/~esr/writings/cathedral-bazaar/**.

The terminology and principles Raymond introduced have become so widespread that the paper is a good starting place for examining many of the principles of free software development, although there is room for debate on certain of his assertions. At any rate, his take on why projects get started is highly persuasive:

Every good work of software starts by scratching a developer's personal itch.

There are exceptions, but in general, new free software is written because someone wants to see a certain problem solved, forever (or at least for the next few years, which is the equivalent of forever in computers). The "return on investment" comes from the convenience of having code do what humans formerly had to do, not from selling copies of the software. Therefore, if the project is to sustain the interest of even one programmer for long enough to reach usability, the project goals must be kept in clear view the entire time, and steady progress must be made throughout the entire initial development stage. The larger and more significant the goals, the longer the project can sustain itself on promise (known in the industry as "vapor") before it must show results. However, if the project doesn't show results within a finite amount of time, people lose interest and move on to another project that has more obvious potential.

Thus, if anyone, including yourself, is to care about the code enough to stick with it, they must first care about the problem the code was written to solve. This is usually not too difficult—after all, you wouldn't have started writing it if you didn't need it for something. The question is, will anybody else be interested?

More likely than not, the answer is "yes." One of the most pleasant surprises to arise from ubiquitous Internet access is the discovery, over and over again, that one's most specialized needs turn out to be shared by tens or hundreds of other people. Your personal itch is unlikely to be unique to you. Chances are there are a few other people out there with the same itch, who may be considering starting a free program themselves. The phenomenon of parallel ideation has long been observed in the older arts and sciences; a certain idea will somehow be "in the air," albeit unspoken, and people independently begin to notice and act on it, all at the same time and without being aware of each other's work. This phenomenon happens in software, too. With greater than the expected statistical frequency, it seems, free software projects designed to solve the same problem will spring up simultaneously. Often, whichever one gets the most success early on wins out by drawing resources away from the others. Because outside contributors are free agents, they turn their attention to whichever code base seems likely to solve their problem first.

This has an obvious implication for you as an initiator of a project: You should look to see if anyone else has already started something similar. Where you look depends largely on the subject domain; you'll probably know the appropriate newsgroups, mailing lists, and Web sites to check for your problem area. Some good generic resources are Freshmeat, a Web site specializing in announcements of new software (**www.freshmeat.net**), the Ask Slashdot archives (**http://slashdot.org**), and the Free Software Foundation's software links (**www.gnu. org/software/**).

If you discover a similar project already under way, you may be better off joining it than starting your own project. It's a matter of determining how closely their goals match yours, examining what they have so far, and possibly asking questions of the authors. If their purposes are very close to yours and they already have running code, you can become a contributor (some work) instead of a primary maintainer (lots of work) and still receive all the benefits of the package.

If you don't find any similar work already under way, the next step is to put your project in public view as soon as the time is right, probably in the very same forums you originally scoured for news of other projects. But when is the time right?

Think about it from the other direction: Is there any reason not to tell others about your code? There is strong pressure to announce to the whole world the moment you start coding. After all, the sooner they know, the sooner they can help out. And, just possibly, the sooner they can stop working on their own half-begun projects to do the same thing.

Resist that pressure. Openness and sharing are wonderful things, but attention is still a nonrenewable resource, and you're in danger of wasting other people's time if you attract them to your project before it's ready. Your reputation is on the line. By telling interested parties that you've started work on a certain program, you've given them the right to expect some running code to play with. If all that is available is a README file, a few rough notes on design, and maybe some skeletal code, these possible contributors will realize there's nothing you've done that they couldn't do themselves in a few hours. Perhaps more importantly, they'll take you less seriously the next time you make an announcement.

On the other hand, if you wait too long, you run the risk of someone else announcing that they have running code that does the same thing as yours. At that point, you'll have to decide whether to throw away everything you've done so far or continue in open, if friendly, competition with the other project. There's another danger to continuing too long in isolation as well: You might miss out on some great contributions—contributions that would have affected the overall design of your code if received early enough.

Release Something Useful

Lest you think all these possibilities exist only in some abstract, theoretical world, here is some actual history from a recent project of mine. In March 1999, I released a small program to the Net. This quite specialized program reformatted the output of the **cvs log** command into the much more readable GNU **ChangeLog** style (covered in later chapters). Although I wasn't completely satisfied with it at the time of release—it lacked several important features—it did perform its basic function without crashing or complaining, and I had a hunch it was something other people would find useful. So I posted it to Ask Slashdot and to an appropriate mailing list (in this case **info-cvs@gnu.org**) and waited for the bug reports and feature suggestions to flow in. They started arriving almost immediately, including the following from Melissa O'Neill (**oneill@cs.sfu.ca**):

```
Hi Karl,
In the spirt of free software, here's a patch to your program to handle
the non-atomicity of CVS checkins better.
Best Regards,
Melissa.
```

```
[patch followed]
```

Her patch, although introduced with little fanfare, actually contained a thorough rewrite of the program's already complicated main loop. It was just the sort of change that you would want to make early in development, rather than later when a lot more dependencies may be affected. Furthermore, in another email, she wrote:

```
From the first time I downloaded CVS, I couldn't believe this support
wasn't there. I resolved to one day write a Perl script to turn cvs
log into something useful, but you beat me to it...
```

The "shared itch" theory had held up wonderfully—not only was the program what she had needed, but she had even been considering writing it herself! Fortunately, she hadn't done any significant coding yet and was able to get everything she needed from my program— and what it lacked, she simply added herself. Over the next week or two, I received 19 separate patches from her, all of which resulted in definite improvements to the code. There were also numerous bug reports, patches, and suggestions from other people (15, to be precise, 14 of whom were complete strangers to me). As a result of all this activity, the program progressed at a far faster rate than would have been possible had I continued working in isolation. Bugs were found and fixed, algorithms improved, and features added—yet my role was mostly to coordinate the changes that others sent in. This was strong confirmation to me both that the program had found its niche—its fireside user community—and that I'd released it at the right time—when it was working but still needed improvement.

The best guideline for an initial release, then, is to post the code when it's far enough along to reliably solve some significant portion of the problem for which it was designed. It should do something useful right away, even if it doesn't yet do everything it's intended to do.

The key word is "reliably." If the program still crashes occasionally, find out why and fix it before your release. You may be anxious to release right away, but delays spent fixing showstopper bugs are almost certainly worth the time. Nothing impresses potential users (and contributors) more than rock-solid stability and graceful handling of error conditions, and nothing scares them away like unexpected crashes. All the glitz and flashy features in the world won't mean a thing if the code's foundation is visibly shaky. (I call this the "just catch it" principle, from a more experienced juggling partner who, on seeing unnecessarily fancy receives attempted and consistently dropped, said, "That's nice, but you know, it always looks better if you catch it.")

The majority of potential contributors often feel that they can patch in a desired missing feature themselves, but that if the fundamental code is fragile, there's no point in their putting new code on top of it. Even the most charitable reaction to crashes is, "Well, I guess it's not really ready for outsiders yet. I'll come back in six months and see what the code looks like."

The importance of releasing runnable code was recently demonstrated by one of the most well-publicized mis-starts in the history of free software. Netscape Communications Corporation announced in January 1998 that they would publicly release the source code to their Navigator Web browser under a license allowing others to modify and redistribute the source code. The news sent a wave of excitement through the free software community. The lack of a good free Web browser had long been a serious problem, and Netscape was claiming that they would solve it in one stroke.

Netscape's sincerity was not faked; they did exactly as they said. However, a year and a half later, the project is a failure by almost any measure. It is still possible that a working Web browser may arise from the tangle of code available from **www.mozilla.org**, but don't hold your breath. Despite the huge demand for a free Web browser and the many programmers willing to contribute their talents to make it happen, the long-awaited Mozilla still does not exist.

What did Netscape do wrong?

Ex-Netscape employee Jamie Zawinski has analyzed the causes of the collapse in some detail at **www.jwz.org/gruntle/nomo.html**, a fascinating essay that offers several reasons for the failure. I'm willing to bet, however, that his Reason Number 2 is the true cause: Their initial release was not running code.

Instead, Netscape released the latest snapshot of their development tree, or as Zawinski put it, "What we released was a large pile of interesting code, but it didn't much resemble something you could actually use." Developers were not treated to an "out of the box" experience; instead, they had to struggle just to get the code to compile, let alone run.

This problem alone may not have been fatal, as long as making Mozilla run was the only way some people could get a working Web browser. But everyone already had a Web browser—usually either Netscape Navigator or Microsoft Internet Explorer—on their computer. These browsers may not have been "free" in the sense of free source code, but they worked well enough and didn't cost any money. So the developers' main "itch" was already being scratched; they all had working Web browsers and were therefore motivated by the somewhat weaker itch to have an Open Source Web browser. Thus, all the people who would otherwise have worked feverishly to ship a working version of Mozilla right away instead felt they had the luxury to turn Mozilla into a textbook-perfect Web browser. In retrospect, the folly seems obvious—no one was really depending on Mozilla to get anything done, so actually shipping it became an infinitely receding priority.

It was a measure of Mozilla's promise, and the intensity of the community's desire for a free Web browser, that many people still contributed. Unfortunately, in software, there is no strength in numbers. The programmers were there, with plenty of technical ability, but they had no compelling reason to make the code work right away; their efforts never focused enough to get the program to run.

It was a costly and probably embarrassing lesson for Netscape, but at least now the rest of us can learn from it: running code—first, last, and always.

Packaging

Getting the program to work is only half the story, however. Although the code itself is the main attraction, the packaging you wrap it in can make a big difference in initial levels of participation. Packaging means at least basic documentation, probably a project home page with a clear description of what the code does and what's required to run it, and a convenient way for the public to get the latest updates to the code. Too often, programmers treat these things as mere decorations and don't devote enough time to providing them. Perhaps it's because of the legendary programmer's distaste for anything that feels like marketing or public relations, or perhaps it's due to a loss of perspective. (When you know your own code front to back, it can be difficult to comprehend that others may need introductory documentation before they can use it.) Whatever the reason, sloppy packaging can seriously detract from a project's attractiveness, which is a shame when the code itself is of good quality. Don't let your project falter because of an unnecessarily steep learning curve for new participants.

The first piece of packaging is the license under which you distribute the code. It may seem trivial, but people can't be confident that your program is really free software until they see its actual terms of copyright.

Free licenses tend to fall into two groups: the GNU General Public License (GPL), and all the others. The GPL insists that not only the code itself but also any derivative works must be distributed under the GPL; thus, it is self-perpetuating and infectious. Others state that the code is free as received but allow derivative works to be distributed under different (and sometimes more restrictive) terms, as long as proper credit is given.

Occasionally, people even write an entirely new license to accompany their software release, designing the license to embody everything they think free software should be (this seems to be the course favored lately by large corporations who have suddenly decided to release code to the public). Writing a custom license is very definitely *not* recommended; for one thing, it's hard to do it right. (Did you use a lawyer? Did you make sure the lawyer really understood your goals in releasing the software this way?) Worse, it's simply tiresome for potential users to have to read and evaluate unfamiliar licenses all the time. Unless you really do have special needs, just stick with one of the standards.

Licensing choices are the subject of fearsomely intense debate among free software advocates, and—discretion being the better part of valor—I'm simply not going to get into that debate here. My favorite license is the GNU GPL. I hope you'll use it for all of your programs, but even if you don't, it probably doesn't matter very much. It is not the details of the license that keep the code free, but the fact that free code has better survival characteristics than non-free code. Even if for some reason you choose to distribute your program under a license allowing non-free derivative works, those non-free descendants are probably doomed to have a shorter lifespan than the free ones. So don't worry about it too much. Just pick a license that ensures everyone else the same rights as you have with respect to the code, or put your code in the public domain if you can't make up your mind and let the dynamics of free software do the rest.

The rest of the packaging tends to be more mundane matters of presentation. Here's an informal checklist I use before releasing new code. I include it here not as a rigid standard, but to give you an idea of the sorts of things that make a project developer-friendly as well as user-friendly.

♦ The code has been tested by at least one person other than its author. Everyone knows that bugs tend to hide from authors, only to reveal themselves in droves as soon as someone else tries the code. Impose on a friend or colleague to give your code at least a cursory test run before you post it to a bunch of strangers on a mailing list or newsgroup.

♦ Documentation is available in an obvious place. It doesn't have to be much at this stage, just a quick summary of the purpose and basic usage of the program. If the project is not overly complex, the documentation need not even be a separate file—it could just be the output from invoking the code with a **-help** option or something like that.

   Also, a special plea, from someone who has seen far too many document formats come and go: If the documentation is in a separate file, use a widely understood, easily searchable format such as plain text or HTML. If you also want to offer PostScript, RTF, PDF, and that sort of thing, that's fine, just as long as those aren't the *only* ways to view the documents. It's possible to alienate an astonishing number of developers in a short amount of time by requiring them to print out a hard copy or download special viewing software just to read the documents. Most of them will depart in frustration rather than continue, reasoning that if the first thing they encounter is so developer-hostile, the rest of the project is likely to be, too.

♦ A project home page or some other central place exists where people can find up-to-date information about the project (a Web page is the norm, though). It introduces the program by first describing the problem that the program was written to solve (so visitors will be able to determine quickly whether they're interested in reading more), then summarizes how the program solves it. The page also lists any unusual system requirements that people may need to run the program and offers links to the documentation, the source code, and any other applicable materials. Finally, the page makes it completely clear that the program is free software, by using the words "free software" or "Open Source" and linking to the actual copyright.

◆ The latest sources can always be retrieved from a clearly designated location. For the latest released version, you can link to it from the home page. For those who need access to the continuously changing development sources, the answer is, of course, CVS. Making the code accessible via a public CVS server allows early enthusiasts to become as involved as they want to be, giving them access to code changes right away instead of making them wait for official releases. (The details of setting up a CVS server to allow anonymous, read-only access are covered in Chapter 4.)

Most users, however, will use the latest versions posted in public forums, for convenience, and because such posted versions are usually thought to be stable and have an implied endorsement from the author. Those who are interested in following the code closely, or perhaps becoming developers themselves, will want and expect continuous access to the latest sources. Access to development sources is also crucial for bug reporters, who will usually update to the latest version of the code and try to reproduce the bug again before they send in a report that is relevant.

◆ The initial release and every release thereafter has a clear version number. This may seem obvious, but you'd be surprised at the number of programs—especially smallish scripts—that are posted without a version number.

The purpose of the number is *not* to mark psychological milestones in the code's progress (although it is traditional for Release 1.0 to signify a stable, workable product, Release 2.0 to be a major improvement over that, and so on). The real purpose of the version number is to give people an easy, unambiguous way to compare two versions of the code and to know which is more recent. To that end, it does not matter if the version numbers convey any information about the degree or significance of the changes between them. Although the difference between Releases 2.0 and 1.0 is usually greater than the difference between Releases 3.90.8 and 3.90.7, this is not a requirement. However, there is a requirement that Release 2.0 be newer than 1.0, and Release 3.101 be newer than 3.99. This consistency is vitally important: When users or developers decide to upgrade to the latest version, they must be able to compare their current version with what's available on the project home page and know instantly whether there are any newer versions available.

Note

Although CVS can increment version numbers for you automatically, this is not necessarily always desirable. The pros and cons of automated version bumping, as well as the mechanism, are covered in Chapter 7.

◆ An email address has been designated for reporting bugs. Although not strictly necessary, I've found that it's often a good idea to separate the bug address from your personal address. When additional developers start to join, you can just add them to a communal bug list, instead of manually forwarding bug reports to them.

A non-bug developers' mailing list can be helpful, too, but you'll probably want to wait until you have several developers trying to communicate with each other. If the project is large and likely to stimulate a lot of early developer interest, you may prefer to have this list address ready before you start.

Don't be surprised if setting up all of this takes as much time as actually writing the code, or perhaps even more. Even though the packaging work may not feel as productive as coding, it will pay off quickly when people join the project and make the pleasant discovery that an infrastructure has already been established. This will give prospective contributors confidence that the project is well run, which in turn makes them more likely to contribute because they'll think their contributions are likely to survive. The more steps you can take to inspire that sort of confidence, the better off the project will be.

Announcing The Program

After you've gone through the checklist and taken care of whatever packaging is appropriate, you're ready to post an announcement to the relevant mailing lists and newsgroups. The convention for such announcements is to have a subject line that looks something like this:

```
Subject: ANN: Genie 1.0, program to take genotype and print out phenotype
```

It's quite important that the subject line be accurate and concise, because most people just scan the subjects of messages in mailing lists and newsgroups and delete everything that doesn't grab their attention.

The body of the announcement should describe the project as clearly and quickly as possible and mention the project home page early on, so interested parties can visit it immediately and bookmark it. If the program consists of just one or two small files, you could include them directly in the announcement message; otherwise, assume that anyone who wants the code will make the trip to the Web site.

That's it. Once the announcement is posted, you can sit back and wait to receive bug reports, feature suggestions, and help requests. The project has now entered its second and lengthiest phase: maintenance.

Running A Project

When the project gets to this stage, you are now the maintainer of an active free software project.

What does that even mean?

Well, we're all still trying to figure that out, actually. For now, I'll summarize a maintainer's responsibilities as follows:

♦ To say "yes."

♦ To say "no."

♦ To code, and help others do the same.

The first two responsibilities, taken together, are probably the most sensitive part of the maintainer's role. In any project with multiple participants, there's no way to avoid occasional disagreements over design, features, or sometimes even the program's very purpose. By accepting ultimate responsibility for the state of the code, the maintainer naturally ends up assuming a degree of authority as well. (There are projects where the maintainership is held equally by a group of people; this scheme is discussed later in the chapter. However, most projects start out with a single person in this role, so that's the situation we'll examine first.)

When the maintainer's decision is to say "yes"—that is, to accept a particular patch or a proposed code change—there is usually no great controversy. Although some developers may feel that the change is for the worse, they usually accept it. After all, the change probably benefits someone, or it wouldn't be proposed. It's difficult to make a forceful argument that some new feature or behavior is undesirable merely because it doesn't fit with the program's overall design.

However, when the maintainer must say "no," care and sensitivity are required. Rejecting a contributor's code or ideas is never easy, especially when someone has spent a long time implementing and testing the changes, but it must be done occasionally if the program is to stay healthy. Good quality control means saying "no"; the only question is how to reject undesirable contributions in a constructive manner.

Luckily, the maintainer starts out with a certain amount of moral authority, and it is generally accepted that the maintainer has the final word in disagreements. In the absence of a more formal decision-making structure, other developers tacitly accept that the maintainer is a benevolent dictator. When no clear consensus can be reached on an issue, the maintainer simply decides by fiat, and that ends the matter (well, it rarely ends the discussion, but at least it settles the question of which direction the code will go).

This may seem surprising for a system that boasts about its democratic and decentralized nature. However, great software, like great art, is rarely created by committee. To resolve disputes quickly, the most efficient way (note that "efficient" does not always mean "best") is to have a designated arbitrator—in other words, a maintainer.

The crucial factor that makes this arrangement acceptable to developers is that the maintainer's authority is based on merit, not ownership. If people disagree strongly enough with the maintainer's decisions, they can make a separate copy of the code and start distributing their own divergent version of the program, one in which their decisions are implemented. This is known as "forking" the code (or sometimes "branching," not to be confused with a literal CVS branch).

A fork is a very serious step. It causes confusion among the program's users, who now have to decide which version of the program is more likely to meet their needs and to survive in the long term. Moreover, a fork can give rise to long-lasting political divisions. As a practical matter, most developers must choose which version to devote their time to (although there are always a few developers who simply go to the extra effort to make their contributions fit both versions).

Fortunately, forks are quite rare, partly because they're so much trouble to undertake, but mainly because the implicit threat of one occurring is usually enough to prevent the maintainer from making decisions that upset a majority of the other developers. Avoiding the possibility of a fork is a strong incentive to be a truly *benevolent* dictator. Your subjects can duplicate your kingdom at any time and remake it in their own image, so you had better pay attention to their opinions!

Benevolence is not just a state of mind; it has quite specific implications for how a maintainer ought to behave. First—and most important—you must always explain the reasons behind your decisions. I'll use an example from a project that I maintain (not because all my decisions are ideal, but because it's the example closest at hand).

I received an email from a user of a program (the same program mentioned before), proposing a feature that struck me as unattractive, at least if implemented strictly according to his descriptions. His proposal concluded:

```
I am sure there will be modifications by [our group] to
the script over time. Is there some way we can work
together?
```

Although the script had benefited immensely from user contributions so far, this seemed a clear place to draw the line. I couldn't make some vague promise to give his changes special consideration or precedence, and I was not willing to include the new feature using his implied implementation. However, just because he had proposed one rejectable feature didn't mean that he might not come up with something useful later on (and in point of fact, attached to the end of his email was a small unrelated patch that corrected a genuine problem in the script). In declining to accept his request, it was important to state my reasons and explain what conditions might make the proposal more acceptable:

```
Hard to say in the abstract; I try to consider each change
individually, based on how useful it would be to how many people.
Making heavy modifications to the script for the specific needs of
only one user or organization wouldn't be good (or maintainable, in
the long run). On the other hand, if there's a generally useful
change that also happens to do what you need, that's great.
```

In other words, I asked him to please come up with an implementation that would provide his desired result but that would also be flexible enough to benefit other users of the script.

This example also demonstrates a very common situation: People often ask a maintainer to accept or reject an idea based only on a vague description. But without an actual patch, or at least a highly technical description of the change, it's usually impossible to determine its worth. In such situations, a standard reply can be something like, "I'm for/against the idea as described for reasons A, B, and C, but my attitude could be changed with a more detailed description or, better yet, a patch."

When the change is not too big, it's not necessarily rude to ask someone to actually implement it before you decide whether it's worth folding into the code. After all, working source code can be viewed as merely the last in a series of increasingly precise behavioral descriptions; to ask for source code is to ask for the most exact possible description of a change, which is sometimes the only way to know if it's worthwhile.

However, if a proposed change is going to require many hours of work, it's understandable that the person would want to know in advance that it will be accepted. In that case, most maintainers typically work with the contributor to produce a specification that resolves all important questions about the nature of the change, while still reminding the contributor that the patch must be reviewed prior to acceptance. This may seem overly harsh, but most developers understand that a maintainer cannot judge a patch without actually reviewing and testing it. Of course, if the maintainer ultimately rejects the patch, she must give the contributor specific reasons.

When rejecting a patch or a proposal, however, the maintainer cannot merely explain why; he or she must explain the reasons politely and without rancor. A contributor's proposals and opinions must be given respect and at least the appearance of consideration when discussed in public forums. Criticisms do not have to be suppressed, but they must be specific, articulately argued, and never personal.

Maintaining a high level of civility while still giving good critiques not only increases the likelihood that that developer will eventually contribute something useful, it also encourages others to contribute, simply because the overall environment will be conducive to high-quality debate, free of personal attacks.

A good maintainer must spend as much time on organizational and social issues as on coding. This may sometimes be a bit of a mismatch with a maintainer's actual skills, as it is well known that the best coders (and, therefore, the ones likely to get code up and running fastest) often devote a disproportionate amount of their minds to programming, leaving correspondingly less available for the niceties of human relations. If you think this describes you, my best advice is to make a conscious decision to read every email and posting that you send out as though you were going to receive it yourself. Like any skill, managing projects gets easier with practice. Most participants don't expect an ambassadorial mastery of high diplomacy; they just want to be treated with the respect due any volunteer.

Tip

While we're on the subject of making a project developer-friendly, it should be noted that Internet-based projects often attract contributors from many different countries. Miscommunication is rare, fortunately; it seems that English has become the language of international software development, and most programmers know enough

English to participate without too much trouble (usually even to the point of being fluent in computer jargon). Whether this is a good thing or not is beyond the scope of this book; Esperanto isn't exactly taking over, and a lot of code and documentation is already written in English. For better or worse most people seem to be following the path of least resistance. However, don't fall into the trap of forgetting who is on a developers mailing list or newsgroup and make a remark that is only comprehensible (or even appropriate) for people from your own country.

Cultivating Technical Judgement

Now that you know how to tell someone diplomatically that his or her change won't be accepted, how do you decide whether to accept it? This is not merely a matter of having the requisite technical judgement, but of demonstrating it in such a way that both you and others are *confident* that you have it.

The answer, perhaps surprisingly, is not to try to be the biggest frog in the pond. You do not need to be a programming guru with vast experience and imposing credentials; indeed, you may well recognize that many of your contributors are far more experienced coders than you are (I've certainly felt that way many times!). What you do need are two things: a clear sense of the program's purpose, and the ability to recognize maintainable solutions.

The first is as much a matter of knowing what the program should not do as what it should. Curiously, when designers err in imagining the scope of their project, they tend to err on the side of inclusiveness rather than restrictiveness. It's extremely tempting to concede no limits, especially early in development; the less actual code has been written, the wider the apparent possibilities for future development.

Unfortunately, a program that does everything probably doesn't do it very well. The best programs, free and otherwise, know the problem they were written to solve and succeed by addressing every aspect of that one problem. Free software starts out with an advantage here, because most free programs were developed because someone wanted to solve a specific problem. When the program later expands beyond that, as it generally will, it's usually because people found a related problem that frequently needed to be solved in conjunction with the original one. (Commercial software, on the other hand, is just made to sell as many copies as possible; this often leads the maintainers to pile on as many features as possible so that there is—theoretically—something for everyone.) A clear understanding of the program's goals, combined with a vigorous fear of software bloat, will aid the maintainer in deciding which changes should be accepted and which shouldn't. Furthermore, that understanding will make it much easier to justify decisions to others.

This need to articulate the program's purpose early in its life may feel overly confining but, in the long run, is really healthy. This statement of purpose doesn't have to be absolutely restrictive; it can evolve over time, in response to unexpected uses. Just such an evolution happened with CVS itself, in fact. Originally, CVS was regarded as only a tool for allowing a group of preselected developers to collaborate. One day, someone combined two of its features (the remote server and read-only repository access) to allow random strangers to check out noncommittable working copies anonymously. As soon as everyone else realized how useful this was, CVS became both a developer-collaboration tool and a software-distribution tool. The expansion was so natural that virtually no objections were raised, and it's safe to say that decisions about CVS's direction will take both aspects into account from now on.

Note that each of those features was driven by real-world usage—not by the maintainer's or developers' idea of what people may or should want. Both the remote server and the read-only repository functionality (which together made anonymous access possible) were implemented because of immediate demand—the code was written to fulfill a need, not the other way around. "Evolution," in the context of free software, is more than just a buzzword. It means that the maintainer is guided by how the program is used in the real world; he or she doesn't try to second-guess reality when deciding what to implement. Even when a program's domain (the range of problems that it can be used to solve) expands, it rarely expands into completely unexpected territory. The border is pushed gently and incrementally, so that at no point does anyone—developer or user—wonder why a particular feature was added or behavior changed.

Thus, the questions to ask yourself when considering whether to implement (or approve) a change are:

♦ Will it benefit a significant percentage of the program's user community?

♦ Does it fit within the program's domain or within a natural, intuitive extension of that domain?

Failure to satisfy one or both of these conditions is reason enough to reject a change. The appropriateness and usefulness of the new functionality is not merely a matter of aesthetics; it has a direct bearing on maintainability. A stretch of code that doesn't get regularly exercised will inevitably suffer bit-rot. Therefore, it's a losing proposition to add a new code path unless you can be confident that it will be executed often enough for any bugs to be found and reported. If no one but the feature's contributor wants or expects a given new feature, then than feature will never be widely used enough to become truly robust.

As far as I know, there's no standard ratio relating the number of changes accepted to the number proposed. You must use your judgement. However, you can also consult with other developers, either on an open discussion list or via private email, when considering a change. In fact, in the most successful projects, the maintainer seems to engage in such consultations regularly. To seek out all points of view on a given change consistently is taken by most developers as a sign of confidence on the maintainer's part. No one expects a maintainer to be an infallible oracle of design wisdom or even to always make inarguably right decisions. People *do* expect a maintainer to be sensitive to the community's opinions, even when she must oppose them, and to provide thorough justification for controversial decisions.

Having clarified in your mind that a particular change is a good idea, you still face the question of whether a contributor's patch to implement this change is technically acceptable.

There is no magic formula to answer this; you just have to roll up your sleeves and dive into the code. It's normal for a maintainer to become quite skilled at reading patches and quite all right for the maintainer to request that **diff**s be sent in the format that he or she finds easiest to read (most likely either context or unified format—respectively, the **-c** or **-u** option to **diff**).

Reviewing patches is not easy. Most patches need at least a little massaging from the maintainer. The mere fact that a patch doesn't apply flawlessly on the first try or even contains a few buglets is probably not enough reason to reject it outright. Instead, you must look over the patch line by line, with the original sources at hand for reference, and decide if it works overall. If it does, you can apply it and manually clean up any loose ends (a detailed description of this process is given in Chapter 7).

It's reasonable to ask your contributors to abide by coding conventions, as long as the demands aren't too burdensome. Two common conventions are:

♦ All patches must be accompanied by log entries (summarizing the changes and making clear what parts of the code are affected).

♦ The changes must adhere to the same indentation standards as the rest of the program. These are a small effort for the developers and greatly reduce the maintainer's "comprehension overhead" when looking at new code.

If you can't easily tell exactly the effects of a change, immediately ask for help, not only from the contributor but from other developers as well. Often, they'll be able to point out things about the change that haven't occurred to you. The great strength of free software, as Eric Raymond said, is that "Given enough eyeballs, all bugs are shallow."

So, Who Is The Maintainer, Really?

Throughout this discussion, a tiny logical inconsistency has been left dangling: We may agree that the maintainer retains his or her position by demonstrated merit, but how is the first maintainer chosen?

The obvious answer is the correct one: In almost all cases, the original author of the software, the one who initially published it to the world, is the first maintainer. Because the first author (or authors) have demonstrated merit by developing the software, in the absence of any adverse indications, people accept this original version of the program as the "canonical" version. In other words, if everyone is downloading the version of the code that you post, that must mean that you're the maintainer!

Thus, the best evidence that someone is the maintainer of a free program lies in the willingness of others to agree that it is so. This is in direct contrast to the world of commercial software. Microsoft, Inc., is the "maintainer" of MS-Word because they have an exclusive and restrictive copyright on the code. No matter how their users (or even employees) feel about their stewardship, they will continue to be the maintainer because they have a permanent legal right to the position.

Rule By Committee

Up to this point, I've been talking as if the maintainer is always a single person. Although most projects start out that way, when a project grows large or important enough, it's not unusual to have a group of developers accepting equal responsibility for the code. Such groups are usually structured, at least nominally, as self-regulating democracies (although in practice, one or two "senior" developers' opinions often informally carry extra weight). Typically, new members are voted on by the existing developers, and the properties that distinguish official developers from the rest of the world are:

♦ CVS **commit** access to the repository

♦ Voting rights (for example, voting on code changes or whether to accept new members)

There's no simple rule defining when it's appropriate to move to this kind of development model. Free software users often feel that once a program has become important to a lot of people, it's not quite proper for everything to depend on one individual. Even when the primary maintenance continues along the benevolent dictator model, it's not uncommon for assistant or backup maintainers to be explicitly designated (Eric Raymond has done this for the "fetchmail" program he maintains, and Linus Torvalds seems to have done the same for the Linux kernel).

CVS itself is group-maintained and even has a description of the development process (see **www.cyclic.com/cvs/dev-policy.html**). Interestingly, the process for approving changes is not heavily formalized; decisions are made by informal consensus, and generally any of the developers can check in contributed changes. New developers are proposed by existing developers and voted on; sometimes developers resign from the group because they've become too busy with other things.

By contrast, the Apache Group (maintainers of the extremely popular Apache Web server) have a little more love for procedure. They vote not only on membership, but also on every change to the software; three positive votes and no negative votes is enough to allow a change to happen. However, even their charter (see **www.apache.org/ABOUT_APACHE.html**) makes it clear that the system really depends on people exercising good judgement and having a healthy respect for the opinions of their peers, rather than on a precise and unambiguous written agreement.

These loose development charters are frequently mistaken for legal documents, but they actually serve a very different purpose. Legal constitutions are usually written with the assumption that the parties involved don't always necessarily want to cooperate, so that part of the constitution's role is to be a contract on which a neutral judge can base arbitration. Free software developer groups, on the other hand, are self-selecting for cooperators. After all, if someone doesn't want to cooperate, they're perfectly free to copy the code and start their own fork. Therefore, everyone in a given developer group is there because they want to be involved; there's no need for the charter to anticipate every possible misinterpretation. If disagreements do arise, people have every motivation to reach a consensus quickly, and they usually do.

Admittedly, dilemmas occasionally can arise from such loose systems. For example, when a developer group splits into two camps because of a major disagreement about some code change, how do you decide which side is the original and which is the fork? Both sides may feel equally legitimate guardians of the program, so each side wants to portray the other as having started a fork. Or what about two developers, both with **commit** access to the sources, who conduct an argument by continually reverting each other's changes—how can the rest of the group stop the cycle? If the two warring developers are equal with everyone else, then strictly speaking, no one has the right to take steps that bar either one of them from doing those things in the repository.

In practice, however, these things rarely happen. For one thing, the consequences of violating these mutually agreed-upon rules are not really very serious. The code won't disappear or stop working just because someone decides to take a step that's not within accepted strictures. A project's procedural regulations do not require the same strict obedience as, say, a nation's, because everyone involved in a project knows that if enough of the developers get disgusted, they'll simply go off and start developing the code on their own. If one developer gets out of hand, the rest are usually quite willing to indulge whatever extra-procedural steps are necessary to solve the problem.

Which method you choose for your project—benevolent dictatorship or ruling council—depends partly on which arrangement you're more comfortable with and partly on what your user community wants. If you're the kind of person who makes a good dictator, and no one seems to mind, then go ahead. If you are more comfortable sharing responsibility and can find others from your developer group willing to share it, then widen the throne. It may feel like you're giving up power, but you're not; with free code, everyone in the world has exactly the same powers. The so-called maintainers really only control mere matters of convenience, such as giving the world an "official" place to download the latest release of the code, submit bug reports, patches, suggestions, and so forth.

Even the phrase "latest release" is slightly misleading. A publicly recognized, generally accepted source for releases of the software exists only because all of the interested and competent developers have coalesced around the same code base (it's in their interests to work together). The code itself is just bit patterns. Anyone can take those patterns, make new ones, and release them to the world, under any name they choose; it doesn't require special permission.

The arrangement that you encourage for running your project should be chosen based solely on what is best for the code. If you decide to share the maintainership—or even hand it off to someone else entirely—you won't really be giving anyone any powers that they didn't already have. You'll just be making it easier for the developers to work together and improve the code. On the other hand, if you think the project will run better if questions are resolved quickly by one person, and you are confident that you are that person, by all means preserve a happy dictatorship. In the long run, the code itself will gravitate toward whichever method is most appropriate for it. If it becomes too large and complex for a single maintainer, you'll begin to feel overloaded and start hearing complaints from users that needed patches aren't getting applied fast enough.

How To Do A Fork, If You Absolutely Must

Even though forks are relatively rare occurrences, it's worth taking a look at how they should be (and generally are) conducted. Not only is it useful knowledge to have in an emergency, but it actually sheds a lot of light on the innately cooperative nature of free software.

First, think long and hard about whether the fork is really necessary. What do you hope to accomplish with it? If the problem is that bugs are not being fixed soon enough in the current version, you should devote your time to being a better bug-fixer within that development group. If the issue is really one of a major disagreement about the direction in which the code should go, a fork may be appropriate. Even then, though, you should ask yourself if you're positive that you can do a better job with the code than the current crew. If the answer is "yes," and you decide to go ahead with the fork, you must face the question of how to present it to the world.

Whatever you do, don't make an announcement that you're angry or frustrated with the current maintainers (even if you are) and that you're forking because you just can't stand it anymore. Instead, politely state the exact nature of the problems you have with the code's current state and apparent future, and what you intend to do (or better yet, have done) differently. These announcements can be posted to the original development mailing list and on your "rival" project home page. You should also set up the forked project exactly as you would any other project, complete with a CVS repository, a bug-reporting address, a developer mailing list, and so on.

The most politically sensitive question is what to call your forked version. To decide that, let's step back a bit and clarify what the original maintainer can reasonably stake a claim to. Although, as we have seen, the whole system rests on the fact that maintainership does not imply ownership, sometimes a maintainer of a free program does own a legal trademark on the program's name. Even when this is not the case, the maintainer may rightfully feel that the reputation earned by the code so far was largely a result of his or her efforts and would be offended if other people began using the same name to distribute their rival code base. In a sense, this constitutes an implied trademark, to be honored until it has been proven beyond a reasonable doubt that the program has moved on to other hands.

There's nothing evil (by which I mean, of course, anti-free-software) about trademarks. Trademarks exist to prevent people from hijacking others' reputations and passing them off as their own. When a piece of free code is distributed under a certain name, that name is associated in users' minds with all the work that the maintainer and developer group have done up to this point. Since your concern is the future of the code itself, not the name under which it's distributed, your goal is not to get people to call your program by that same name right away, but merely to get them to use the code.

Therefore, the rule for someone considering starting a divergent branch is to only fork the code, not the name. If you run off and start distributing a rival version of program Foo, and you call your program "Foo" as well, it will only cause confusion among users and make other developers suspicious of your sense of civility. If you have the slightest doubt about whether your fork is the diverging one, err on the side of caution and assume it is. It's only polite.

Of course, you want people to know that your new distribution is based on the software they've known from past releases and is applicable to a very similar problem domain. One solution is to give the new code a name that makes clear exactly what's going on. You can try "Rogue Foo," "Foo, Branch Edition," and so on, or use a mostly unrelated name but explain clearly in the distribution and on the project home page that it is a descendant of the Foo program.

Neither of these solutions is particularly elegant, but that's okay. The fork will either die out quickly or end up supplanting the new program. If it dies out, it doesn't matter that for a short while it existed with an awkward name. If it ends up taking over from the old distribution in the minds of the user community, and you're absolutely secure that that has happened, you can start calling it "Foo" again. After some time has passed, most people will forget that the fork ever happened, and any name confusion will be over. Remember, though, that the onus is on you to prove the new code's merit, so don't adopt the old name until the user community has made its preference for the forked version utterly clear. In cases where both the fork and its parent continue to exist side by side for a long time, eventually your program's name will acquire a reputation of its own, one that is associated in people's minds with precisely what your program actually does.

Choosing a nonconflicting name is one of the elements of a civilized fork, but not the only one. It should also be remembered that there is absolutely no reason to treat the original maintainer and his or her allied developers as enemies. If you think they're technically competent, you should even automatically make them full-fledged developers with **commit** access in the forked version. Whether or not they ever use the access, the message is clear— you are emphasizing that your goals are the same as theirs; your only disagreement is about how to achieve them.

Conversely, if you are the maintainer of a program from which a fork is diverging, there are also certain standards of behavior. No matter how you feel about the matter personally, don't criticize the instigators publicly. They came to their conclusions honestly, and although you may disagree, the issue of which version is better will be decided by the user community in the end. If the forkers had **commit** access to the original repository before, don't change that. Wish them luck and monitor their progress. If at some point you see that their version of the program really is doing a better job than yours, make a public statement that you now consider them to be the official maintainers, close down your version, and move on to other things.

In short, although a fork may feel like a hostile act, it does not have to be that way in practice. In fact, it would be contrary to the spirit of free software to make it so. It may seem like an unrealistically idealized view of human nature to think that people could cooperate in such circumstances, but in fact they do, because cooperation serves everyone better than competition. One of the most well-known forks is the GNU Emacs/XEmacs divergence, now several years old, which occurred due to technical and organizational disagreements about how to produce the best possible text editor. Both versions are still going strong; all of the maintainers also state that they would like to see a re-merge happen someday, if the disagreements can ever be resolved. Most interestingly, the XEmacs team actively tracks changes to GNU Emacs and incorporates them into XEmacs. Meanwhile, on the GNU Emacs side, the maintainer (Richard Stallman) publicly admits that there's a lot of good code in XEmacs that he'd like to incorporate into GNU Emacs, if only certain organizational hurdles could be overcome.

This is not the behavior of fierce and implacable enemies; it's more like rival climbers ascending by different routes on opposite sides of a mountain, while trading information by radio and hoping to see each other at the summit soon.

Changing Maintainers

Not all maintainership changes happen because of a disagreement. Sometimes, someone just gets too busy, or too tired, to continue being responsible for a program. When that happens, it is incumbent on the maintainer to abide by yet another convention, well summarized by Eric Raymond, "When you lose interest in a program, your last duty to it is to hand it off to a competent successor."

You can advertise for a new maintainer on the current developer list; usually someone will come forward. If no one does, you can try posting a resignation announcement to the appropriate mailing lists and newsgroups, requesting that interested parties contact you about taking over. From those who express interest, you should determine, as best you can, which of them is most likely to have the technical and organizational competence—and the time— to do a good job. The reason to take such care is that the world will very likely accept whomever you designate as the official maintainer; you don't want to let all those users down.

Of course, it's always possible that no one will volunteer. If you are determined to stop working on the code, and no one else shows signs of taking over, the code enters a kind of limbo state, where it is not being actively developed but continues to be available. When asked about it, users say, "Oh, yeah, I still use it, but I think it's not being maintained anymore." The project has reached an end, although not necessarily *the* end.

Stasis

Free software projects never really disappear, not completely. Usually, there are too many copies of the code spread around the world for a given project to become literally unrecoverable. However, as the last known maintainer, you have a special responsibility to keep an archive of the latest version of the code, just in case someone with an eye toward restarting development ever asks you for it. (I neglected to keep an archive of a particularly large and complex project once. A few years after when I'd mostly stopped thinking about it, someone emailed me that he was interested in trying it out and possibly reviving it. I had to respond, to my immense chagrin, that I couldn't find a copy of it anywhere, and he went away disappointed. I don't know if he ever found a copy from somewhere else.)

If possible, you should preserve the project home page and download links, with a notice stating that the project is no longer in active development and that potential new maintainers are invited to propose themselves. Whether you ever hear more about it depends on how important the code is to its users. As time passes, the code will bit-rot, displaying funny behaviors or otherwise showing signs of age as it's run in newer and newer environments. Eventually, its users will band together to save it, if they really need it. If they don't, it was probably time to move on to something else anyway.

Knowing What We Don't Know

At the risk of repeating myself, I must state again that this account of the free software development process should be taken with a grain—maybe an entire shaker—of salt. I've tried to describe and analyze the way I've seen most successful projects work, but that doesn't mean it's the only way they can work. In addition to experimenting with the code itself, I hope you'll be encouraged to experiment with the *process* of running projects. One of the nicest things about CVS is that it functions as a safety net for your source code—it ensures that you can't lose any of the work you've done so far. That frees you and your co-developers to explore many methods of collaboration. When you find one that works for you, use it. It doesn't matter if it flies in the face of every piece of advice written here: if it works, it works. That is the final proof of any development method.

Chapter 4
CVS Repository Administration

The Administrator's Role

In Chapter 2, you learned enough CVS to use it effectively as a project participant. If you're going to be a project maintainer, however, you'll need to know how to install CVS and administer repositories. In this chapter, we'll throw back the curtain and look in detail at how the repository is structured, and how CVS uses it. You'll learn all the major steps CVS goes through during updates and commits, and how you can modify its behavior. By understanding *how* CVS works, you'll also be able to trace problems to their causes, and fix them in maintainable ways.

This may sound very involved, but remember that CVS has already proven quite long-lived, and will probably be around for many years to come. Whatever you learn now will be useful for a long time. CVS also tends to become more indispensable the more you use it. If you're going to be that dependent on something (and trust me, you are), it's worth really getting to know it.

With that in mind, let's begin at the beginning: putting CVS on your system.

Getting And Installing CVS

In many cases, you won't have to go out and get CVS, because it will already be on your system. If you run one of the major Linux or FreeBSD distributions, it's probably already installed in /usr/bin or some other likely location. If not, Red Hat Linux users can usually find an RPM (Red Hat Package) for the latest, or nearly latest, version of CVS in their distributions. And Debian users can install the latest Debian package with these commands:

```
floss$ apt-get update
floss$ apt-get install cvs
```

If CVS isn't already on your machine, you'll probably have to build it from source. If you're a non-Unix user, you'll probably find it easier to get a prebuilt binary for your operating system (more on that later). Fortunately, CVS is fully "autoconfiscated"—that is, it uses the GNU autoconfiguration mechanism, making compilation from source surprisingly easy.

Getting And Building CVS Under Unix

As of this writing, there are two canonical sites from which you can download CVS. One is the Free Software Foundation's FTP site, **ftp://ftp.gnu.org/gnu/cvs/**, which offers CVS as an official GNU tool. The other is Cyclic Software's download site. Cyclic Software is, if not the maintainer of CVS, then the "maintainer of the maintainers," by providing a repository server and download access for users and developers. They distribute releases from **http://download.cyclic.com/pub/**.

Either location is fine. In the following example, I use Cyclic Software's site. If you point your FTP client (probably your Web browser) there, you'll see a list of directories, something like this:

```
Index of /pub
    cvs-1.10.5/         18-Feb-99 21:36      -
    cvs-1.10.6/         17-May-99 10:34      -
    cvs-1.10/           09-Dec-98 17:26      -
    macintosh/          23-Feb-99 00:53      -
    os2/                09-Dec-98 17:26      -
    packages/           09-Dec-98 17:26      -
    rcs/                09-Dec-98 17:26      -
    tkcvs/              09-Dec-98 17:26      -
    training/           09-Dec-98 17:26      -
    unix/               09-Dec-98 17:26      -
    vms/                09-Dec-98 17:26      -
```

Pay attention to the directories beginning with "cvs-" (you can ignore most of the others). As you can see, there are three cvs- directories, which means that you're already faced with a choice: Get the designated "stable" release, or go with a newer (but less-tested) interim release. The stable releases have only one decimal point, as in "cvs-1.10," whereas the interim releases have minor version increments tacked on the end, as in "1.10.5."

Note

The GNU site usually only offers the major releases, not the interim ones, so you won't see all of this if you get CVS from there.

In general, the interim releases have been pretty safe, and sometimes contain fixes to bugs that were found in the major release. Your best policy is to go with the highest interim release, but if you encounter any problems with it, be prepared to drop back to the previous release, as many times as necessary.

The highest release listed in the earlier example is cvs-1.10.6. Entering that directory, we see this:

```
Index of /pub/cvs-1.10.6
   cvs-1.10.6.tar.gz      17-May-99 08:44    2.2M
```

That's it—the full source code to CVS. Just download it to your machine, and you're ready to build. At this point, if you're already familiar with the standard build process for GNU tools, you know what to do and probably don't need to read anything between here and the section "Anatomy Of A CVS Distribution". On the other hand, if you're not sure how to proceed, then read on....

The following compilation instructions and examples assume that you have a fairly standard distribution of Unix. Any of the free versions of Unix (for example, FreeBSD or Linux) should work with no problem, as should the major commercial Unix versions (such as SunOS/ Solaris, AIX, HP-UX, or Ultrix). Even if these instructions don't work for you exactly as written, don't give up hope. Although covering the details of compiling on every operating system is beyond the scope of this book, I'll give some pointers to other help resources later in this chapter.

Anyway, to proceed with the compilation, first unpack the tar file using GNU gunzip and tar (if you don't have these installed on your system, you can get gunzip from **ftp://ftp.gnu.org/ gnu/gzip/** and GNU's version of tar from **ftp://ftp.gnu.org/gnu/tar/**):

```
floss$ gunzip cvs-1.10.6.tar.gz
floss$ tar xvf cvs-1.10.6.tar
```

You'll see a lot of file names fly by on your screen.

Now you have a new directory on your machine—cvs-1.10.6—and it is populated with the CVS source code. Go into that directory and configure CVS for your system, by using the provided **configure** script:

```
floss$ cd cvs-1.10.6
floss$  ./configure
creating cache ./config.cache
checking for gcc... gcc
checking whether we are using GNU C... yes
checking whether gcc accepts -g... yes
checking how to run the C preprocessor... gcc -E
  (etc)
```

When the **configure** command finishes, the source tree will know everything it needs to know about compiling on your machine. The next step is to type:

```
floss$ make
```

(You will probably need to do that last step as the superuser.) You'll see lots of output fly by, then type:

```
floss$ make install
```

You'll see yet more output fly by; when it's all over, CVS will be installed on your system.

By default, the CVS executable will end up as /usr/local/bin/cvs. This assumes you have a decent make program installed on your system (again, if you don't have one, get the GNU project's make from **ftp://ftp.gnu.org/gnu/make/**).

If you want CVS to install to a location other than /usr/local/bin, you should change how you run the initial configuration step. For example,

```
floss$ ./configure --prefix=/usr
```

results in CVS being installed as /usr/bin/cvs (it always ends up as *PREFIX*/bin/cvs). The default prefix is /usr/local, which is fine for most installations.

> **Note**
> *Note To Experienced Users: Although older versions of CVS consisted of more than just an executable in that they depended on having RCS installed as well, this has not been the case since Version 1.10. Therefore, you don't need to worry about any libraries or executables other than cvs itself.*

If you just intend to use CVS to access remote repositories, the preceding is all you need to do. If you also plan to serve a repository from *this* system, a few additional steps are necessary, which are covered later in this chapter.

Getting And Installing CVS Under Windows

Unless you're truly religious about having the source code to your executable, you don't need to compile CVS from source on your Windows box. Unlike Unix, the necessary compilation tools probably do not already exist on your system, so a source build would involve first going out and getting those tools. Because such a project is beyond the scope of this book, I'll just give instructions for getting a precompiled CVS binary.

First, note that Windows binary distributions of CVS are usually made only for major releases of CVS—not for the interim releases—and are not found on the GNU FTP site. So you'll need to go to Cyclic Software's download site, where in the major version directory, **http://download.cyclic.com/pub/cvs-1.10/**, you'll see an extra subdirectory

```
Index of /pub/cvs-1.10
   cvs-1.10.tar.gz          14-Aug-98 09:35    2.4M
   windows/
```

inside of which is a ZIP file:

```
Index of /pub/cvs-1.10/windows
   cvs-1.10-win.zip        14-Aug-98 10:10    589k
```

This ZIP file contains a binary distribution of CVS. Download and extract that ZIP file:

```
floss$ unzip cvs-1.10-win.zip

Archive:  cvs-1.10-win.zip
  inflating: cvs.html
  inflating: cvs.exe
  inflating: README
  inflating: FAQ
  inflating: NEWS
  inflating: patch.exe
  inflating: win32gnu.dll
```

The README there contains detailed instructions. For most installations, they can be summarized as follows: Put all of the EXE and DLL files in a directory in your PATH. Additionally, if you're going to be using the **pserver** method to access a remote repository, you may need to put the following in your C:\AUTOEXEC.BAT file and reboot:

```
set HOME=C:
```

This tells CVS where to store the .cvspass file.

CVS running under Windows cannot currently serve repositories to remote machines; it can be a client (connecting to remote repositories), and operate in local mode (using a repository on the same machine). For the most part, this book assumes that CVS under Windows is operating as a client. However, it shouldn't be too hard to set up a local repository under Windows after reading the Unix-oriented instructions in the rest of this chapter.

If you are only accessing remote repositories, you may not even need to run CVS. There is a tool called WinCvs that implements only the client-side portion of CVS. It is distributed separately from CVS itself but, like CVS, is freely available under the GNU General Public License. More information is available from **www.wincvs.org**.

Getting And Installing CVS On A Macintosh

CVS is available for the Macintosh, but not as part of the main distribution. At the moment, there are actually three separate Macintosh CVS clients available:

- *MacCvs*—**www.wincvs.org**

- *MacCVSClient*—**www.glink.net.hk/~jb/MacCVSClient** or **www.cyclic.com/ maccvsclient/**

- *MacCVS Pro*—**www.maccvs.org**

Frankly, I have no idea which one is best. Try them all, not necessarily in the order given, and see which one you like. MacCVS Pro seems to be under active development. MacCvs is apparently a companion project of WinCVS and shares a home page with it. (As of this writing, a notice on the WinCVS page states, "Development of MacCvs will be resumed soon," whatever that means.)

Limitations Of The Windows And Macintosh Versions

The Windows and Macintosh distributions of CVS are generally limited in functionality. They can all act as clients, meaning that they can contact a repository server to obtain a working copy, commit, update, and so on. But they can't serve repositories themselves. If you set it up right, the Windows port can use a local-disk repository, but it still can't serve projects from that repository to other machines. In general, if you want to have a network-accessible CVS repository, you must run the CVS server on a Unix box.

Anatomy Of A CVS Distribution

The preceding instructions are designed to get you up and running quickly, but there's a lot more inside a CVS source distribution than just the code. Here's a quick road map to the source tree, so you'll know which parts are useful resources and which can be ignored.

Informational Files

In the top level of the distribution tree, you'll find several files containing useful information (and pointers to further information). They are, in approximate order of importance:

- *NEWS*—This file lists the changes from one release to the next, in reverse chronological order (that is, most recent first). If you've already been using CVS for a while and have just upgraded to a new version, you should look at the NEWS file to see what new features are available. Also, although most changes to CVS preserve backward compatibility, noncompatible changes do occur from time to time. It's better to read about them here than be surprised when CVS doesn't behave the way you expect it to.

- *BUGS*—This file contains exactly what you think it does: a list of known bugs in CVS. They usually aren't show-stoppers, but you should read over them whenever you install a new release.

- *DEVEL-CVS*—This file is the CVS "constitution." It describes the process by which changes are accepted into the main CVS distribution and the procedures through which a person becomes a CVS developer. You don't really need to read it if you just want to use CVS; however, it's highly interesting if you want to understand how the mostly uncoordinated efforts of people scattered across the globe coalesce into a working, usable piece of software. And of course, it's required reading if you plan to submit a patch (be it a bug fix or new feature) to CVS.

♦ *HACKING*—Despite its name, the HACKING file doesn't say much about the design or implementation of CVS. It's mainly a guide to coding standards and other technical "administrivia" for people thinking of writing a patch to CVS. It can be thought of as an addendum to the DEVEL-CVS file. After you understand the basic philosophy of CVS development, you must read the HACKING file to translate that into concrete coding practices.

♦ *FAQ*—This is the CVS "Frequently Asked Questions" document. Unfortunately it has a rather spotty maintenance history. David Grubbs took care of it until 1995, then he (presumably) got too busy and it languished for a while. Eventually, in 1997, Pascal Molli took over maintenance. Molli also didn't have time to maintain it by hand, but at least he found time to put it into his automated FAQ-O-Matic system, which allows the public to maintain the FAQ in a decentralized manner (basically, anyone can edit or add entries via a Web form). This was probably a good thing, in that at least the FAQ was once again being maintained; however, its overall organization and quality control are not on the same level as if a person were maintaining it.

The master version of the FAQ is always available from Molli's Web site (**www.loria.fr/ ~molli/cvs-index.html**, under the link "Documentation"). The FAQ file shipped with CVS distributions is generated automatically from that FAQ-O-Matic database, so by the time it reaches the public it's already a little bit out of date. Nevertheless, it can be quite helpful when you're looking for hints and examples about how to do something specific (say, merging a large branch back into the trunk or resurrecting a removed file). The best way to use it is as a reference document; you can bring it up in your favorite editor and do text searches on terms that interest you. Trying to use it as a tutorial would be a mistake—it's missing too many important facts about CVS to serve as a complete guide.

Subdirectories

The CVS distribution contains a number of subdirectories. In the course of a normal installation, you won't have to navigate among them, but if you want to go poking around in the sources, it's nice to know what each one does. Here they are:

```
contrib/
diff/
doc/
emx/
lib/
man/
os2/
src/
tools/
vms/
windows-NT/
zlib/
```

The majority of these can be ignored. The emx/, os2/, vms/, and windows-NT/ subdirectories all contain operating-system-specific source code, which you would only need if you're actually trying to debug a code-level problem in CVS (an unlikely situation, though not unheard of). The diff/ and zlib/ subdirectories contain CVS's internal implementations of the diff program and the GNU gzip compression library, respectively. (CVS uses the latter to reduce the number of bits it has to send over the network when accessing remote repositories.)

The contrib/ and tools/ subdirectories contain free third-party software meant to be used with CVS. In contrib/, you will find an assortment of small, specialized shell scripts (read contrib/README to find out what they do). The tools/ subdirectory used to contain contributed software, but now contains a README file, which says in part:

```
This subdirectory formerly contained tools that can be used with CVS.
In particular, it used to contain a copy of pcl-cvs version 1.x.
Pcl-cvs is an Emacs interface to CVS.

If you are looking for pcl-cvs, we'd suggest pcl-cvs version 2.x, at:
    ftp://ftp.weird.com/pub/local/
```

The PCL-CVS package it's referring to is very handy, and I'll have more to say about it in Chapter 10.

The src/ and lib/ subdirectories contain the bulk of the CVS source code, which involves the CVS internals. The main data structures and commands are implemented in src/, whereas lib/ contains small code modules of general utility that CVS uses.

The man/ subdirectory contains the CVS man pages (intended for the Unix online manual system). When you ran **make install**, they were incorporated into your Unix system's regular man pages, so you can type

```
floss$ man cvs
```

and get a rather terse introduction and subcommand reference to CVS. Although useful as a quick reference, the man pages may not be as up to date or complete as the Cederqvist manual (see the next section); however, the man pages are more likely to be incomplete than actually wrong, if it's any comfort.

The Cederqvist Manual

That leaves the doc/ subdirectory, whose most important inhabitant is the famed Cederqvist. These days, it's probably a stretch to call it "the Cederqvist." Although Per Cederqvist (of Signum Support, Linkoping Sweden, **www.signum.se**) wrote the first version around 1992, it has been updated since then by many other people. For example, when contributors add a new feature to CVS, they usually also document it in the Cederqvist.

The Cederqvist manual is written in Texinfo format, which is used by the GNU project because it's relatively easy to produce both online and printed output from it (in Info and

PostScript formats, respectively). The Texinfo master file is doc/cvs.texinfo, but CVS distributions come with the Info and PostScript pregenerated, so you don't have to worry about running any Texinfo tools yourself.

Although the Cederqvist can be used as an introduction and tutorial, it is probably most useful as a reference document. For that reason, most people browse it online instead of printing it out (although the PostScript file is doc/cvs.ps, for those with paper to spare). If this is the first time you've installed CVS on your system, you'll have to take an extra step to make sure the manual is accessible online.

The Info files (doc/cvs.info, doc/cvs.info-1, doc/cvs.info-2, and so on) were installed for you when you ran **make install**. Although the files were copied into the system's Info tree, you may still have to add a line for CVS to the Info table of contents, the "Top" node. (This will only be necessary if this is the first time CVS has been installed on your system; otherwise, the entry from previous installations should already be in the table of contents.)

If you've added new Info documentation before, you may be familiar with the process. First figure out where the Info pages were installed. If you used the default installation (in /usr/local/), then the Info files are /usr/local/info/cvs.info*. If you installed using

```
floss$ ./configure --prefix=/usr
```

the files ended up as /usr/info/cvs.*. After you locate the files, you'll need to add a line for CVS to the Info table of contents, which is in a file named dir in that directory (so in the latter case, it would be /usr/info/dir). If you don't have root access, ask your system administrator to do it. Here is an excerpt from dir before the reference to CVS documentation was added:

```
* Bison: (bison).        The Bison parser generator.
* Cpp: (cpp).            The GNU C preprocessor.
* Flex: (flex).          A fast scanner generator
```

And here is the same region of dir afterwards:

```
* Bison: (bison).        The Bison parser generator.
* Cpp: (cpp).            The GNU C preprocessor.
* Cvs: (cvs).            Concurrent Versions System
* Flex: (flex).          A fast scanner generator
```

The format of the line is very important. You must include the asterisk, spaces, and colon in "*** Cvs:**" and the parentheses and period in "**(cvs).**" after it. If any of these elements are missing, the Info dir format will be corrupt, and you'll be unable to read the Cederqvist.

Once the manual is installed and referred to from the table of contents, you can read it with any Info-compatible browser. The ones most likely to be installed on a typical Unix system are either the command-line Info reader, which can be invoked this way if you want to go straight to the CVS pages

```
floss$ info cvs
```

and the one within Emacs, which is invoked by typing

```
M-x info
```

or

```
C-h i
```

Take whatever time is necessary to get the Cederqvist set up properly on your system when you install CVS; it will pay off many times down the road when you need to look something up.

Other Sources Of Information

In addition to the Cederqvist, the FAQ, and the other files in the distribution itself, there are Internet resources devoted to CVS. If you're going to administrate a CVS server, you'll probably want to join the info-cvs mailing list. To subscribe, send email to **info-cvs-request@gnu.org** (the list itself is **info-cvs@gnu.org**). Traffic can be medium to heavy, around 10 to 20 emails a day, most of them questions seeking answers. The majority of these can be deleted without reading (unless you want to help people by answering their questions, which is always nice), but every now and then someone will announce the discovery of a bug or announce a patch that implements some feature you've been wanting.

You can also join the formal bug report mailing list, which includes every bug report sent in. This probably isn't necessary, unless you intend to help fix the bugs, which would be great, or you're terrifically paranoid and want to know about every problem other people find with CVS. If you do want to join, send email to **bug-cvs-request@gnu.org**.

There's also a Usenet newsgroup, **comp.software.config-mgmt**, which is about version control and configuration management systems in general, in which there is a fair amount of discussion about CVS.

Finally, there are at least three Web sites devoted to CVS. Cyclic Software's **www.cyclic.com** has been CVS's informal home site for a few years, and probably will continue to be for the foreseeable future. Cyclic Software also provides server space and Net access for the repository where the CVS sources are kept. The Cyclic Web pages contain comprehensive links to experimental patches for CVS, third-party tools that work with CVS, documentation, mailing list archives, and just about everything else. If you can't find what you need in the distribution, **www.cyclic.com** is the place to start looking.

Two other good sites are Pascal Molli's **www.loria.fr/~molli/cvs-index.html** and Sean Dreilinger's **http://durak.org/cvswebsites/**. The biggest attraction at Molli's site is, of course, the FAQ, but it also has links to CVS-related tools and mailing list archives. Dreilinger's site specializes in information about using CVS to manage Web documents and also has a CVS-specific search engine.

Starting A Repository

Once the CVS executable is installed on your system, you can start using it right away as a client to access remote repositories, following the procedures described in Chapter 2. However, if you want to serve revisions from your machine, you have to create a repository there. The command to do that is

```
floss$ cvs -d /usr/local/newrepos init
```

where **/usr/local/newrepos** is a path to wherever you want the repository to be (of course, you must have write permission to that location, which may imply running the command as the root user). It may seem somewhat counterintuitive that the location of the new repository is specified before the **init** subcommand instead of after it, but by using the **-d** option, it stays consistent with other CVS commands.

The command will return silently after it is run. Let's examine the new directory:

```
floss$ ls -ld /usr/local/newrepos
drwxrwxr-x   3 root      root             1024 Jun 19 17:59 /usr/local/newrepos/
floss$ cd /usr/local/newrepos
floss$ ls
CVSROOT
floss$ cd CVSROOT
floss$ ls
checkoutlist       config,v        history      notify       taginfo,v
checkoutlist,v     cvswrappers     loginfo      notify,v     verifymsg
commitinfo         cvswrappers,v   loginfo,v    rcsinfo      verifymsg,v
commitinfo,v       editinfo        modules      rcsinfo,v
config             editinfo,v      modules,v    taginfo

floss$
```

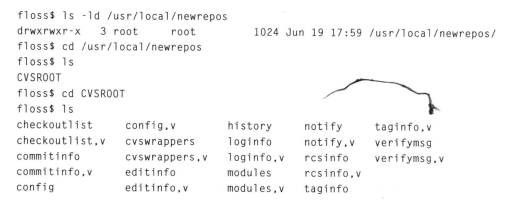

The single subdirectory in the new repository—CVSROOT/—contains various administrative files that control CVS's behavior. Later on, we'll examine those files one by one; for now, the goal is just to get the repository working. In this case, "working" means users can import, check out, update, and commit projects.

Note

*Don't confuse the CVSROOT environment variable introduced in Chapter 2 with this CVSROOT subdirectory in the repository. They are unrelated—it is an unfortunate coincidence that they share the same name. The former is a way for users to avoid having to type **-d <repository-location>** every time they use CVS; the latter is the administrative subdirectory of a repository.*

Once the repository is created, you must take care of its permissions. CVS does not require any particular, standardized permission or file ownership scheme; it merely needs write access to the repository. However—partly for security reasons, but mainly for your own sanity as an administrator—I *highly* recommend that you take the following steps:

1. Add a Unix group "cvs" to your system. Any users who need to access the repository should be in this group. For example, here's the relevant line from my machine's /etc/ group file:

```
cvs:*:105:kfogel,sussman,jimb,noel,lefty,fitz,craig,anonymous,jrandom
```

2. Make the repository's group ownership and permissions reflect this new group:

```
floss$ cd /usr/local/newrepos
floss$ chgrp -R cvs .
floss$ chmod ug+rwx . CVSROOT
```

Now any of the users listed in that group can start a project by running **cvs import**, as described in Chapter 2. **Checkout, update**, and **commit** should work as well. They can also reach the repository from remote locations by using the **:ext:** method, assuming that they have rsh or ssh access to the repository machine. (You may have noticed that the **chgrp** and **chmod** commands in that example gave *write* access to a user named "anonymous," which is not what one would expect. The reason is that even anonymous, read-only repository users need system-level write access, so that their CVS processes can create temporary lockfiles inside the repository. CVS enforces the "read-only" restriction of anonymous access not through Unix file permissions, but by other means, which will be covered shortly.)

If your repository is intended to serve projects to the general public, where contributors won't necessarily have accounts on the repository machine, you should set up the password-authenticating server now. It's necessary for anonymous read-only access, and it's also probably the easiest way to grant commit access to certain people without giving them full accounts on the machine.

The Password-Authenticating Server

Before running through the steps needed to set up the password server, let's examine how such connections work in the abstract. When a remote CVS client uses the **:pserver:** method to connect to a repository, the client is actually contacting a specific port number on the server machine—specifically, port number 2401 (which is 49 squared, if you like that sort of thing). Port 2401 is the designated default port for the CVS pserver, although one could arrange for a different port to be used as long as both client and server agree on it.

The CVS server is not actually waiting for connections at that port—the server won't get started up until a connection actually arrives. Instead, the Unix inetd (InterNET Daemon) program is listening on that port, and needs to know that when it receives a connection request there, it should start up the CVS server and connect it to the incoming client.

This is accomplished by modifying inetd's configuration files: /etc/services and /etc/inetd.conf. The services file maps raw port numbers to service names and then inetd.conf tells inetd what to do for a given service name.

First, put a line like this into /etc/services (after checking to make sure it isn't already there):

```
cvspserver 2401/tcp
```

Then in /etc/inetd.conf, put this:

```
cvspserver stream tcp nowait root /usr/local/bin/cvs cvs \
  --allow-root=/usr/local/newrepos pserver
```

(In the actual file, this should be all one long line, with no backslash.) If your system uses tcpwrappers, you may want to use something like this instead:

```
cvspserver stream tcp nowait root /usr/sbin/tcpd /usr/local/bin/cvs \
  --allow-root=/usr/local/newrepos pserver
```

Now, restart inetd so it notices the changes to its configuration files (if you don't know how to restart the daemon, just reboot the machine—that will work too).

That's enough to permit connections, but you'll also want to set up special CVS passwords—separate from the users' regular login passwords—so people can access the repository without compromising overall system security.

The CVS password file is CVSROOT/passwd in the repository. It was not created by default when you ran **cvs init**, because CVS doesn't know for sure that you'll be using pserver. Even if the password file had been created, CVS would have no way of knowing what usernames and passwords to create. So, you'll have to create one yourself; here's a sample CVSRoot/passwd file:

```
kfogel:rKa5jzULzmhOo
anonymous:XR4EZcEsOszik
melissa:tGX1fS8sun6rY:pubcvs
```

The format is as simple as it looks. Each line is:

```
<USERNAME>:<ENCRYPTED_PASSWORD>:<OPTIONAL_SYSTEM_USERNAME>
```

The extra colon followed by an optional system username tells CVS that connections authenticated with USERNAME should run as the system account SYSTEM_USERNAME—in other words, that CVS session would only be able to do things in the repository that someone logged in as SYSTEM_USERNAME could do.

If no system username is given, USERNAME must match an actual login account name on the system, and the session will run with that user's permissions. In either case, the encrypted password should not be the same as the user's actual login password. It should be an independent password used only for CVS pserver connections.

The password is encrypted using the same algorithm as the standard Unix system passwords stored in /etc/passwd. You may be wondering at this point, how does one acquire an encrypted version of a password? For Unix system passwords, the **passwd** command takes care of the encryption in /etc/passwd for you. Unfortunately, there is no corresponding **cvs passwd** command (it has been proposed several times, but no one's gotten around to writing it—perhaps you'll do it?).

This is an inconvenience, but only a slight one. If nothing else, you can always temporarily change a regular user's system password using **passwd**, cut and paste the encrypted text from /etc/passwd into CVSROOT/passwd, and then restore the old password.

Note

On some systems, the encrypted passwords are found in /etc/shadow and are readable only by root.

That scheme is workable but rather cumbersome. It would be much easier to have a command-line utility that takes a plain text password as its argument and outputs the encrypted version. Here is such a tool, written in Perl:

```perl
#!/usr/bin/perl

srand (time());
my $randletter = "(int (rand (26)) + (int (rand (1) + .5) % 2 ? 65 : 97))";
my $salt = sprintf ("%c%c", eval $randletter, eval $randletter);
my $plaintext = shift;
my $crypttext = crypt ($plaintext, $salt);

print "${crypttext}\n";
```

I keep the preceding script in /usr/local/bin/cryptout.pl:

```
floss$ ls -l /usr/local/bin/cryptout.pl

-rwxr-xr-x   1   root   root   265   Jun 14 20:41 /usr/local/bin/cryptout.pl
floss$ cryptout.pl "some text"
sB3A79YDX5L4s

floss$
```

If I took the output of this example and used it to create the following entry in CVSROOT/passwd

```
jrandom:sB3A79YDX5L4s:craig
```

then someone could connect to the repository with the following command:

```
remote$ cvs -d :pserver:jrandom@floss.red-bean.com:/usr/local/newrepos login
```

They could then type "some text" as their password and thereafter be able to execute CVS commands with the same access privileges as the system user "craig."

If someone attempts to authenticate with a username and password that don't appear in CVSROOT/passwd, CVS will check to see if that username and password are present in /etc/passwd. If they are (and if the password matches, of course), CVS will grant access. It behaves this way for the administrator's convenience, so that separate CVSROOT/passwd entries don't have to be set up for regular system users. However, this behavior is also a security hole, because it means that if one of those users does connect to the CVS server, her regular login password will have crossed over the network in cleartext, potentially vulnerable to the eyes of password sniffers. A bit further on, you'll learn how to turn off this "fallback" behavior, so that CVS consults only its own passwd file. Whether you leave it on or off, you should probably force any CVS users who also have login accounts to maintain different passwords for the two functions.

Although the passwd file authenticates for the whole repository, with a little extra work you can still use it to grant project-specific access. Here's one method:

Suppose you want to grant some remote developers access to project "foo," and others access to project "bar," and you don't want developers from one project to have commit access to the other. You can accomplish this by creating project-specific user accounts and groups on the system and then mapping to those accounts in the CVSROOT/passwd file.

Here's the relevant excerpt from /etc/passwd

```
cvs-foo:*:600:600:Public CVS Account for Project Foo:/usr/local/cvs:/bin/false
cvs-bar:*:601:601:Public CVS Account for Project Bar:/usr/local/cvs:/bin/false
```

and from /etc/group

```
cvs-foo:*:600:cvs-foo
cvs-bar:*:601:cvs-bar
```

and, finally, CVSROOT/passwd:

```
kcunderh:rKa5jzULzmhOo:cvs-foo
jmankoff:tGX1fS8sun6rY:cvs-foo
brebard:cAXVPNZN6uFH2:cvs-foo
xwang:qp5lsf7nzRzfs:cvs-foo
dstone:JDNNF6HeX/yLw:cvs-bar
twp:g1UHEM8KhcbO6:cvs-bar
ffranklin:cG6/6yXbS9BHI:cvs-bar
yyang:YoEqcCeCUqlvQ:cvs-bar
```

Some of the CVS usernames map onto the system user account cvs-foo and some onto cvs-bar. Because CVS runs under the user ID of the system account, you just have to make sure that the relevant parts of the repository are writeable only by the appropriate users and groups. If you just make sure that the user accounts are locked down pretty tight (no valid login password, /bin/false as the shell), then this system is reasonably secure (but see later in this chapter about CVSROOT permissions!). Also, CVS does record changes and log messages under the CVS username, not the system username, so you can still tell who is responsible for a given change.

Anonymous Access Via The Password-Authenticating Server

So far we've only seen how to use the password-authenticating server to grant normal full access to the repository (although admittedly one can restrict that access through carefully arranged Unix file permissions). Turning this into anonymous, read-only access is a simple step: You just have to add a new file, or possibly two, in CVSROOT/. The files' names are "readers" and "writers"—the former containing a list of usernames who can only read the repository, the latter users who can read and write.

If you list a username in CVSROOT/readers, that user will have only read access to all projects in the repository. If you list a username in CVSROOT/writers, that user will have write access, and every pserver user *not* listed in writers will have read-only access (that is, if the writers file exists at all, it implies read-only access for all those not listed in it). If the same username is listed in both files, CVS resolves the conflict in the more conservative way: the user will have read-only access.

The format of the files is very simple: one user per line (don't forget to put a newline after the last user). Here is a sample readers file:

```
anonymous
splotnik
guest
jbrowse
```

Note that the files apply to CVS usernames, not system usernames. If you use user aliasing in the CVSROOT/passwd file (putting a system username after a second colon), the leftmost username is the one to list in a readers or writers file.

Just to be painfully accurate about it, here is a formal description of the server's behavior in deciding whether to grant read-only or read-write access:

If a readers file exists and this user is listed in it, then she gets read-only access. If a writers file exists and this user is not listed in it, then she also gets read-only access (this is true even if a readers file exists but that person is not listed there). If that person is listed in both, she gets read-only access. In all other cases, that person gets full read-write access.

Thus, a typical repository with anonymous CVS access has this (or something like it) in CVSROOT/passwd

```
anonymous:XR4EZcEsOszik
```

this (or something like it) in /etc/passwd

```
anonymous:!:1729:105:Anonymous CVS User:/usr/local/newrepos:/bin/false
```

and this in CVSROOT/readers:

```
anonymous
```

And, of course, the aforementioned setup in /etc/services and /etc/inetd.conf. That's all there is to it!

Note that some older Unix systems don't support usernames longer than eight characters. One way to get around this would be to call the user "anon" instead of "anonymous" in CVSROOT/passwd and in the system files, because people often assume that anon is short for anonymous anyway. But it might be better to put something like this into the CVSROOT/passwd file

```
anonymous:XR4EZcEsOszik:cvsanon
```

(and then of course use "cvsanon" in the system files). That way, you'd be able to publish a repository address that uses "anonymous," which is more or less standard now. People accessing the repository with

```
cvs -d :pserver:anonymous@cvs.foobar.com:/usr/local/newrepos (etc...)
```

would actually run on the server as cvsanon (or whatever). But they wouldn't need to know or care about how things are set up on the server side—they'd only see the published address.

Repository Structure Explained In Excruciating Detail

The new repository still has no projects in it. Let's re-run the initial import from Chapter 2, watching what happens to the repository. (For simplicity's sake, all commands will assume that the CVSROOT environment variable has been set to /usr/local/newrepos, so there's no need to specify the repository with **-d** on imports and checkouts.)

```
floss$ ls /usr/local/newrepos
CVSROOT/
floss$ pwd
/home/jrandom/src/
floss$ ls
myproj/
floss$ cd myproj
floss$ cvs import -m "initial import into CVS" myproj jrandom start
N myproj/README.txt
```

```
N myproj/hello.c
cvs import: Importing /usr/local/newrepos/myproj/a-subdir
N myproj/a-subdir/whatever.c
cvs import: Importing /usr/local/newrepos/myproj/a-subdir/subsubdir
N myproj/a-subdir/subsubdir/fish.c
cvs import: Importing /usr/local/newrepos/myproj/b-subdir
N myproj/b-subdir/random.c

No conflicts created by this import

floss$ ls /usr/local/newrepos
CVSROOT/  myproj/
floss$ cd /usr/local/newrepos/myproj
floss$ ls
README.txt,v  a-subdir/      b-subdir/      hello.c,v
floss$ cd a-subdir
floss$ ls
subsubdir/      whatever.c,v
floss$ cd ..

floss$
```

Before the import, the repository contained only its administrative area, CVSROOT. After the import, a new directory—myproj—appeared. The files and subdirectories inside that new directory look suspiciously like the project we imported, except that the files have the suffix ",v." These are RCS-format version control files (the ",v" stands for "version"), and they are the backbone of the repository. Each RCS file stores the revision history of its corresponding file in the project, including all branches and tags.

You do not need to know any of the RCS format to use CVS (although there is an excellent writeup included with the source distribution, see doc/RCSFILES). However, a basic understanding of the format can be of immense help in troubleshooting CVS problems, so we'll take a brief peek into one of the files, hello.c,v. Here are its contents:

```
head      1.1;
branch    1.1.1;
access    ;
symbols   start:1.1.1.1 jrandom:1.1.1;
locks     ; strict;
comment   @ * @;


1.1
date      99.06.20.17.47.26;  author jrandom;  state Exp;
branches 1.1.1.1;
next;
```

```
1.1.1.1
date      99.06.20.17.47.26;  author jrandom;  state Exp;
branches ;
next;

desc
@@


1.1
log
@Initial revision
@
text
@#include <stdio.h>

void
main ()
{
  printf ("Hello, world!\n");
}
@


1.1.1.1
log
@initial import into CVS
@
text
@@
```

Whew! Most of that you can ignore; don't worry about the relationship between 1.1 and 1.1.1.1, for example, or the implied 1.1.1 branch—they aren't really significant from a user's or even an administrator's point of view. What you should try to grok is the overall format. At the top is a collection of header fields:

```
head      1.1;
branch    1.1.1;
access    ;
symbols   start:1.1.1.1 jrandom:1.1.1;
locks     ; strict;
comment   @ * @;
```

Farther down in the file are groups of meta-information about each revision (but still not showing the contents of that revision), such as:

```
1.1
date      99.06.20.17.47.26;  author jrandom;  state Exp;
```

```
branches 1.1.1.1;
next     ;
```

And finally, the log message and text of an actual revision:

```
1.1
log
@Initial revision
@
text
@#include <stdio.h>

void
main ()
{
  printf ("Hello, world!\n");
}
@


1.1.1.1
log
@initial import into CVS
@
text
@@
```

If you look closely, you'll see that the first revision's contents are stored under the heading 1.1, but that the log message there is "Initial revision," whereas the log message we actually used at import time was "initial import into CVS," which appears farther down, under Revision 1.1.1.1. You don't need to worry about this discrepancy right now. It happens because imports are a special circumstance: In order to make repeated imports into the same project have a useful effect, **import** actually places the initial revision on both the main trunk *and* on a special branch (the reasons for this will become clearer when we look at vendor branches in Chapter 6). For now, you can treat 1.1 and 1.1.1.1 as the same thing.

The file becomes even more revealing after we commit the first modification to hello.c:

```
floss$ cvs -Q co myproj
floss$ cd myproj
floss$ emacs hello.c
    (make some changes to the file)

floss$ cvs ci -m "print goodbye too"
cvs commit: Examining .
cvs commit: Examining a-subdir
cvs commit: Examining a-subdir/subsubdir
cvs commit: Examining b-subdir
```

```
Checking in hello.c;
/usr/local/newrepos/myproj/hello.c,v  <--  hello.c
new revision: 1.2; previous revision: 1.1
done
```

If you look at hello.c,v in the repository now, you can see the effect of the **commit**:

```
head    1.2;
access;
symbols
        start:1.1.1.1 jrandom:1.1.1;
locks; strict;
comment   @ * @;


1.2
date    99.06.21.01.49.40;   author jrandom;   state Exp;
branches;
next    1.1;


1.1
date    99.06.20.17.47.26;   author jrandom;   state Exp;
branches
        1.1.1.1;
next    ;


1.1.1.1
date    99.06.20.17.47.26;   author jrandom;   state Exp;
branches;
next    ;


desc
@@


1.2
log
@print goodbye too
@
text
@#include <stdio.h>

void
main ()
{
  printf ("Hello, world!\n");
  printf ("Goodbye, world!\n");
}
@
```

```
1.1
log
@Initial revision
@
text
@d7 1
@

1.1.1.1
log
@initial import into CVS
@
text
@@
```

Now the full contents of Revision 1.2 are stored in the file, and the text for Revision 1.1 has been replaced with the cryptic formula:

```
d7 1
```

The **d7 1** is a diff code that means "starting at line 7, delete 1 line." In other words, to derive Revision 1.1, delete line 7 from Revision 1.2! Try working through it yourself. You'll see that it does indeed produce Revision 1.1—it simply does away with the line we added to the file.

This demonstrates the basic principle of RCS format: It stores only the differences between revisions, thereby saving a lot of space compared with storing each revision in full. To go backwards from the most recent revision to the previous one, it patches the later revision using the stored diff. Of course, this means that the further back you travel in the revision history, the more patch operations must be performed (for example, if the file is on Revision 1.7 and CVS is asked to retrieve Revision 1.4, it has to produce 1.6 by patching backwards from 1.7, then 1.5 by patching 1.6, then 1.4 by patching 1.5). Fortunately, old revisions are also the ones least often retrieved, so the RCS system works out pretty well in practice: The more recent the revision, the cheaper it is to obtain.

As for the header information at the top of the file, you don't need to know what all of it means. However, the effects of certain operations show up very clearly in the headers, and a passing familiarity with them may prove useful.

When you commit a new revision on the trunk, the "head" label is updated (note how it became 1.2 in the preceding example, when the second revision to hello.c was committed). When you add a file as binary or tag it, those operations are recorded in the headers as well. As an example, we'll add foo.jpg as a binary file and then tag it a couple of times:

```
floss$ cvs add -kb foo.jpg
cvs add: scheduling file 'foo.jpg' for addition
```

```
cvs add: use 'cvs commit' to add this file permanently
floss$ cvs -q commit -m "added a random image; ask jrandom@red-bean.com why"
RCS file: /usr/local/newrepos/myproj/foo.jpg,v
done
Checking in foo.jpg;
/usr/local/newrepos/myproj/foo.jpg,v  <--  foo.jpg
initial revision: 1.1
done
floss$ cvs tag some_random_tag foo.jpg
T foo.jpg
floss$ cvs tag ANOTHER-TAG foo.jpg
T foo.jpg
floss$
```

Now examine the header section of foo.jpg,v in the repository:

```
head    1.1;
access;
symbols
      ANOTHER-TAG:1.1
      some_random_tag:1.1;
locks; strict;
comment   @# @;
expand    @b@;
```

Notice the **b** in the **expand** line at the end—it's due to our having used the **-kb** flag when adding the file, and means the file won't undergo any keyword or newline expansions, which would normally occur during checkouts and updates if it were a regular text file. The tags appear in the **symbols** section, one tag per line—both of them are attached to the first revision, since that's what was tagged both times. (This also helps explain why tag names can only contain letters, numbers, hyphens, and underscores. If the tag itself contained colons or dots, the RCS file's record of it might be ambiguous, because there would be no way to find the textual boundary between the tag and the revision to which it is attached.)

RCS Format Always Quotes @ Signs

The @ symbol is used as a field delimiter in RCS files, which means that if one appears in the text of a file or in a log message, it must be quoted (otherwise, CVS would incorrectly interpret it as marking the end of that field). It is quoted by doubling—that is, CVS always interprets @@ as "literal @ sign," never as "end of current field." When we committed foo.jpg, the log message was

```
"added a random image; ask jrandom@red-bean.com why"
```

which is stored in foo.jpg,v like this:

```
1.1
log
@added a random image; ask jrandom@@red-bean.com why
@
```

The @ sign in **jrandom@@red-bean.com** will be automatically unquoted whenever CVS
retrieves the log message:

```
floss$ cvs log foo.jpg
RCS file: /usr/local/newrepos/myproj/foo.jpg,v
Working file: foo.jpg
head: 1.1
branch:
locks: strict
access list:
symbolic names:
      ANOTHER-TAG: 1.1
      some_random_tag: 1.1
keyword substitution: b
total revisions: 1;        selected revisions: 1
description:
----------------------------
revision 1.1
date: 1999/06/21 02:56:18;  author: jrandom;  state: Exp;
added a random image; ask jrandom@red-bean.com why
============================================================================

floss$
```

The only reason you should care is that if you ever find yourself hand-editing RCS files (a
rare circumstance, but not unheard of), you must remember to use double @ signs in revision contents and log messages. If you don't, the RCS file will be corrupt and will probably
exhibit strange and undesirable behaviors.

Speaking of hand-editing RCS files, don't be fooled by the permissions in the repository:

```
floss$ ls -l
total 6
-r--r--r--  1 jrandom    users         410 Jun 20 12:47 README.txt,v
drwxrwxr-x  3 jrandom    users        1024 Jun 20 21:56 a-subdir/
drwxrwxr-x  2 jrandom    users        1024 Jun 20 21:56 b-subdir/
-r--r--r--  1 jrandom    users         937 Jun 20 21:56 foo.jpg,v
-r--r--r--  1 jrandom    users         564 Jun 20 21:11 hello.c,v

floss$
```

(For those not fluent in Unix **ls** output, the "-r--r--r--" lines on the left essentially mean that the files can be read but not changed.) Although the files appear to be read-only for everyone, the directory permissions must also be taken into account:

```
floss$ ls -ld .
drwxrwxr-x   4 jrandom    users          1024 Jun 20 22:16 ./
floss$
```

The myproj/ directory itself—and its subdirectories—are all writeable by the owner (jrandom) and the group (users). This means that CVS (running as jrandom, or as anyone in the users group) can create and delete files in those directories, even if it can't directly edit files already present. CVS edits an RCS file by making a separate copy of it, so you should also make all of your changes in a temporary copy, and then replace the existing RCS file with the new one. (But please don't ask why the files themselves are read-only—there are historical reasons for that, having to do with the way RCS works when run as a standalone program.)

Incidentally, having the files' group be "users" is probably not what you want, considering that the top-level directory of the repository was explicitly assigned group "cvs." You can correct the problem by running this command inside the repository:

```
floss$ cd /usr/local/newrepos
floss$ chgrp -R cvs myproj
```

Unfortunately, the usual Unix file-creation rules govern which group is assigned to new files that appear in the repository, so once in a while you may need to run **chgrp** or **chmod** on certain files or directories in the repository. There are no hard and fast rules about how you should structure repository permissions; it just depends on who is working on what projects.

What Happens When You Remove A File

When you remove a file from a project, it doesn't just disappear. CVS must be able to retrieve such files when you request an old snapshot of the project. Instead, the file gets put in the "Attic," literally:

```
floss$ pwd
/home/jrandom/src/myproj
floss$ ls /usr/local/newrepos/myproj/
README.txt,v  a-subdir/     b-subdir/      foo.jpg,v   hello.c,v
floss$ rm foo.jpg
floss$ cvs rm foo.jpg
cvs remove: scheduling 'foo.jpg' for removal
cvs remove: use 'cvs commit' to remove this file permanently
floss$ cvs ci -m "Removed foo.jpg" foo.jpg
Removing foo.jpg;
/usr/local/newrepos/myproj/foo.jpg,v  <--  foo.jpg
```

```
new revision: delete; previous revision: 1.1
done
floss$ cd /usr/local/newrepos/myproj/
floss$ ls
Attic/        README.txt,v  a-subdir/      b-subdir/     hello.c,v
floss$ cd Attic
floss$ ls
foo.jpg,v
floss$
```

In each repository directory of a project, the presence of an Attic/ subdirectory means that at least one file has been removed from that directory (this means that you shouldn't use directories named Attic in your projects). CVS doesn't merely move the RCS file into Attic/, however; it also commits a new revision into the file, with a special revision state of "dead." Here's the relevant section from Attic/foo.jpg,v:

```
1.2
date     99.06.21.03.38.07;    author jrandom;    state dead;
branches;
next          1.1;
```

If the file is later brought back to life, CVS has a way of recording that it was dead at some point in the past and is now alive again.

This means that if you want to restore a removed file, you can't just take it out of the Attic/ and put it back into the project. Instead, you have to do something like this in a working copy:

```
floss$ pwd
/home/jrandom/src/myproj
floss$ cvs -Q update -p -r 1.1 foo.jpg > foo.jpg
floss$ ls
CVS/        README.txt   a-subdir/   b-subdir/   foo.jpg      hello.c
floss$ cvs add -kb foo.jpg
cvs add: re-adding file foo.jpg (in place of dead revision 1.2)
cvs add: use 'cvs commit' to add this file permanently
floss$ cvs ci -m "revived jpg image" foo.jpg
Checking in foo.jpg;
/usr/local/newrepos/myproj/foo.jpg,v  <-- foo.jpg
new revision: 1.3; previous revision: 1.2
done
floss$ cd /usr/local/newrepos/myproj/
floss$ ls
Attic/             a-subdir/      foo.jpg,v
README.txt,v  b-subdir/      hello.c,v
floss$ ls Attic/
floss$
```

There's a lot more to know about RCS format, but this is sufficient for a CVS adminstrator to maintain a repository. It's quite rare to actually edit an RCS file; you'll usually just have to tweak file permissions in the repository, at least if my own experience is any guide. Nevertheless, when CVS starts behaving truly weirdly (rare, but not completely outside the realm of possibility), you may want to actually look inside the RCS files to figure out what's going on.

The CVSROOT/ Administrative Directory

The files in newrepos/CVSROOT/ are not part of any project, but are used to control CVS's behavior in the repository. The best way to edit those files is to check out a working copy of CVSROOT, just like a regular project:

```
floss$ cvs co CVSROOT
cvs checkout: Updating CVSROOT
U CVSROOT/checkoutlist
U CVSROOT/commitinfo
U CVSROOT/config
U CVSROOT/cvswrappers
U CVSROOT/editinfo
U CVSROOT/loginfo
U CVSROOT/modules
U CVSROOT/notify
U CVSROOT/rcsinfo
U CVSROOT/taginfo
U CVSROOT/verifymsg
floss$
```

We'll take the files in their approximate order of importance. Note that each of the files comes with an explanatory comment at the beginning (the comment convention is the same across all of them: A "#" sign at the beginning of the line signifies a comment, and CVS ignores such lines when parsing the files). Remember that any change you make to the administrative files in your checked out working copy won't affect CVS's behavior until you commit the changes.

Tip

If you're extremely security conscious, you may want to arrange the Unix-level permissions on CVSROOT to be different from permissions elsewhere in the repository, in order to have fine-grained control over who can commit changes to CVSROOT. As you'll see a little later, being able to modify the files in CVSROOT essentially gives any CVS user—even remote ones—the ability to run arbitrary commands on the repository machine.

The config File

The config file allows you to configure certain global behavioral parameters. It follows a very strict format

```
PARAMETER=VALUE
(etc)
```

with no extra spaces allowed. For example, here is a possible config file:

```
SystemAuth=yes
TopLevelAdmin=no
PreservePermissions=no
```

(An absent entry would be equivalent to "no.")

The **SystemAuth** parameter governs whether CVS should look in the system passwd file if it fails to find a given username in the CVSROOT/passwd file. CVS distributions are shipped with this set to "no" to be conservative about your system's security.

TopLevelAdmin tells CVS whether to make a sibling CVS/ directory when it checks out a working copy. This CVS/ directory would not be *inside* the working copy, but rather next to it. It might be convenient to turn this on if you tend (and your repository's users tend) to check out many different projects from the same repository. Otherwise, you should leave it off, as it can be disconcerting to see an extra CVS/ directory appear where you don't expect it.

PreservePermissions governs whether to preserve file permissions and similar metadata in the revision history. This is a somewhat obscure feature that probably isn't worth describing in detail. See the node "Special Files" in the Cederqvist if you're interested.

Tip

"Node" is Texinfo-speak for a particular location within an Info document. To go to a node while reading Info, just type "g" followed by the name of the node, from anywhere inside the document.

LockDir is also a rarely used feature. In special circumstances, you may want to tell CVS to create its lockfiles somewhere other than directly in the project subdirectories, in order to avoid permission problems. These lockfiles keep CVS from tripping over itself when multiple operations are performed on the same repository directory simultaneously. Generally, you never need to worry about them, but sometimes users may have trouble updating or checking out from a repository directory because they're unable to create a lockfile (even on read-only operations, CVS needs to create a lockfile to avoid situations where it could end up reading while another invocation of CVS is writing). The usual fix for this is to change repository permissions, but when that's not feasible, the **LockDir** parameter can come in handy.

There are no other parameters at this time, but future versions of CVS may add new ones; you should always check the Cederqvist or the distribution config file itself for updates.

The modules File

In modules, you can define aliases and alternate groupings for projects in the repository. The most basic module line is of the form:

```
MODULE_NAME   DIRECTORY_IN_REPOSITORY
```

for example,

```
mp    myproj
asub  myproj/a-subdir
```

(The paths given on the right are relative to the top of the repository.) This gives developers an alternate name by which to check out a project or a portion of a project:

```
floss$ cvs co mp
cvs checkout: Updating mp
U mp/README.txt
U mp/foo.jpg
U mp/hello.c
cvs checkout: Updating mp/a-subdir
U mp/a-subdir/whatever.c
cvs checkout: Updating mp/a-subdir/subsubdir
U mp/a-subdir/subsubdir/fish.c
cvs checkout: Updating mp/b-subdir
U mp/b-subdir/random.c
```

or

```
floss$ cvs -d /usr/local/newrepos/ co asub
cvs checkout: Updating asub
U asub/whatever.c
cvs checkout: Updating asub/subsubdir
U asub/subsubdir/fish.c
```

Notice how in both cases the module's name became the name of the directory created for the working copy. In the case of asub, it didn't even bother with the intermediate myproj/ directory, but created a top-level asub/ instead, even though it came from myproj/a-subdir in the repository. Updates, commits, and all other CVS commands will behave normally in those working copies—the only thing unusual about them are their names.

By putting file names after the directory name, you can define a module consisting of just some of the files in a given repository directory. For example

```
readme  myproj  README.txt
```

and

```
no-readme  myproj  hello.c  foo.jpg
```

would permit the following checkouts, respectively:

```
floss$ cvs -q co readme
U readme/README.txt
floss$ cvs -q co no-readme
U no-readme/hello.c
U no-readme/foo.jpg
floss$
```

You can define a module that will include multiple repository directories by using the **-a** (for "alias") flag, but note that the directories will get them checked out under their original names. For example, this line

```
twoproj  -a  myproj  yourproj
```

would allow you to do this (assuming that both myproj/ and yourproj/ are in the repository):

```
floss$ cvs co twoproj
U myproj/README.txt
U myproj/foo.jpg
U myproj/hello.c
U myproj/a-subdir/whatever.c
U myproj/a-subdir/subsubdir/fish.c
U myproj/b-subdir/random.c
U yourproj/README
U yourproj/foo.c
U yourproj/some-subdir/file1.c
U yourproj/some-subdir/file2.c
U yourproj/some-subdir/another-subdir/blah.c
```

The name "twoproj" was a convenient handle to pull in both projects, but it didn't affect the names of the working copies. (There is no requirement that alias modules refer to multiple directories, by the way; we could have omitted twoproj, in which case myproj would still have been checked out under the name "myproj.")

Modules can even refer to other modules, by prefixing them with an ampersand:

```
mp    myproj
asub  myproj/a-subdir
twoproj -a myproj yourproj
tp  &twoproj
```

Doing a checkout of tp would have exactly the same result as the checkout of twoproj did.

There are a few other tricks you can do with modules, most of them less frequently used than the ones just presented. See the node **modules** in the Cederqvist for information about them.

The commitinfo, loginfo, And rcsinfo Files

Most of the other administrative files provide programmatic "hooks" into various parts of the commit process (for example, the ability to validate log messages or file states before permitting the **commit**, or the ability to notify a group of developers whenever a **commit** happens in a certain directory of the repository).

The files generally share a common syntax. Each line is of the form:

```
REGULAR_EXPRESSION     PROGRAM_TO_RUN
```

The regular expression will be tested against the directory into which the **commit** is taking place (with the directory name relative to the top of the repository). If it matches, the designated program will be run. The program will be passed the names of each of the files in the **commit**; it can do whatever it likes with those names, including opening up the files and examining their contents. If the program returns with a nonzero exit status, the **commit** is prevented from taking place.

> **Tip**
>
> *Regular expressions being a system for concisely describing classes of strings. If you aren't familiar with regular expressions, you can get by with the following short summary: "foo" would match any file whose name contains the string "foo", and "foo.*bar" would match any file whose name contains "foo", followed by any number of characters, followed by the string "bar". That's because normal substrings match themselves, but "." and "*" are special. "." matches any character, and "*" means match any number of the preceding character, including zero. The "^" and "$" signs mean match at the beginning and end of the string, respectively; thus, "^foo.*bar.*baz$" would match any string beginning with "foo", containing "bar" somewhere in the middle, and ending with "baz". That's all we'll go into here; this summary is a very abbreviated subset of full regular expression syntax.*

Here are some example commitinfo lines:

```
^a-subdir*     /usr/local/bin/check-asubdir.sh
ou             /usr/local/bin/validate-project.pl
```

So any **commit** into myproj/a-subdir/ would match the first line, which would then run the check-asubdir.sh script. A **commit** in any project whose name (actual repository directory name, not necessarily module name) contained the string "ou" would run the validate-project.pl script, *unless* the **commit** had already matched the previous a-subdir line.

In place of a regular expression, the word **DEFAULT** or **ALL** may be used. The **DEFAULT** line (or the first **DEFAULT** line, if there are more than one) will be run if no regular expression matches, and each of the **ALL** lines will be run in addition to any other lines that may match.

> **Note**
>
> *The file names passed to the program do not refer to RCS files—they point to normal files, whose contents are exactly the same as the working-copy files being committed. The only unusual aspect is that CVS has them temporarily placed inside the repository, so they'll be available to programs running on the machine where the repository is located.*

The loginfo file is similar to commitinfo, except that instead of acting on the files' contents, it acts on the log message. The left side of the loginfo file contains regular expressions, including possibly **DEFAULT** and **ALL** lines. The program invoked on the right side receives the log message on its standard input; it can do whatever it wants with that input.

The program on the right side can also take an arbitrary number of command-line arguments. One of those arguments can be a special "%" code, to be expanded by CVS at runtime, as follows:

```
%s      ------>        name(s) of the file(s) being committed
%V      ------>        revision number(s) before the commit
%v      ------>        revision number(s) after the commit
```

The expansion always begins with the path to the repository (done for backward-compatibility), followed by the per-file information. For example, if the files committed were foo, bar, and baz, then **%s** would expand into

```
/usr/local/newrepos  foo  bar  baz
```

whereas **%V** would expand to show their old revision numbers

```
/usr/local/newrepos  1.7  1.134  1.12
```

and **%v** their new revision numbers:

```
/usr/local/newrepos  1.8  1.135  1.13
```

There can only be one "%" expression per line in the loginfo file. If you want to use more than one of the codes, you must enclose them in curly braces after the "%" sign—this will expand them into a series of comma-separated sublists, each containing the corresponding information for one file in the commit. For instance, **%{sv}** would expand to

```
/usr/local/newrepos  foo,1.8  bar,1.135  baz,1.13
```

whereas **%{sVv}** would expand to

```
/usr/local/newrepos  foo,1.7,1.8  bar,1.134,1.135  baz,1.12,1.13
```

(You may have to look carefully to distinguish the commas from the periods in those examples.)

Here is a sample loginfo file:

```
^myproj$    /usr/local/newrepos/CVSROOT/log.pl -m myproj-devel@foobar.com %s
ou          /usr/local/bin/ou-notify.pl  %{sv}
DEFAULT     /usr/local/bin/default-notify.pl  %{sVv}
```

In the first line, any commit in the myproj subdirectory of the repository invokes "log.pl," passing it an email address (to which log.pl will send a mail containing the log message), followed by the repository, followed by all the files in the commit.

In the second line, any commit in a repository subdirectory containing the string "ou" will invoke the (imaginary) "ou-notify.pl" script, passing it the repository followed by the file names and new revision numbers of the files in the commit.

The third line invokes the (equally imaginary) default-notify.pl script for any commit that didn't match either of the two previous lines, passing it all possible information (path to repository, file names, old revisions, and new revisions).

Commit Emails

The loginfo file is how one sets up commit emails—automated emails that go out to everyone working on a project whenever a commit takes place. (It may seem counterintuitive that this is done in loginfo instead of commitinfo, but the point is that one wants to include the log message in the email). The program to do the mailing—contrib/log.pl in the CVS source distribution—can be installed anywhere on your system. I customarily put it in the repository's CVSROOT/ subdirectory, but that's just a matter of taste.

You may need to edit log.pl a bit to get it to work on your system, possibly changing the first line to point to your Perl interpreter, and maybe changing this line

```
$mailcmd = "| Mail -s 'CVS update: $modulepath'";
```

to invoke your preferred mailer, which may or may not be named "Mail". Once you've got it set the way you like it, you can put lines similar to these into your loginfo:

```
listerizer CVSROOT/log.pl %s -f CVSROOT/commitlog -m listerizer@red-bean.com
RoadMail   CVSROOT/log.pl %s -f CVSROOT/commitlog -m roadmail@red-bean.com
bk/*score  CVSROOT/log.pl %s -f CVSROOT/commitlog -m bkscore-devel@red-bean.com
```

The %s expands to the names of the files being committed; the -f option to log.pl takes a file name, to which the log message will be appended (so CVSROOT/commitlog is an ever-growing file of log messages); and the -m flag takes an email address, to which log.pl will send a message about the commit. The address is usually a mailing list, but you can specify the -m option as many times as necessary in one log.pl command line.

The verifymsg And rcsinfo Files

Sometimes you may just want a program to automatically verify that the log message conforms to a certain standard and to stop the **commit** if that standard is not met. This can be accomplished by using "verifymsg," possibly with some help from "rcsinfo."

The verifymsg file is the usual combination of regular expressions and programs. The program receives the log message on standard input; presumably it runs some checks to verify that the log message meets certain criteria, then it exits with status zero or nonzero. If the latter, the **commit** will fail.

Meanwhile, the left side of rcsinfo has the usual regular expressions, but the right side points to template files instead of programs. A template file might be something like this

```
Condition:
Fix:
Comments:
```

or some other collection of fields that a developer is supposed to fill out to form a valid log message. The template is not very useful if everyone commits using the **-m** option explicitly, but many developers prefer not to do that. Instead, they run

```
floss$ cvs commit
```

and wait for CVS to automatically fire up a text editor (as specified in the **EDITOR** environment variable). There they write a log message, then save the file and exit the editor, after which CVS continues with the **commit**.

In that scenario, an rcsinfo template would insert itself into the editor before the user starts typing, so the fields would be displayed along with a reminder to fill them in. Then when the user commits, the appropriate program in verifymsg is invoked. Presumably, it will check that the message does follow that format, and its exit status will reflect the results of its inquiry (with zero meaning success).

As an aid to the verification programs, the path to the template from the rcsinfo file is appended as the last argument to the program command line in verifymsg; that way, the program can base its verification process on the template itself, if desired.

Note that when someone checks out a working copy to a remote machine, the appropriate rcsinfo template file is sent to the client as well (it's stored in the CVS/ subdirectory of the working copy). However, this means that if the rcsinfo file on the server is changed after that, the client won't see the changes without re-checking out the project (merely doing an update won't work).

Note also that in the verifymsg file, the **ALL** keyword is not supported (although **DEFAULT** still is). This is to make it easier to override default verification scripts with subdirectory-specific ones.

The taginfo File

What loginfo does for log messages, taginfo does for tags. The left side of taginfo is regular expressions, as usual, and the right side is programs. Each program is automatically handed arguments when CVS **tag** is invoked, in this order:

```
arg 1:          tag name
arg 2:          operation ("add" => tag, "mov" => tag -F, "del" => tag -d)
arg 3:          repository
arg 4, 5, etc:  file revision [file revision ...]
```

If the program returns nonzero, the tag is aborted.

We haven't covered the **-F** option to **tag** before now, but it's exactly what the above implies: a way to move a tag from one revision to another. For example, if the tag "Known_Working" is attached to Revision 1.7 of a file and you want it attached to Revision 1.11 instead, you'd do this

```
cvs tag -r 1.11 -F Known_Working foo.c
```

which removes the tag from 1.7, or wherever it was previously in that file, and puts it at 1.11.

The cvswrappers File

The redundantly-named cvswrappers file gives you a way to specify that certain files should be treated as binary, based on their file name. CVS does not assume that all .jpg files are JPG image data, for example, so it doesn't automatically use **-kb** when adding JPG files. Nonetheless, certain projects would find it very useful to simply designate all JPG files as binary. Here is a line in cvswrappers to do that:

```
*.jpg -k 'b'
```

The '**b**' is separate and in quotes because it's not the only possible RCS keyword expansion mode; one could also specify '**o**', which means not to expand $ sign keywords but to do newline conversion. However, '**b**' is the most common parameter.

There are a few other modes that can be specified from the wrappers file, but they're for such rare situations that they're probably not worth documenting here (translation: your author has never had to use them). See the node "Wrappers" in the Cederqvist if you're curious.

The editinfo File

This file is obsolete, even though it's still included in distributions. Just ignore it.

The notify File

This file is used in conjunction with CVS's "watch" features, which are described in Chapter 6. Nothing about it will make sense until you understand what watches are (they're a useful but non-essential feature), so see Chapter 6 for details about this file and about watches.

The checkoutlist File

If you look inside CVSROOT/, you'll see that working copies of the files exist side by side with their RCS revision files:

```
floss$ ls /usr/local/newrepos/CVSROOT
checkoutlist      config,v        history       notify       taginfo
checkoutlist,v    cvswrappers     loginfo       notify,v     taginfo,v
commitinfo        cvswrappers,v   loginfo,v     passwd       verifymsg
commitinfo,v      editinfo        modules       rcsinfo      verifymsg,v
config            editinfo,v      modules,v     rcsinfo,v

floss$
```

CVS only pays attention to the working versions, not the RCS files, when it's looking for guidance on how to behave. Therefore, whenever you **commit** your working copy of CVSROOT/ (which might, after all, even be checked out to a different machine), CVS automatically updates any changed files in the repository itself. You will know that this has happened because CVS will print a message at the end of such commits:

```
floss$ cvs ci -m "added mp and asub modules" modules
Checking in modules;
/usr/local/newrepos/CVSROOT/modules,v  <--  modules
new revision: 1.2; previous revision: 1.1
done
cvs commit: Rebuilding administrative file database
```

CVS automatically knows about the standard administrative files, and will rebuild them in CVSROOT/ as necessary. If you decide to put custom files in CVSROOT/ (such as programs or rcsinfo template files), you'll have to tell CVS explicitly to treat them the same way.

That's the purpose of the checkoutlist file. It has a different format from most of the files we've looked at so far

```
FILENAME     ERROR_MESSAGE_IF_FILE_CANNOT_BE_CHECKED_OUT
```

for example,

```
log.pl          unable to check out / update log.pl in CVSROOT

bugfix.tmpl     unable to check out / update bugfix.tmpl in CVSROOT
```

Certain files in CVSROOT are traditionally not kept under revision control. One such is the history file, which keeps a running record of all actions in the repository, for use by the **cvs history** command (which lists checkout, update, and tag activity for a given file or project directory). Incidentally, if you just remove the history file, CVS will obligingly stop keeping that log.

> **Tip**
>
> *Sometimes the history file is the cause of permission problems, and the easiest way to solve them is to either make it world-writeable or just remove it.*

Another "unrevisioned" administrative file is passwd, the assumption being that having it checked out over the network might compromise the passwords (even though they're encrypted). You'll have to decide based on your own security situation whether you want to add passwd to checkoutlist or not; by default, it is not in checkoutlist.

Two final notes about the CVSROOT/ directory: It is possible, if you make a big enough mistake, to commit an administrative file that is broken in such a way as to prevent any commits from happening at all. If you do that, naturally you won't be able to commit a fixed version of the administrative file! The solution is to go in and hand-edit the repository's working copy of the administrative file to correct the problem; the whole repository may stay inaccessible until you do that.

Also, for security's sake, make sure your CVSROOT/ directory is only writeable by users you trust (by "trust," I mean you trust both their intentions and their ability not to compromise their password). The *info files give people the ability to invoke arbitrary programs, so anyone who can commit or edit files in the CVSROOT/ directory can essentially run any command on the system. That's something you should always keep in mind.

Finding Out More

Although this chapter tries to give a complete introduction to installing and administering CVS, I've left out things that are either too rarely used to be worth mentioning or already well documented in the Cederqvist manual. The latter category includes setting up the other remote access methods: RSH/SSH, kserver (Kerberos 4), and GSSAPI (which includes Kerberos 5, among other things). It should be noted that nothing special needs to be done for RSH/ SSH connections, other than making sure that the user in question can log into the repository machine using RSH or SSH. If they can and CVS is installed on both client and server, and they have the right permissions to use the repository directly from the server machine, then they should be able to access the repository remotely via the :ext: method.

Descriptions of certain specialized features of CVS have been deferred to later chapters, so they can be introduced in contexts where their usefulness is obvious. General CVS trouble-shooting tips are found in Chapter 8.

Although it's not necessary to read the entire Cederqvist manual, you should familiarize yourself with it; it will be an invaluable reference tool. If for some reason you don't have Info working on your machine and don't want to print the manual, you can browse it online at **http://durak.org/cvswebsites/doc/** or **www.loria.fr/~molli/cvs/doc/cvs_toc.html**.

Chapter 5

Designing For Decentralized Development

The Importance Of Software Design

If you glance along the shelves of any bookstore with a decent computer section, you'll see approximately ten million volumes (well, maybe a slight exaggeration) on the subject of software design. The reason for this could be that software design is extremely important, or perhaps it means that no one really knows how to do it! Although design is rarely defined, it is a respected and sought-after skill among programmers. We've all heard sentences like "Yeah, she's a good coder, but she lacks design sense," uttered in such a way that, despite the initial compliment, the overall sense is more disparaging than not.

But what is design? It can be defined in a number of ways, but for this book, let's just agree that software design is about *comprehensibility*—that is, it's the part of programming concerned with making programs understandable and maintainable by humans.

Good design does not:

♦ Make programs run more efficiently in terms of memory usage or speed.

♦ Improve the quality or accuracy of their output.

Good design does:

♦ Make the general plan of the program easy to grasp. When the program is "graspable," it means that for any given behavior of the software, a person can find the region of source code that controls it.

- Enable a programmer to figure out the cause of a bug quickly.

- Help design-sensitive programmers immediately to see only one or two plausible ways to fit in a new feature, instead of an infinity of equally possible (and equally nonintuitive) implementations.

It cannot be emphasized too much that comprehensibility is a concern of people, not code. The code couldn't care less whether, from a human's point of view, it is clean and beautiful or tangled and knotty. The code is not even aware that such properties exist. By the time the computer runs it, the code has been transformed (compiled) into a numbingly long string of machine instructions, from which the original plan of the source code can be discerned only with great effort, by very patient programmers. Software does not run any better because it has been divided into intuitive modules or because its data structures have been segregated by role and documented. These benefit only people, not machines.

Thus, good design actually has little to do with the quality of the program as seen by the end user. Many computer users are happily depending on software that, although stable and well built to all outward appearances, would probably make an experienced programmer blanch with fright were its internals exposed to public inspection.

Proprietary Software Design Vs. Free Software Design

Of course, only proprietary software has hidden internals. The inner mechanisms of free software are constantly exposed and studied. You might think that this would make good design even more important for free software, but (as far as I can tell) it doesn't work out that way. Free programs do tend toward classically "good" design over the long haul, but their authors are usually less concerned with well-structured design at inception than authors of proprietary programs are.

Why? One reason is that a commercial software vendor can afford to make a high initial investment in the code, confident that it will be paid for by sales over the long run. That means the initial design stage can be heavily subsidized. In addition, the more maintainable the program, the less costly it will be for the company to produce each upgrade. Another reason may be that the senior programmers at proprietary software companies often have advanced degrees in computer science or software engineering, so they come with the traditional academic preference for solid foundations. In a sense, a program is a mathematical construct or proof, so if it does not proceed clearly from well-established premises, it is not quite academically acceptable.

Formal qualifications and theoretical correctness seem to hold less influence in the free software world, however. Admittedly, there is a tremendous amount of discussion among free software enthusiasts about what constitutes good design, but what one sees in chat groups and mailing lists is not always an accurate indication of what's happening on the coding front. When it comes to successful free software projects, clean design—although desirable—is of secondary importance to simply running reliably on a wide variety of platforms. Some reasons for this are:

♦ In a free project, many small initial investments are made at different times by various contributors, instead of a single massive initial investment on the part of one organization. These individual contributors became involved in the first place because of their interest in what the code does (as opposed to an interest in earning their salary or gaining the approval of the project leader). Their first job is to install and run the code, not peruse it. If they're able to get it up and running, they'll almost automatically be inclined to evaluate the program's design more charitably anyway.

♦ The majority of contributors to free software have no need to carefully inspect the code, although that is really the only way to develop a truly informed opinion about a program's design. New contributors usually just want some small, incremental addition to the program's behavior (after all, if they could only obtain their desired results by making major changes to the program, they would probably write something from scratch themselves or find a more appropriate project to join). For such quick, minor changes, the best strategy is generally for them to dive in and start hacking. There usually isn't time—or, to be honest, inclination—to take a broad survey of the code and then make changes in the most theoretically pleasing way.

However, the triumph of practice over theory in free software is indicative of something deeper than mere time constraints. Although everyone agrees that programs should be easy to understand and modify, no two people will agree on exactly what that means in terms of actual code layout and data structures. Often, a design that looked good when the project started may turn out to be unwieldy and obstructive one year and several thousand lines of code later. It's just not possible to predict how the software will perform in the real world. Given the choice, most programmers would postpone as many design decisions as possible until after the code has seen some real use.

In free projects, they can do just that—the program needs to run, but it doesn't need to be mature or settled. Commercial software has to be not only usable, but polished and professional, right from the first release. Polished, professional software does not confuse (or stimulate) the user by suggesting alternative uses or unexpected applications; instead, it tries to do exactly what its marketing plan says it does. Thus, its design must be relatively complete from the very beginning of the project. Free programs can postpone design decisions for as long as the developers are comfortable; commercial programs generally cannot.

Cost Issues

The vendor of commercial software is also concerned with controlling the total cost of producing the software over the long term, including post-release maintenance and upgrades. The additional effort and expense involved in creating a sound design is justified because it minimizes expensive rewrites or workarounds later on. Even though a careful, comprehensive design probably means a steeper learning curve for developers (who will need to familiarize themselves with the master plan before doing anything to the code), this extra effort usually pays off for the vendor in the long run.

Free software projects, though, are not really concerned with minimizing the total "cost" over the entire lifetime of a project. Instead, they're concerned with minimizing the cost to any one contributor at any one time. Sharp, immediate impediments to modification—say, having to understand a complex master plan—impose a high initial cost on participation. However, constant but low-key hassles, such as dealing with a slightly disorganized code base in which it's relatively easy to find what you're looking for even when you can't tell quite how it relates to everything else, are not likely to discourage anyone from participating. (Volunteers may be psychologically more comfortable with loose designs, too. People are more inclined to jump in and start hacking if they don't feel like they may be upsetting some delicate and intricate master plan.)

Design Invariants

Free software projects tend to settle at the outset on a very small number of invariants ("We're going to organize everything around a text-buffer structure" or "The records will be kept in an SQL-compatible database"). This allows the project to get started without complete chaos, and then the rest of the project can grow around those decisions. Indeed, I'd go so far as to say that the two most valuable skills a designer can have in the free software world are:

♦ Knowing which invariants will prove fertile rather than constricting

♦ Knowing what questions *don't* have to be answered right away

Refusing to design prematurely is an open acknowledgment that we just don't know what the world will do with our code. Our imaginations are limited and our intellects puny when faced with such highly complex situations. Who can calculate the outcomes of hundreds or thousands of user-program interactions, especially when the users have access to the source code? It's better to devote our resources to increasing the code's adaptability than to anticipating every future direction of development.

The important thing, then, is not to come up with the perfect design at the start, but to design the software to be evolvable. Partly, of course, this is simply a matter of the developers keeping an open mind, but it's also a matter of how the code is organized. This organization constitutes a kind of message to future developers, in which you make clear which parts of the code are design invariants and which are not. Most parts of the code are not invariants—they are quick decisions made to get things up and running, and don't claim to be the best solution.

(Even the so-called invariants are subject to reconsideration. But if the original developers' judgement was reasonably sound, then the assumptions they saw as structurally defining usually also turn out to be sound. Those assumptions could, theoretically, be changed, but changing them to accommodate some new design often requires an effort equivalent to rewriting the entire program from scratch. Therefore, in practice, the core of the code evolves much more slowly than the rest, and rarely loses its basic design.)

Code Design

When it comes to concrete design organization, there are good practices, but no universally agreed-on best practices (at least not yet). So I'm just going to describe some methods that I've seen work in the past—but don't hesitate to experiment liberally.

I'm not going to discuss design principles that are universally accepted as equally applicable to both open and closed source projects. Thousands of books are available explaining the necessity of avoiding unnecessary duplication of code, breaking the project into manageable components with clear entry and exit points, and many other useful guidelines. This chapter is about open source software design, not design in general.

Dividing Certainties From Uncertainties

First, document the core assumptions of your code. Save this information in a file that is easily accessible (for example, in a file called "DESIGN" at the top level of the project). This file should describe the code only at a very general level. Detailed descriptions of the central data structures, for example, should be included in comments in header or source files, so they can be updated as the structures evolve. The design document gives an overview of the project's overall shape as it was first conceived. If the assumptions stated there are general enough to remain more or less invariable, then you won't have to worry about the document becoming obsolete, and it may only rarely need to be changed at all.

A design document makes it much easier for new developers to grasp the project as a whole entity. Once they understand the basic design, everything else they examine in the project will have a ready-made framework to fit into.

Note

Beware if the design document becomes too large. You may be including noncentral assumptions, which are likely to change quickly. Then that portion of your document would be out of date, which is even worse than not being there at all. Here's a good strategy for avoiding this: If you find yourself going back into the design document to revise a section in more than a minor way, consider removing that section entirely. The design document is intended to include only written-in-stone truths, not field reports that require revision from time to time.

The corollary to having a few clear central assumptions is that the rest of the project—the majority of the code—should not be written in stone. This means acknowledging (in comments in the code or perhaps via a mailing list) that some procedure could have been done a different way, and might even be better if done that way. When you've written a piece of code in the quickest way possible, it's rare for it to also be the most efficient implementation. That's okay for the first release—the quicker way is often preferable. However, including a comment in the code at that point may encourage people to try alternatives if that portion of the code becomes a bottleneck.

Here are some general points about writing for distributed developers:

♦ Write your code to be clear and self-explanatory because you're not going to be there to train new arrivals. The clarity of the code has a direct bearing on how much other people will be able to understand and modify it. A navigable plan is better than an all-encompassing but complex one.

♦ Write every line of code as though you're taking part in a conversation with the other developers—which you are, although the conversation is stretched out across time, and some of the people you're conversing with may not even have joined the project yet. You are not on stage—your goal is not for them to see a flawless performance, but for them to understand what you were thinking when you wrote the code. You want to make them feel confident that they're as cognizant of all the major issues as you were when you wrote it. When people feel comfortable in a region of code, they'll feel they have a right to change it, which is exactly what you want.

♦ Don't be afraid to leave comments expressing doubt or second thoughts about what you've done in the code, any more than you would hesitate to say such things in a conversation. Later, when others are wondering why you wrote the code a particular way, they'll see your comments, revealing that you also entertained thoughts of doing it another way. This will reassure them that they're onto something, and make them less hesitant to improve the code there. (Although comments may not traditionally be considered part of a program's design, they do interact with the design when they indicate how closely a certain part of the source is connected to the overall plan.)

♦ Use syntax-sensitive indentation throughout the source code. Most programmers expect this of publicly distributed code nowadays, and they may be confused or even misread parts of the code if it's not indented consistently.

Dividing Code Into Files And Directories

Turning our attention to the next level of organization, let's consider the arrangement of files and directories.

How you divide up the code semantically (data structures, calling conventions, and so on) is very much a matter of taste, of course. But the best way to divide the code up *physically*, in my experience, is to use shallow directory hierarchies, at least at the beginning of a project. Partly this is due to the odd way CVS removes obsolete directories: It doesn't remove them, it just has a special-case feature for making them vanish from the working copy once all their files have been removed. (The directories are still there, lurking in the repository, taking up space, and occasionally confusing people who forget to pass the **-P** option to **cvs update** to prune them out.) The fewer directories that you create at the beginning of the project, the less frequently you will have to remove directories later on.

There is another reason to avoid creating a lot of subdirectories starting a project. Sometimes, people are tempted to "over-hierarchize" as a way of making statements about the structure of the code (as an extreme example, putting all the networking code into a net subdirectory, all the printing code into a print subdirectory , and so on). The problem with this is that you usually can't *know* at the start of the project which parts will turn out to be natural modules later on. Maybe the printing code will turn out to be just one of many output drivers, and end up belonging in an outputs subdirectory that gets added to the project later, or maybe it will go away entirely, with the printing functions handed off to an external library instead. If contributors' organizational ideas are biased by an artificially imposed directory hierarchy, they may be slow to see alternatives that would be immediately obvious under a looser arrangement. Absence of structure is a message that says, "We don't know yet how everything will turn out, so we're waiting for the proper arrangements to suggest themselves."

Placing portions of the code into subdirectories is helpful when the time is ripe, just don't be overeager to feel that the time is ripe. A file's position in a hierarchy is really less important than an understanding of what the file actually does.

Also, a minor technical advantage to having most of the project in one directory is that the files are slightly more convenient to navigate. Fewer keystrokes are required to call up a new source file, and basic search tools (such as grep in Unix) can easily be invoked on all the files in the project.

Dividing Code Into Modules

The semantic layout of the code—the division of the code into modules or subprograms, each performing a discrete portion of the whole task for which the software was designed— is related to the physical layout, but is harder to generalize about because it can be so different from project to project.

Modules can help keep the code robust, even code that is in the busy hands of random contributors who may have varying levels of experience and competence. The point of a module is to group all of the code for a given subsystem into a definite set of files, so that when you change one part of that code, you know where to look for dependencies that may need to compensate for the change. Commonly, all the code in a given module will share certain data structures, and those data structures will be used nowhere else in the program— the module is entirely responsible for maintaining their integrity and understanding what each of those data structures means.

Access to a module is usually done through designated entry points—functions (or, sometimes, exported variables) that the rest of the program knows to use when it wants something from the module. All of the code outside the module scrupulously avoids ever referring to any part of the module not explicitly advertised as an entry point. Indeed, many modern programming languages make it possible to render the module's internals actually invisible to the rest of the program, and you should take advantage of those features whenever possible. Although this may seem restrictive, it's actually liberating, because it means anyone can rewrite the internals of the module to an arbitrary degree (say, to use better algorithms) without disturbing the external code that depends on the module. As long as the entry points remain the same—that is, keeping the same names, taking the same arguments, and returning the same sorts of values—what goes on inside the module is nobody's business but the module's.

As far as it goes, this advice is applicable to any kind of software project. What's different for open source projects is how modules are treated *politically*. In a closely managed project with a programming team that is more or less set (that is to say, most proprietary software projects), responsibility for the various modules tends to be fairly formalized, with most or all changes to a given module going through that module's maintainer. From a management perspective, this makes a lot of sense: You know the programmer is going to be there for a long time, because it's her job, so she becomes the house expert in the intricacies of that module. Meanwhile, the rest of the team can treat the module as a "black box" and be spared the necessity of learning its code. Also, it's easier to measure a programmer's contribution when their coding isn't mixed and diluted with everyone else's.

A free software team is not optimized for this particular kind of efficiency, however, because they don't know how long a given member will be around nor how much time that member will be able to devote to the project this week (or month, or whatever). Although there is sometimes a "responsible party" for a certain module, it's a much looser kind of responsibility, and anyone on the team will generally feel free to make changes to the module (or they will if the project is socially healthy and the programmers are free of destructive territorial instincts). When the module doesn't provide quite the interface needed by outside code, the person working on the calling code will often jump into the module and *make* it provide the missing feature.

I am indebted to Jim Blandy for identifying this borderlessness as one of the distinguishing characteristics of free software. Several years ago he was discussing some technical issues with another programmer while I listened. The programmer was complaining that one of the major modules of a certain free program didn't provide a well-designed interface to the rest of the code and this deficiency was causing him to have to write things in an awkward way. Jim raised his eyebrows archly and said with righteous fervor, "Well, change the provider, then! Isn't that the free software way?" Absolutely. This is especially true when the code is kept in CVS or some other version control system; the worst thing that can happen if someone makes an ill-advised change to a module is that the change will have to be reverted. It's no big deal—and probably a valuable learning experience for the programmer.

In some ways, it may be less efficient when everyone has to know a little bit about the module, as opposed to having one person be the official expert and gatekeeper. However, free projects optimize in favor of a distributed burden, lessening the vulnerability of the module to any one person's schedule (or lapse in judgement for that matter). Over time, the module and its callers will slowly find their way to a polished balance that lies somewhere between a perfectly opaque "black box" that reveals nothing about its inner workings and a perfectly controllable engine that needs to be told how to do every little thing. This balance will be the right one, because the same people who use the module also have the opportunity to tune it. There can be no self-delusion about the intuitiveness of its interface or the efficiency of its implementation, because any sufficiently dissatisfied user of the module will do whatever is necessary to fix it.

Evolution-Centered Design

There is an obvious analogy between software development and biological evolution. Free programs often end up resembling living organisms, and can be compared to nonfree programs in roughly the same way that natural organisms can be compared to manufactured machines. Anyone with an engineering bent who spends some time studying living creatures is usually surprised by the extreme inconsistency of natural selection's design sense. A beautiful and intuitive—to our sensibilities—solution (say, having an internal skeleton) may be used in a totally inappropriate way at certain places in the code (say, the reshaping of ancient jawbones into part of our hearing apparatus, where they serve a purpose completely unrelated to issues of rigidity or load-bearing). But beauty and appropriateness are only meaningful to us as we consider the results from an aesthetic point of view. For the evolved creature, the only thing that matters is that things work well enough for the creature to survive and reproduce (and we do hear, after all).

The dynamics of free software survival are largely the same: If the code runs well, it will be copied more; if it doesn't, it will be copied less or not at all. If you work with such software long enough, you may even find your ideas about good design changing to accommodate all sorts of solutions that, while they may seem odd and unexpected at first glance, turn out in practice to work very well. Although the idea of letting the software largely design itself is not new, it also has not received the kind of attention I think it deserves. I even made some attempts to coin a catchy new word for evolution-centered design, but none of them turned out very well ("Designolution"? "Evolvitechture"?) So we'll have to discuss the fundamental concept of evolutionary design using an eight-syllable phrase to refer to it (unless someone wants to contribute a new one).

Evolutionary design really is qualitatively different from top-down, master-plan-based design, the kind that dominates the proprietary software industry. It's not that top-down programs don't also evolve, but that their authors aren't depending on evolution to make major decisions for them. They have other sources of guidance (contractual requirements, focus groups, magazine reviews, company politics, and presumably even user feedback) for the program's future. As an evolutionary force, however, these sources pale in comparison to having users indicate their preferences by directly hacking on the code. Even if a user botches a modification and someone else has to rewrite it, the fact that they tried at all sends the developers a clear message that the change was very important to someone. When hordes of random strangers start using your code, you soon discover where the preference lines truly fall. How do people *really* want the software to behave? You'll find out just by watching what they code; it's better than any focus group.

Comprehensibility—good design—is just one more evolving property. Although immediate usefulness may cause people to start working on a program, overall maintainability probably does a lot to keep them there. If the program didn't slowly become more navigable and more developer-friendly over time, you'd have to wonder what was wrong. The people working on it have every reason to organize it well, and experience with the code gives them the knowledge they need to do so.

The most beautiful example I know of evolutionary design has nothing to do with software; in fact, it probably never happened. You may have heard the story about the architect of a university campus, who deliberately left pedestrian paths out of his design and specified that grass be planted everywhere. When the university's board of directors inquired about this seemingly major omission, he smiled and said, "Wait." After a year had passed, he returned to campus, observed the routes along which the grass had been most trampled by students, and ordered concrete paths to be built along those routes.

I've heard this tale now about three different architects and three different campuses, which leads me to believe it's only an urban legend. Anyway, everyone knows that professional architects don't behave like that. Nevertheless, it always sounded like a brilliant idea to me: Don't tell the students where to walk; instead find out where they *do* walk and make it more convenient for them to do what they do already. Don't tell reality how you want it to behave, but *ask* it how it behaves instead. The architect laid down some core assumptions—the buildings—but then let a supposedly major design choice essentially decide itself, by watching how the system flowed around the invariants.

With software, which is far more malleable and cooperative than grass and concrete, you have the opportunity to do this sort of thing every day. But we're trained not to. We're taught to try and hold the entire project in our minds at once, to have a master plan, and to shape the project to fit the plan. I think a lot of software would be better off if people let it design itself (or rather, if they paid more attention to what reality, in the form of users and contributors, told them about their software).

Principles Of Free Software Design

That being said, let me turn around now and offer some inviolable principles of design, ones that are especially important for free software.

Don't Limit Input

When accepting input, tolerate no arbitrary limits on the size of the data (this applies to all kinds of input: streams, file contents, file names, prompted command lines from the user, and so on). This is one of the best-known of the GNU Coding Standards (which are all worth reading—you can find them at **www.gnu.org/prep/standards_toc.html**). It's partly motivated by security concerns (nonobvious limits on input length can result in buffer-overflow bugs—if you don't know what that means, just take my word for it that it's something you want to avoid).

A ban on arbitrary limits is important for your program to remain evolvable. You can't predict what kind of input people will send or for what purpose. What if the description slot in some data structure ends up being used to hold a full JPEG image instead of the short textual description of a person's face it was originally meant to hold? At the time the data structure was designed, no one could foresee that it would one day be used to store images (which typically require much more storage than text). Nevertheless, if the receiving area is dynamically allocated to be as large as the incoming data, there won't be a problem. Avoidance of arbitrary limits automatically makes the code more robust in the face of unexpected input, and the code becomes more extensible because developers don't have to worry whether parts of the input will inexplicably disappear when stored in certain locations.

In addition to tolerating data of any size, the program should, for the same reasons, tolerate data of any type. In other words, it shouldn't modify a binary data stream (by zeroing the high bit of each byte, for instance, as some programs have been known to do), unless munging the data in that way is part of the program's purpose. Always leave the data as you found it, like a good camper.

Note

Neither of these injunctions should be taken to mean that the program has to know how to interpret any kind of data it sees. If the code expects plain text and doesn't know what to do with a JPEG image, that's fine. The issue is not so much that people will suddenly start storing images where they formerly stored text, as that they may make modifications to the program that depend on it being able to store an image where it formerly stored text. If they proceed under this assumption, only to discover that most of each image is missing because the data structure silently truncated it, they'll feel—rightly—that an implicit promise has been broken. The software doesn't have to handle every conceivable input; it just shouldn't close any doors to the possibility of receiving every conceivable input.

Use A Consistent Interface

When the program has to interact with the outside world—for example, via file formats or network protocols—it's important that it present a consistent interface. These interfaces must actually be more carefully planned for free software than for proprietary software. Free third-party tools tend to spring up very quickly to augment free programs, and the authors of those tools don't want to constantly rewrite them to cope with changing interfaces. (Commercial software companies can afford to have someone responsible for tracking format changes in other vendors' products and advising programmers on how to compensate for them. This won't happen with volunteer programmers—instead, they'll just stop interfacing with your software and start interfacing with someone else's.)

This means that formats and protocols need to be planned thoroughly in advance; otherwise, you may discover later that you have unintentionally built unexpected and inconvenient limitations into them. For example, one of the first programs I wrote was an extension to the Emacs text editor that allowed users to set "bookmarked" locations in text files (just like the bookmark feature found in most Web browsers today). Obviously, the bookmarks had to be stored in a file on disk between Emacs sessions, so I whipped up what I thought was a sufficiently powerful file format and wrote code to write it out and read it back in.

As the software acquired a respectable user base, I began to get emails from people suggesting additional information that could be stored with each bookmark (annotations, for example). Certain of these suggestions were made with such regularity that I knew the software really ought to incorporate them. Unfortunately, I hadn't left any space in my file format for storing annotations or any of the other new information. I hadn't even taken the most basic step of leaving an "escape hatch" slot in each entry that I could toggle on to indicate the presence of additional information not accounted for by the original format.

Eventually, I resorted to an inelegant solution that at least allowed compatibility in both directions: I made up a special "version stamp" that would appear at the beginning of the record file, telling the software what version of the format that this file used. An absent version stamp was decreed to mean Version 1, corresponding to the first release of the software. The newer versions of the software were given special code to convert Version 1 format files to Version 2. (And if that all sounds like a great pain in the neck, let me assure you it was!)

Version 2 was a much better-designed format, allowing essentially arbitrary numbers of key-value pairs. For the sake of forward-compatibility, the software was now free to simply ignore any keys it didn't understand. Because of this flexibility, Version 3 of the format will probably never be needed. But I could have saved many hours of time and effort by doing things the Version 2 way right from the start. (Then again, I seem to be in august company. Microsoft Word's native document format apparently changes quite a bit from one release to the next of the software, to the point where the latest versions of Word actually cannot read some files written by the earliest versions).

Document Data Structures

When commenting, it's usually better to document data structures, as opposed to the code that uses the data structures. It may seem counterintuitive to document the "nouns" of a program before the "verbs," but most people seem to be able to figure out the dynamic portions of the code, once they know the layout and purpose of the data on which it operates. So if you're writing code, put a description by each field in a data structure, directly in the file that defines the structure. If you're reading code, look at the header files first; the rest of the code will then usually make much more sense.

Make It Portable

Make portability a priority. Obviously, this gets easier when you have more participants, testing the software in more environments. However, it also means that you'll have to take their word for it when they tell you that a certain way of doing things won't work on their computer. Normally this is no big deal, but sometimes it can mean substantial changes are required to make the software run in that environment. (For example, such a situation may happen if you release a thread-based program that makes use of a thread library peculiar to your operating system. In that case, it simply won't run anywhere else and must be changed to use some version of threading that works on both your machine and on the new person's.)

When this happens, and the platform is one you hoped to support eventually anyway, don't hesitate at all to accept the necessary changes. Every time a new platform is added to the list of where the code can run, you gain everyone who works on that platform as potential users. This is too good an opportunity to pass up, no matter how fond you were of the original, nonportable implementation.

If your project is somewhat complex and you want it to be very widely used, especially in the Unix world, consider using GNU **autoconf**. This allows you to "abstract out" nonportable aspects of your code and test, at build time on each platform, how each aspect is implemented there. The initial autoconfiscation (yes, that's the verb) of a project can be a bit daunting, but once it's done, many thorny issues are handled for you, because **autoconf** already knows about the most commonly encountered differences between various flavors of Unix. See **www.gnu.org/software/autoconf/autoconf.html** for more information.

The preceding points are more about adhering to certain well-tested conventions than about having any grand architectural vision for the program. But it is about as far as I'm willing to go in suggesting how to do robust large-scale design in a world where programs frequently end up with both unexpected uses and unexpected users. Naturally, if you really want to write a program in a certain way, do it—part of the reason for writing software is the pleasure of testing out ideas in running code. However, don't ignore evidence that the design may not be working exactly as expected (and with any reasonably complex program there are bound to be discrepancies between your vision and its realization in software).

If you're set on making your program perfect and beautiful, don't expect anyone else to hack on it. They'll be too afraid of making a mess in your nice, clean room. On the other hand, if your goal is a useful program and not a clean room, you can expect your preconceptions of the project's future to be constantly shaken up by contributors. When a lot of developers participate in a project, the resulting design often ends up representing a compromise, a mixture of styles and solutions, weighted in favor of those who do the most coding. This may seem like rough justice, but it has the advantage of tuning the implementation to those who must interact with it the most—that is, the biggest contributors.

When In Doubt, Abstain

It may only be a slight exaggeration to say that the basic principle of open source design is "Don't." Design only what you absolutely must to get the code running or to express a firm belief you have about how the software must be to succeed. Leave the rest to evolution. Sure, you may end up with something very different from what you originally set out to produce, but is that so bad? You will be freed from the limits of your imagination, and that's a substantial reward in itself.

Chapter 6
Advanced CVS

Beyond The Basics

Now that we've covered the basic concepts of CVS usage and repository administration, we'll look at how CVS can be incorporated into the entire process of development. The fundamental CVS working cycle—checkout, update, commit, update, commit, and so on—was demonstrated by the examples in Chapter 2. This chapter elaborates on the cycle and discusses how CVS can be used to help developers communicate, give overviews of project activity and history, isolate and reunite different branches of development, and automate frequently performed tasks. Some of the techniques covered introduce new CVS commands, but many merely explain better ways to use commands that you already know.

CVS As Telephone

A major benefit of using CVS on a project is that it can function as a communications device as well as a record-keeper. This section concentrates on how CVS can be used to keep participants informed about what's going on in a project. As is true with other aspects of CVS, these features reward cooperation. The participants must want to be informed; if people choose not to use the communications features, there's nothing CVS can do about it.

"Watches": Knowing Who's Working On What, When

In its default behavior, CVS treats each working copy as an isolated sandbox. No one knows what you're doing in your working copy until you commit your changes. In turn, you don't know what others are doing in theirs—except via the usual methods of communication, such as shouting down the hallway, "Hey, I'm going to work on parse.c now. Let me know if you're editing it so we can avoid conflicts!"

This informality works for projects where people have a general idea of who's responsible for what. However, this process can break down when a large number of developers are active in all parts of a code base and want to avoid conflicts. In such cases, they frequently have to cross each others' areas of responsibility but can't shout down the hallway at each other because they're geographically distributed.

A feature of CVS called "watches" provides developers with a way to notify each other about who is working on what files at a given time. By "setting a watch" on a file, a developer can have CVS notify her if anyone else starts to work on that file. The notifications are normally sent via email, although it is possible to set up other notification methods.

To use watches, you must modify one or two files in the repository administrative area, and developers must add some extra steps to the usual checkout/update/commit cycle. The changes on the repository side are fairly simple: You may need to edit the CVSROOT/notify file so that CVS knows how notifications are to be performed. You may also have to add lines to the CVSROOT/users file, which supplies external email addresses.

On the working copy side, developers have to tell CVS which files they want to watch so that CVS can send them notifications when someone else starts editing those files. They also need to tell CVS when they start or stop editing a file, so CVS can send out notifications to others who may be watching. The following commands are used to implement these extra steps:

♦ **cvs watch**

♦ **cvs edit**

♦ **cvs unedit**

Note

*The command **watch** differs from the usual CVS command pattern in that it requires further subcommands, such as **cvs watch add...**, **cvs watch remove...**, and so on.*

In the following example, we'll look at how to turn on watches in the repository and then how to use watches from the developer's side. The two example users, jrandom and qsmith, each have their own separate working copies of the same project; the working copies may even be on different machines. As usual, all examples assume that the **$CVSROOT** environment variable has already been set, so there's no need to pass **-d <REPOS>** to any CVS commands.

Enabling Watches In The Repository

First, the CVSROOT/notify file must be edited to turn on email notification. One of the developers can do this, or the repository administrator can if the developers don't have permission to change the repository's administrative files. In any case, the first thing to do is check out the administrative area and edit the notify file:

```
floss$ cvs -q co CVSROOT
U CVSROOT/checkoutlist
U CVSROOT/commitinfo
U CVSROOT/config
U CVSROOT/cvswrappers
U CVSROOT/editinfo
U CVSROOT/loginfo
U CVSROOT/modules
U CVSROOT/notify
U CVSROOT/rcsinfo
U CVSROOT/taginfo
U CVSROOT/verifymsg
floss$ cd CVSROOT
floss$ emacs notify
...
```

When you edit the notify file for the first time, you'll see something like this:

```
# The "notify" file controls where notifications from watches set by
# "cvs watch add" or "cvs edit" are sent. The first entry on a line is
# a regular expression which is tested against the directory that the
# change is being made to, relative to the $CVSROOT. If it matches,
# then the remainder of the line is a filter program that should contain
# one occurrence of %s for the user to notify, and information on its
# standard input.
#
# "ALL" or "DEFAULT" can be used in place of the regular expression.
#
# For example:
# ALL mail %s -s "CVS notification"
```

All you really need to do is uncomment the last line by removing the initial "#" mark. Although the notify file provides the same flexible interface as the other administrative files, with regular expressions matching against directory names, the truth is that you almost never want to use any of that flexibility. The only reason to have multiple lines, with each line's regular expression matching a particular part of the repository, would be if you wanted to use a different notification method for each project. However, normal email is a perfectly good notification mechanism, so most projects just use that.

To specify email notification, the line

```
ALL mail %s -s "CVS notification"
```

should work on any standard Unix machine. This command causes notifications to be sent as emails with the subject line "CVS notification" (the special expression **ALL** matches any directory, as usual). Having uncommented that line, **commit** the notify file so the repository is aware of the change:

```
floss$ cvs ci -m "turned on watch notification"
cvs commit: Examining .
Checking in notify;
/usr/local/newrepos/CVSROOT/notify,v  <--  notify
new revision: 1.2; previous revision: 1.1
done
cvs commit: Rebuilding administrative file database
floss$
```

Editing the notify file in this way may be all that you'll need to do for watches in the repository. However, if there are remote developers working on the project, you may need to edit the CVSROOT/users file, too. The purpose of the users file is to tell CVS where to send email notifications for those users who have external email addresses. The format of each line in the users file is:

```
CVS_USERNAME:EMAIL_ADDRESS
```

For example,

```
qsmith:quentinsmith@farawayplace.com
```

The CVS username at the beginning of the line corresponds to a CVS username in CVSROOT/password (if present and the pserver access method is being used), or failing that, the server-side system username of the person running CVS. Following the colon is an external email address to which CVS should send watch notifications for that user.

Unfortunately, as of this writing, the users file does not exist in the stock CVS distribution. Because it's an administrative file, you must not only create, **cvs add**, and commit it in the usual way, but also add it to CVSROOT/checkoutlist so that a checked-out copy is always maintained in the repository.

Here is a sample session demonstrating this:

```
floss$ emacs checkoutlist
  ... (add the line for the users file) ...
floss$ emacs users
  ... (add the line for qsmith) ...
floss$ cvs add users
floss$ cvs ci -m "added users to checkoutlist, qsmith to users"
```

```
cvs commit: Examining .
Checking in checkoutlist;
/usr/local/newrepos/CVSROOT/checkoutlist,v  <--  checkoutlist
new revision: 1.2; previous revision: 1.1
done
Checking in users;
/usr/local/newrepos/CVSROOT/users,v  <--  users
new revision: 1.2; previous revision: 1.1
done
cvs commit: Rebuilding administrative file database
floss$
```

It's possible to use expanded-format email addresses in CVSROOT/users, but you have to be careful to encapsulate all whitespace within quotes. For example, the following will work

```
qsmith:"Quentin Q. Smith <quentinsmith@farawayplace.com>"
```

or

```
qsmith:'Quentin Q. Smith <quentinsmith@farawayplace.com>'
```

However, this will not work:

```
qsmith:"Quentin Q. Smith" <quentinsmith@farawayplace.com>
```

When in doubt, you should test by running the command line given in the notify file manually. Just replace the **%s** in

```
mail %s -s "CVS notification"
```

with what you have following the colon in users. If it works when you run it at a command prompt, it should work in the users file, too.

When it's over, the checkout file will look like this:

```
# The "checkoutlist" file is used to support additional version controlled
# administrative files in $CVSROOT/CVSROOT, such as template files.
#
# The first entry on a line is a filename which will be checked out from
# the corresponding RCS file in the $CVSROOT/CVSROOT directory.
# The remainder of the line is an error message to use if the file cannot
# be checked out.
#
# File format:
#
```

```
#          [<whitespace>]<filename><whitespace><error message><end-of-line>
#
# comment lines begin with '#'

users    Unable to check out 'users' file in CVSROOT.
```

The users file will look like this:

```
qsmith:quentinsmith@farawayplace.com
```

Now that the repository is set up for watches, let's look at what developers need to do in their working copies.

Using Watches In Development

First, a developer checks out a working copy and adds herself to the list of watchers for one of the files in the project:

```
floss$ whoami
jrandom
floss$ cvs -q co myproj
U myproj/README.txt
U myproj/foo.gif
U myproj/hello.c
U myproj/a-subdir/whatever.c
U myproj/a-subdir/subsubdir/fish.c
U myproj/b-subdir/random.c
floss$ cd myproj
floss$ cvs watch add hello.c
floss$
```

The last command, **cvs watch add hello.c**, tells CVS to notify jrandom if anyone else starts working on hello.c (that is, it adds jrandom to hello.c's watch list). For CVS to send notifications as soon as a file is being edited, the user who is editing it has to announce the fact by running **cvs edit** on the file first. CVS has no other way of knowing when someone starts working on a file. Once checkout is done, CVS isn't usually invoked until the next update or commit, which happens after the file has already been edited:

```
paste$ whoami
qsmith
paste$ cvs -q co myproj
U myproj/README.txt
U myproj/foo.gif
U myproj/hello.c
U myproj/a-subdir/whatever.c
U myproj/a-subdir/subsubdir/fish.c
```

```
U myproj/b-subdir/random.c
paste$ cd myproj
paste$ cvs edit hello.c
paste$ emacs hello.c
...
```

When qsmith runs **cvs edit hello.c**, CVS looks at the watch list for hello.c, sees that jrandom is on it, and sends email to jrandom telling her that qsmith has started editing the file. The email even appears to come from qsmith:

```
From: qsmith
Subject: CVS notification
To: jrandom
Date: Sat, 17 Jul 1999 22:14:43 -0500

myproj hello.c
--
Triggered edit watch on /usr/local/newrepos/myproj
By qsmith
```

Furthermore, every time that qsmith (or anyone) commits a new revision of hello.c, jrandom will receive another email:

```
myproj hello.c
--
Triggered commit watch on /usr/local/newrepos/myproj
By qsmith
```

After receiving these emails, jrandom may want to update hello.c immediately to see what qsmith has done, or perhaps she'll email qsmith to find out why he's working on that file. Note that nothing forced qsmith to remember to run **cvs edit**—presumably he did it because he wanted jrandom to know what he was up to (anyway, even if he forgot to do **cvs edit**, his commits would still trigger notifications). The reason to use **cvs edit** is that it notifies watchers *before* you start to work on a file. The watchers can contact you if they think there may be a conflict, before you've wasted a lot of time.

CVS assumes that anyone who runs **cvs edit** on a file wants to be added to the file's watch list, at least temporarily, in case someone else starts to edit it. When qsmith ran **cvs edit**, he became a watcher of hello.c. Both he and jrandom would have received notification if a third party had run **cvs edit** on that file (or committed it).

However, CVS also assumes that the person editing the file only wants to be on its watch list while he or she is editing it. Such users are taken off the watch list when they're done editing. If they prefer to be permanent watchers of the file, they would have to run **cvs watch add**. CVS makes a default assumption that someone is done editing when he or she commits a file (until the next time, anyway).

Anyone who gets on a file's watch list solely by virtue of having run **cvs edit** on that file is known as a "temporary watcher" and is taken off the watch list as soon as she commits a change to the file. If she wants to edit it again, she has to rerun **cvs edit**.

CVS's assumption that the first commit ends the editing session is only a best guess, of course, because CVS doesn't know how many commits the person will need to finish their changes. The guess is probably accurate for "one-off" changes—changes where someone just needs to make one quick fix to a file and commit it. For more prolonged editing sessions involving several commits, users should add themselves permanently to the file's watch list:

```
paste$ cvs watch add hello.c
paste$ cvs edit hello.c
paste$ emacs hello.c
...
paste$ cvs commit -m "print hello in Sanskrit"
```

Even after the commit, qsmith remains a watcher of hello.c because he ran **watch add** on it. (By the way, qsmith will not receive notification of his own edits; only other watchers will. CVS is smart enough not to notify you about actions that you took.)

Ending An Editing Session

If you don't want to commit but want to explicitly end an editing session, you can do so by running **cvs unedit**:

```
paste$ cvs unedit hello.c
```

But beware! This does more than just notify all watchers that you're done editing—it also offers to revert any uncommitted changes that you've made to the file:

```
paste$ cvs unedit hello.c
hello.c has been modified; revert changes? y
paste$
```

If you answer "y", CVS undoes all your changes and notifies watchers that you're not editing the file anymore. If you answer "n", CVS keeps your changes and also keeps you registered as an editor of the file (so no notification goes out—in fact, it's as if you never ran **cvs unedit** at all). The possibility of CVS undoing all of your changes at a single keystroke is a bit scary, but the rationale is easy to understand: If you declare to the world that you're ending an editing session, then any changes you haven't committed are probably changes you don't mean to keep. At least, that's the way CVS sees it. Needless to say, be careful!

Controlling What Actions Are Watched

By default, watchers are notified about three kinds of action: edits, commits, and unedits. However, if you only want to be notified about, say, commits, you can restrict notifications by adjusting your watch with the **-a** flag (*a* for action):

```
floss$ cvs watch add -a commit hello.c
```

Or if you want to watch edits and commits but don't care about unedits, you could pass the **-a** flag twice:

```
floss$ cvs watch add -a edit -a commit hello.c
```

Adding a watch with the **-a** flag will never cause any of your existing watches to be removed. If you were watching for all three kinds of actions on hello.c, running

```
floss$ cvs watch add -a commit hello.c
```

has no effect—you'll still be a watcher for all three actions. To remove watches, you should run

```
floss$ cvs watch remove hello.c
```

which is similar to **add** in that, by default, it removes your watches for all three actions. If you pass **-a** arguments, it removes only the watches you specify:

```
floss$ cvs watch remove -a commit hello.c
```

This means that you want to stop receiving notifications about commits but continue to receive notifications about edits and unedits (assuming you were watching edits and unedits to begin with, that is).

There are two special actions you can pass to the **-a** flag: **all** or **none**. The former means all actions that are eligible for watching (edits, commits, and unedits, as of this writing), and the latter means none of these. Because CVS's default behavior, in the absence of **-a**, is to watch all actions, and because watching **none** is the same as removing yourself from the watch list entirely, it's hard to imagine a situation in which it would be useful to specify either of these two special actions. However, **cvs edit** also takes the **-a** option, and in this case, it can be useful to specify **all** or **none**. For example, someone working on a file very briefly may not want to receive any notifications about what other people do with the file. Thus, this command

```
paste$ whoami
qsmith
paste$ cvs edit -a none README.txt
```

causes watchers of README.txt to be notified that qsmith is about to work on it, but qsmith would *not* be added as a temporary watcher of README.txt during his editing session (which he normally would have been), because he asked not to watch any actions.

Remember that you can only affect your own watches with the **cvs watch** command. You may stop watching a certain file yourself, but that won't change anyone else's watches.

Finding Out Who's Watching What

Sometimes you may want to know who's watching before you even run **cvs edit** or want to see who is editing what without adding yourself to any watch lists. Or you may have forgotten exactly what your own status is. After setting and unsetting a few watches and committing some files, it's easy to lose track of what you're watching and editing.

CVS provides two commands to show who's watching and who's editing files—**cvs watchers** and **cvs editors**:

```
floss$ whoami
jrandom
floss$ cvs watch add hello.c
floss$ cvs watchers hello.c
hello.c jrandom  edit unedit  commit
floss$ cvs watch remove -a unedit hello.c
floss$ cvs watchers hello.c
hello.c jrandom  edit commit
floss$ cvs watch add README.txt
floss$ cvs watchers
README.txt       jrandom edit     unedit  commit
hello.c jrandom edit     commit
floss$
```

Notice that the last **cvs watchers** command doesn't specify any files and, therefore, shows watchers for all files (all those that have watchers, that is).

All of the **watch** and **edit** commands have this behavior in common with other CVS commands. If you specify file names, they act on those files. If you specify directory names, they act on everything in that directory and its subdirectories. If you don't specify anything, they act on the current directory and everything underneath it, to as many levels of depth as are available. For example (continuing with the same session):

```
floss$ cvs watch add a-subdir/whatever.c
floss$ cvs watchers
README.txt       jrandom edit     unedit  commit
hello.c jrandom edit     commit
a-subdir/whatever.c        jrandom edit     unedit  commit
floss$ cvs watch add
floss$ cvs watchers
README.txt       jrandom edit     unedit  commit
foo.gif jrandom edit     unedit  commit
hello.c jrandom edit     commit  unedit
a-subdir/whatever.c        jrandom edit     unedit  commit
a-subdir/subsubdir/fish.c        jrandom edit     unedit  commit
b-subdir/random.c        jrandom edit     unedit  commit
floss$
```

The last two commands made jrandom a watcher of every file in the project and then showed the watch list for every file in the project, respectively. The output of **cvs watchers** doesn't always line up perfectly in columns because it mixes tab stops with information of varying length, but the lines are consistently formatted:

```
[FILENAME] [whitespace] WATCHER [whitespace] ACTIONS-BEING-WATCHED...
```

Now watch what happens when qsmith starts to edit one of the files:

```
paste$ cvs edit hello.c
paste$ cvs watchers
README.txt         jrandom edit      unedit   commit
foo.gif jrandom edit      unedit   commit
hello.c jrandom edit      commit   unedit
        qsmith  tedit     tunedit  tcommit
a-subdir/whatever.c        jrandom edit      unedit   commit
a-subdir/subsubdir/fish.c        jrandom edit      unedit   commit
b-subdir/random.c        jrandom edit      unedit   commit
```

The file hello.c has acquired another watcher: qsmith himself (note that the file name is not repeated but is left as white space at the beginning of the line—this would be important if you ever wanted to write a program that parses **watchers** output). Because he's editing hello.c, qsmith has a "temporary watch" on the file; it goes away as soon as he commits a new revision of hello.c. The prefix "**t**" in front of each of the actions indicates that these are temporary watches. If qsmith adds himself as a regular watcher of hello.c as well

```
paste$ cvs watch add hello.c
README.txt         jrandom edit      unedit   commit
foo.gif jrandom edit      unedit   commit
hello.c jrandom edit      commit   unedit
        qsmith  tedit     tunedit  tcommit edit     unedit   commit
a-subdir/whatever.c        jrandom edit      unedit   commit
a-subdir/subsubdir/fish.c        jrandom edit      unedit   commit
b-subdir/random.c        jrandom edit      unedit   commit
```

he is listed as both a temporary watcher and a permanent watcher. You may think that the permanent watch status would simply override the temporary, so that the line would look like this:

```
        qsmith  edit      unedit   commit
```

However, CVS can't just replace the temporary watches because it doesn't know in what order things happen. Will qsmith remove himself from the permanent watch list before ending his editing session, or will he finish the edits while still remaining a watcher? If the former, the edit/unedit/commit actions disappear while the tedit/tunedit/tcommit ones remain; if the latter, the reverse would happen.

Anyway, that side of the watch list is usually not of great concern. Most of the time, what you want to do is run

```
floss$ cvs watchers
```

or

```
floss$ cvs editors
```

from the top level of a project and see who's doing what. You don't really need to know the details of who cares about what actions: the important things are people and files.

Reminding People To Use Watches

You've probably noticed that the watch features are utterly dependent on the cooperation of all the developers. If someone just starts editing a file without first running **cvs edit**, no one else will know about it until the changes get committed. Because **cvs edit** is an additional step, not part of the normal development routine, people can easily forget to do it.

Although CVS can't force someone to use **cvs edit**, it does have a mechanism for reminding people to do so—the **watch on** command:

```
floss$ cvs -q co myproj
U myproj/README.txt
U myproj/foo.gif
U myproj/hello.c
U myproj/a-subdir/whatever.c
U myproj/a-subdir/subsubdir/fish.c
U myproj/b-subdir/random.c
floss$ cd myproj
floss$ cvs watch on hello.c
floss$
```

By running **cvs watch on hello.c**, jrandom causes future checkouts of myproj to create hello.c read-only in the working copy. When qsmith tries to work on it, he'll discover that it's read-only and be reminded to run **cvs edit** first:

```
paste$ cvs -q co myproj
U myproj/README.txt
U myproj/foo.gif
U myproj/hello.c
U myproj/a-subdir/whatever.c
U myproj/a-subdir/subsubdir/fish.c
```

```
U myproj/b-subdir/random.c
paste$ cd myproj
paste$ ls -l
total 6
drwxr-xr-x    2 qsmith      users          1024 Jul 19 01:06 CVS/
-rw-r--r--    1 qsmith      users            38 Jul 12 11:28 README.txt
drwxr-xr-x    4 qsmith      users          1024 Jul 19 01:06 a-subdir/
drwxr-xr-x    3 qsmith      users          1024 Jul 19 01:06 b-subdir/
-rw-r--r--    1 qsmith      users           673 Jun 20 22:47 foo.gif
-r--r--r--    1 qsmith      users           188 Jul 18 01:20 hello.c
paste$
```

When he does so, the file becomes read-write. He can then edit it, and when he commits, it becomes read-only again:

```
paste$ cvs edit hello.c
paste$ ls -l hello.c
-rw-r--r--    1 qsmith      users           188 Jul 18 01:20 hello.c
paste$ emacs hello.c
   ...
paste$ cvs commit -m "say hello in Aramaic" hello.c
Checking in hello.c;
/usr/local/newrepos/myproj/hello.c,v  <--  hello.c
new revision: 1.12; previous revision: 1.11
done
paste$ ls -l hello.c
-r--r--r--    1 qsmith      users           210 Jul 19 01:12 hello.c
paste$
```

His edit and commit will send notification to all watchers of hello.c. Note that jrandom isn't necessarily one of them. By running **cvs watch on hello.c**, jrandom did not add herself to the watch list for that file; she merely specified that it should be checked out read-only. People who want to watch a file must remember to add themselves to its watch list—CVS cannot help them with that.

Turning on watches for a single file may be the exception. Generally, it's more common to turn on watches project-wide:

```
floss$ cvs -q co myproj
U myproj/README.txt
U myproj/foo.gif
U myproj/hello.c
U myproj/a-subdir/whatever.c
U myproj/a-subdir/subsubdir/fish.c
```

```
U myproj/b-subdir/random.c
floss$ cd myproj
floss$ cvs watch on
floss$
```

This action amounts to announcing a policy decision for the entire project: "Please use **cvs edit** to tell watchers what you're working on, and feel free to watch any file you're interested in or responsible for." Every file in the project will be checked out read-only, and thus people will be reminded that they're expected to use **cvs edit** before working on anything.

Curiously, although checkouts of watched files make them read-only, updates do not. If qsmith had checked out his working copy *before* jrandom ran **cvs watch on**, his files would have stayed read-write, remaining so even after updates. However, any file he commits after jrandom turns watching on will become read-only. If jrandom turns off watches

```
floss$ cvs watch off
```

qsmith's read-only files do not magically become read-write. On the other hand, after he commits one, it will not revert to read-only again (as it would have if watches were still on).

It's worth noting that qsmith could, were he truly devious, make files in his working copy writeable by using the standard Unix **chmod** command, bypassing **cvs edit** entirely

```
paste$ chmod u+w hello.c
```

or if he wanted to get everything in one fell swoop:

```
paste$ chmod -R u+w .
```

There is nothing CVS can do about this. Working copies by their nature are private sandboxes—the watch features can open them up to public scrutiny a little bit, but only as far as the developer permits. Only when a developer does something that affects the repository (such as commits) is her privacy unconditionally lost.

The relationship among **watch add**, **watch remove**, **watch on**, and **watch off** probably seems a bit confusing. It may help to summarize the overall scheme: **add** and **remove** are about adding or removing users from a file's watch list; they don't have anything to do with whether files are read-only on checkout or after commits. **on** and **off** are only about file permissions. They don't have anything to do with who is on a file's watch list; rather, they are tools to help remind developers of the watch policy by causing working-copy files to become read-only.

All of this may seem a little inconsistent. In a sense, using watches works against the grain of CVS. It deviates from the idealized universe of multiple developers editing freely in their working copies, hidden from each other until they choose to commit. With watches, CVS gives developers convenient shortcuts for informing each other of what's going on in their working copies; however, it has no way to enforce observation policies, nor does it have a definitive concept of what constitutes an editing session. Nevertheless, watches can be helpful in certain circumstances if developers work with them.

What Watches Look Like In The Repository

In the interests of stamping out black boxes and needless mystery, let's take a quick look at how watches are implemented in the repository. We'll only take a quick look, though, because it's not pretty.

When you set a watch

```
floss$ pwd
/home/jrandom/myproj
floss$ cvs watch add hello.c
floss$ cvs watchers
hello.c jrandom edit     unedit  commit
floss$
```

CVS records it in the special file, CVS/fileattr, in the appropriate repository subdirectory:

```
floss$ cd /usr/local/newrepos
floss$ ls
CVSROOT/    myproj/
floss$ cd myproj
floss$ ls
CVS/            a-subdir/       foo.gif,v
README.txt,v  b-subdir/       hello.c,v
floss$ cd CVS
floss$ ls
fileattr
floss$ cat fileattr
Fhello.c        _watchers=jrandom>edit+unedit+commit
floss$
```

The fact that fileattr is stored in a CVS subdirectory in the repository does not mean that the repository has become a working copy. It's simply that the name "CVS" was already reserved for bookkeeping in the working copy, so CVS can be sure no project will ever need a subdirectory of that name in the repository.

I won't describe the format of fileattr formally; you can probably grok it pretty well just by watching it change from command to command:

```
floss$ cvs watch add hello.c
floss$ cat /usr/local/newrepos/myproj/CVS/fileattr
Fhello.c        _watchers=jrandom>edit+unedit+commit
```

```
floss$ cvs watch add README.txt
floss$ cat /usr/local/newrepos/myproj/CVS/fileattr
Fhello.c        _watchers=jrandom>edit+unedit+commit
FREADME.txt     _watchers=jrandom>edit+unedit+commit
floss$ cvs watch on hello.c
floss$ cat /usr/local/newrepos/myproj/CVS/fileattr
Fhello.c        _watchers=jrandom>edit+unedit+commit;_watched=
FREADME.txt     _watchers=jrandom>edit+unedit+commit
floss$ cvs watch remove hello.c
floss$ cat /usr/local/newrepos/myproj/CVS/fileattr
Fhello.c        _watched=
FREADME.txt     _watchers=jrandom>edit+unedit+commit
floss$ cvs watch off hello.c
floss$ cat /usr/local/newrepos/myproj/CVS/fileattr
FREADME.txt     _watchers=jrandom>edit+unedit+commit
floss$
```

Edit records are stored in fileattr, too. Here's what happens when qsmith adds himself as an editor:

```
paste$ cvs edit hello.c

floss$ cat /usr/local/newrepos/myproj/CVS/fileattr
Fhello.c        _watched=;_editors=qsmith>Tue Jul 20 04:53:23 1999 GMT+floss\
+/home/qsmith/myproj;_watchers=qsmith>tedit+tunedit+tcommit
FREADME.txt     _watchers=jrandom>edit+unedit+commit
```

Finally, note that CVS removes fileattr and the CVS subdirectory when there are no more watchers or editors for any of the files in that directory:

```
paste$ cvs unedit

floss$ cvs watch off
floss$ cvs watch remove
floss$ cat /usr/local/newrepos/myproj/CVS/fileattr
cat: /usr/local/newrepos/myproj/CVS/fileattr: No such file or directory
floss$
```

It should be clear after this brief exposure that the details of parsing fileattr format are better left to CVS. The main reason to have a basic understanding of the format—aside from the inherent satisfaction of knowing what's going on behind the curtain—is if you try to write an extension to the CVS watch features or debug some problem in them. It's sufficient to know that you shouldn't be alarmed if you see CVS/ subdirectories popping up in your repository. They're the only safe place CVS has to store meta-information such as watch lists.

Log Messages And Commit Emails

Commit emails are notices sent out at commit time, showing the log message and files involved in the commit. They usually go to all project participants and sometimes to other interested parties. The details of setting up commit emails were covered in Chapter 4, so I won't repeat them here. I have noticed, however, that commit emails can sometimes result in unexpected side effects to projects, effects that you may want to take into account if you set up commit emails for your project.

First, be prepared for the messages to be mostly ignored. Whether people read them depends, at least partly, on the frequency of commits in your project. Do developers tend to commit one big change at the end of the day, or many small changes throughout the day? The closer your project is to the latter, the thicker the barrage of tiny commit notices raining down on the developers all day long, and the less inclined they will be to pay attention to each message.

This doesn't mean the notices aren't useful, just that you shouldn't count on every person reading every message. It's still a convenient way for people to keep tabs on who's doing what (without the intrusiveness of watches). When the emails go to a publicly subscribable mailing list, they are a wonderful mechanism for giving interested users (and future developers!) a chance to see what happens in the code on a daily basis.

You may want to consider having a designated developer who watches all log messages and has an overview of activity across the entire project (of course, a good project leader will probably be doing this anyway). If there are clear divisions of responsibility—say, certain developers are "in charge of" certain subdirectories of the project—you could do some fancy scripting in CVSROOT/loginfo to see that each responsible party receives specially marked notices of changes made in their area. This will help ensure that the developers will at least read the email that pertains to their subdirectories.

A more interesting side effect happens when commit emails aren't ignored. People start to use them as a realtime communications method. Here's the kind of log message that can result:

```
Finished feedback form; fixed the fonts and background colors
on the home page. Whew! Anyone want to go to Mon Lung for lunch?
```

There's nothing wrong with this, and it makes the logs more fun to read over later. However, people need to be aware that log messages, such as the following, are not only distributed by email but is also preserved forever in the project's history. For example, griping about customer specifications is a frequent pastime among programmers; it's not hard to imagine someone committing a log message like this one, knowing that the other programmers will soon see it in their email:

```
Truncate four-digit years to two-digits in input. What the customer
wants, the customer gets, no matter how silly & wrong. Sigh.
```

This makes for an amusing email, but what happens if the customer reviews the logs some-day? (I'll bet similar concerns have led more than one site to set up CVSROOT/loginfo so that it invokes scripts to guard against offensive words in log messages!)

The overall effect of commit emails seems to be that people become less willing to write short or obscure log messages, which is probably a good thing. However, they may need to be reminded that their audience is anyone who might ever read the logs, not just the people receiving commit emails.

Changing A Log Message After It's Been Committed

Just in case someone does commit a regrettable log message, CVS enables you to rewrite logs after they've been committed. It's done with the **-m** option to the **admin** command (this command is covered in more detail later in this chapter) and allows you to change one log message (per revision, per file) at a time. Here's how it works:

```
floss$ cvs admin -m 1.7:"Truncate four-digit years to two in input." date.c
RCS file: /usr/local/newrepos/someproj/date.c,v
done
floss$
```

The original, offensive log message that was committed with revision 1.7 has been replaced with a perfectly innocent—albeit duller—message. (Don't forget the colon separating the revision number from the new log message.)

If the bad message was committed into multiple files, you'll have to run **cvs admin** sepa-rately for each one, because the revision number is different for each file. Therefore, this is one of the few commands in CVS that requires you to pass a single file name as argument:

```
floss$ cvs admin -m 1.2:"very boring log message" hello.c README.txt foo.gif
cvs admin: while processing more than one file:
cvs [admin aborted]: attempt to specify a numeric revision
floss$
```

Confusingly, you get the same error if you pass no file names (because CVS then assumes all the files in the current directory and below are implied arguments):

```
floss$ cvs admin -m 1.2:"very boring log message"
cvs admin: while processing more than one file:
cvs [admin aborted]: attempt to specify a numeric revision
floss$
```

(As is unfortunately often the case with CVS error messages, you have to see things from CVS's point of view before the message makes sense!)

Invoking **admin -m** actually changes the project's history, so use it with care. There will be no record that the log message was ever changed—it will simply appear as if that revision had been originally committed with the new log message. No trace of the old message will be left anywhere (unless you saved the original commit email).

Although its name might seem to imply that only the designated CVS administrator can use it, in fact anyone can run **cvs admin**, as long as they have write access to the project in question. Nevertheless, it is best used with caution; the ability to change a project's history is mild compared with other potentially damaging things it can do. See Chapter 9 for more about **admin**, as well as a way to restrict its use.

Getting Rid Of A Working Copy

In typical CVS usage, the way to get rid of a working copy directory tree is to remove it like any other directory tree:

```
paste$ rm -rf myproj
```

However, if you eliminate your working copy this way, other developers will not know that you have stopped using it. CVS provides a command to relinquish a working copy explicitly. Think of **release** as the opposite of **checkout**—you're telling the repository that you're done with the working copy now. Like **checkout**, **release** is invoked from the parent directory of the tree:

```
paste$ pwd
/home/qsmith/myproj
paste$ cd ..
paste$ ls
myproj
paste$ cvs release myproj
You have [0] altered files in this repository.
Are you sure you want to release directory 'myproj': y
paste$
```

If there are any uncommitted changes in the repository, the release fails, meaning that it just lists the modified files and otherwise has no effect. Assuming the tree is clean (totally up to date), **release** records in the repository that the working copy has been released.

You can also have **release** automatically delete the working tree for you, by passing the **-d** flag:

```
paste$ ls
myproj
paste$ cvs release -d myproj
You have [0] altered files in this repository.
Are you sure you want to release (and delete) directory 'myproj: y
paste$ ls
paste$
```

As of CVS version 1.10.6, the **release** command is not able to deduce the repository's location by examining the working copy (this is because **release** is invoked from above the working copy, not within it). You must pass the **-d <REPOS>** global option or make sure that your CVSROOT environment variable is set correctly. (This bug may be fixed in future versions of CVS.)

The Cederqvist claims that if you use **release** instead of just deleting the working tree, people with watches set on the released files will be notified just as if you had run **unedit**. However, I tried to verify this experimentally, and it does not seem to be true.

A Bird's Eye View Of Project History

In Chapter 4, I briefly mentioned the **cvs history** command. This command displays a summary of all **checkouts**, **commits**, **updates**, **rtags**, and **releases** done in the repository (at least, since logging was enabled by the creation of the CVSROOT/history file in the repository). You can control the format and contents of the summary with various options.

The first step is to make sure that logging is enabled in your repository. The repository administrator should first make sure there is a history file

```
floss$ cd /usr/local/newrepos/CVSROOT
floss$ ls -l history
ls: history: No such file or directory
floss$
```

and if there isn't one, create it, as follows:

```
floss$ touch history
floss$ ls -l history
-rw-r--r--   1 jrandom    cvs            0 Jul 22 14:57 history
floss$
```

This history file also needs to be writeable by everyone who uses the repository, otherwise they'll get an error every time they try to run a CVS command that modifies that file. The easiest way is simply to make the file world-writeable:

```
floss$ chmod a+rw history
floss$ ls -l history
-rw-rw-rw-   1 jrandom    cvs            0 Jul 22 14:57 history
floss$
```

Note
*If the repository was created with the **cvs init** command, the history file already exists. You may still have to fix its permissions, however.*

The rest of these examples assume that history logging has been enabled for a while, so that data has had time to accumulate in the history file.

The output of **cvs history** is somewhat terse (it's probably intended to be parsed by programs rather than humans, although it is readable with a little study). Let's run it once and see what we get:

```
paste$ pwd
/home/qsmith/myproj
paste$ cvs history -e -a
O 07/25 15:14 +0000 qsmith  myproj =mp=     ~/*
M 07/25 15:16 +0000 qsmith  1.14 hello.c    myproj == ~/mp
U 07/25 15:21 +0000 qsmith  1.14 README.txt myproj == ~/mp
G 07/25 15:21 +0000 qsmith  1.15 hello.c    myproj == ~/mp
A 07/25 15:22 +0000 qsmith  1.1  goodbye.c  myproj == ~/mp
M 07/25 15:23 +0000 qsmith  1.16 hello.c    myproj == ~/mp
M 07/25 15:26 +0000 qsmith  1.17 hello.c    myproj == ~/mp
U 07/25 15:29 +0000 qsmith  1.2  goodbye.c  myproj == ~/mp
G 07/25 15:29 +0000 qsmith  1.18 hello.c    myproj == ~/mp
M 07/25 15:30 +0000 qsmith  1.19 hello.c    myproj == ~/mp
O 07/23 03:45 +0000 jrandom myproj =myproj= ~/src/*
F 07/23 03:48 +0000 jrandom        =myproj= ~/src/*
F 07/23 04:06 +0000 jrandom        =myproj= ~/src/*
M 07/25 15:12 +0000 jrandom 1.13 README.txt myproj == ~/src/myproj
U 07/25 15:17 +0000 jrandom 1.14 hello.c    myproj == ~/src/myproj
M 07/25 15:18 +0000 jrandom 1.14 README.txt myproj == ~/src/myproj
M 07/25 15:18 +0000 jrandom 1.15 hello.c    myproj == ~/src/myproj
U 07/25 15:23 +0000 jrandom 1.1  goodbye.c  myproj == ~/src/myproj
U 07/25 15:23 +0000 jrandom 1.16 hello.c    myproj == ~/src/myproj
U 07/25 15:26 +0000 jrandom 1.1  goodbye.c  myproj == ~/src/myproj
G 07/25 15:26 +0000 jrandom 1.17 hello.c    myproj == ~/src/myproj
M 07/25 15:27 +0000 jrandom 1.18 hello.c    myproj == ~/src/myproj
C 07/25 15:30 +0000 jrandom 1.19 hello.c    myproj == ~/src/myproj
M 07/25 15:31 +0000 jrandom 1.20 hello.c    myproj == ~/src/myproj
M 07/25 16:29 +0000 jrandom 1.3  whatever.c myproj/a-subdir == ~/src/myproj
paste$
```

There, isn't that clear?

Before we examine the output, notice that the invocation included two options: -e and -a. When you run **history**, you almost always want to pass options telling it what data to report and how to report it. In this respect, it differs from most other CVS commands, which usually do something useful when invoked without any options. In this example, the two flags meant "everything" (show every kind of event that happened) and "all" (for all users), respectively.

Another way that **history** differs from other commands is that, although it is usually invoked from within a working copy, it does not restrict its output to that working copy's project. Instead, it shows all history events from all projects in the repository—the working copy merely serves to tell CVS from which repository to retrieve the history data. (In the preceding example, the only history data in that repository is for the "myproj" project, so that's all we see.)

The general format of the output is:

```
CODE DATE USER [REVISION] [FILE] PATH_IN_REPOSITORY ACTUAL_WORKING_COPY_NAME
```

The code letters refer to various CVS operations, as shown in Table 6.1.

For operations (such as **checkout**) that are about the project as a whole rather than about individual files, the revision and file are omitted, and the repository path is placed between the equal signs.

Although the output of the **history** command was designed to be compact, parseable input for other programs, CVS still gives you a lot of control over its scope and content. The options shown in Table 6.2 control what types of events get reported.

Table 6.1   The meaning of the code letters.

Letter	Meaning
O	Checkout
T	Tag
F	Release
W	Update (no user file, remove from entries file)
U	Update (file overwrote unmodified user file)
G	Update (file was merged successfully into modified user file)
C	Update (file was merged, but has conflicts with modified user file)
M	Commit (from modified file)
A	Commit (an added file)
R	Commit (the removal of a file)
E	Export (see Chapter 9)

Table 6.2   Options to filter by event type.

Option	Meaning
-m MODULE	Show historical events affecting **MODULE**.
-c	Show commit events.
-o	Show checkout events.
-T	Show tag events.
-x CODE(S)	Show all events of type **CODE** (one or more of **OTFWUGCMARE**).
-e	Show all types of events, period. Once you have selected what type of events you want reported, you can filter further with the options shown in Table 6.3.

Table 6.3   Options to filter by user.

Option	Meaning
-a	Show actions taken by all users
-w	Show only actions taken from within this working copy
-l	Show only the last time this user took the action
-u USER	Show records for **USER**

A Bird's Eye View, With Telescope:
The **annotate** Command

If the **history** command gives an overview of project activity, the **annotate** command is a way of attaching a zoom lens to the view. With **annotate**, you can see who was the last person to touch each line of a file, and at what revision they touched it:

```
floss$ cvs annotate
Annotations for README.txt
***************
1.14        (jrandom  25-Jul-99): blah
1.13        (jrandom  25-Jul-99): test 3 for history
1.12        (qsmith   19-Jul-99): test 2
1.11        (qsmith   19-Jul-99): test
1.10        (jrandom  12-Jul-99): blah
1.1         (jrandom  20-Jun-99): Just a test project.
1.4         (jrandom  21-Jun-99): yeah.
1.5         (jrandom  21-Jun-99): nope.
Annotations for hello.c
***************
1.1         (jrandom  20-Jun-99): #include <stdio.h>
1.1         (jrandom  20-Jun-99):
1.1         (jrandom  20-Jun-99): void
1.1         (jrandom  20-Jun-99): main ()
1.1         (jrandom  20-Jun-99): {
1.15        (jrandom  25-Jul-99):   /* another test for history */
1.13        (qsmith   19-Jul-99):   /* random change number two */
1.10        (jrandom  12-Jul-99):   /* test */
1.21        (jrandom  25-Jul-99):   printf ("Hellooo, world!\n");
1.3         (jrandom  21-Jun-99):   printf ("hmmm\n");
1.4         (jrandom  21-Jun-99):   printf ("double hmmm\n");
1.11        (qsmith   18-Jul-99):   /* added this comment */
1.16        (qsmith   25-Jul-99):   /* will merge these changes */
1.18        (jrandom  25-Jul-99):   /* will merge these changes too */
1.2         (jrandom  21-Jun-99):   printf ("Goodbye, world!\n");
1.1         (jrandom  20-Jun-99): }
Annotations for a-subdir/whatever.c
***************
```

```
1.3            (jrandom  25-Jul-99): /* A completely non-empty C file. */
Annotations for a-subdir/subsubdir/fish.c
***************
1.2            (jrandom  25-Jul-99): /* An almost completely empty C file. */
Annotations for b-subdir/random.c
***************
1.1            (jrandom  20-Jun-99): /* A completely empty C file. */
floss$
```

The output of **annotate** is pretty intuitive. On the left are the revision number, developer, and date on which the line in question was added or last modified. On the right is the line itself, as of the current revision. Because every line is annotated, you can actually see the entire contents of the file, pushed over to the right by the annotation information.

If you specify a revision number or tag, the annotations are given as of that revision, meaning that it shows the most recent modification to each line at or before that revision. This is probably the most common way to use annotations—examining a particular revision of a single file to determine which developers were active in which parts of the file.

For example, in the output of the previous example, you can see that the most recent revision of hello.c is 1.21, in which jrandom did something to the line:

```
printf ("Hellooo, world!\n");
```

One way to find out what she did is to **diff** that revision against the previous one:

```
floss$ cvs diff -r 1.20 -r 1.21 hello.c
Index: hello.c
===================================================================
RCS file: /usr/local/newrepos/myproj/hello.c,v
retrieving revision 1.20
retrieving revision 1.21
diff -r1.20 -r1.21
9c9
<   printf ("Hello, world!\n");
--
>   printf ("Hellooo, world!\n");
floss$
```

Another way to find out, while still retaining a file-wide view of everyone's activity, is to compare the current annotations with the annotations from a previous revision:

```
floss$ cvs annotate -r 1.20 hello.c
Annotations for hello.c
***************
```

```
1.1         (jrandom  20-Jun-99): #include <stdio.h>
1.1         (jrandom  20-Jun-99):
1.1         (jrandom  20-Jun-99): void
1.1         (jrandom  20-Jun-99): main ()
1.1         (jrandom  20-Jun-99): {
1.15        (jrandom  25-Jul-99):   /* another test for history */
1.13        (qsmith   19-Jul-99):   /* random change number two */
1.10        (jrandom  12-Jul-99):   /* test */
1.1         (jrandom  20-Jun-99):   printf ("Hello, world!\n");
1.3         (jrandom  21-Jun-99):   printf ("hmmm\n");
1.4         (jrandom  21-Jun-99):   printf ("double hmmm\n");
1.11        (qsmith   18-Jul-99):   /* added this comment */
1.16        (qsmith   25-Jul-99):   /* will merge these changes */
1.18        (jrandom  25-Jul-99):   /* will merge these changes too */
1.2         (jrandom  21-Jun-99):   printf ("Goodbye, world!\n");
1.1         (jrandom  20-Jun-99): }
floss$
```

Although the **diff** reveals the textual facts of the change more concisely, the annotation may be preferable because it places them in their historical context by showing how long the previous incarnation of the line had been present (in this case, all the way since revision 1.1). That knowledge can help you decide whether to look at the logs to find out the motivation for the change:

```
floss$ cvs log -r 1.21 hello.c
RCS file: /usr/local/newrepos/myproj/hello.c,v
Working file: hello.c
head: 1.21
branch:
locks: strict
access list:
symbolic names:
        random-tag: 1.20
        start: 1.1.1.1
        jrandom: 1.1.1
keyword substitution: kv
total revisions: 22;    selected revisions: 1
description:
----------------------------
revision 1.21
date: 1999/07/25 20:17:42;  author: jrandom;  state: Exp;  lines: +1 -1
say hello with renewed enthusiasm
=============================================================================
floss$
```

In addition to **-r**, you can also filter annotations using the **-D DATE** option:

```
floss$ cvs annotate -D "5 weeks ago" hello.c
Annotations for hello.c
***************
1.1          (jrandom   20-Jun-99): #include <stdio.h>
1.1          (jrandom   20-Jun-99):
1.1          (jrandom   20-Jun-99): void
1.1          (jrandom   20-Jun-99): main ()
1.1          (jrandom   20-Jun-99): {
1.1          (jrandom   20-Jun-99):   printf ("Hello, world!\n");
1.1          (jrandom   20-Jun-99): }
floss$ cvs annotate -D "3 weeks ago" hello.c
Annotations for hello.c
***************
1.1          (jrandom   20-Jun-99): #include <stdio.h>
1.1          (jrandom   20-Jun-99):
1.1          (jrandom   20-Jun-99): void
1.1          (jrandom   20-Jun-99): main ()
1.1          (jrandom   20-Jun-99): {
1.1          (jrandom   20-Jun-99):   printf ("Hello, world!\n");
1.3          (jrandom   21-Jun-99):   printf ("hmmm\n");
1.4          (jrandom   21-Jun-99):   printf ("double hmmm\n");
1.2          (jrandom   21-Jun-99):   printf ("Goodbye, world!\n");
1.1          (jrandom   20-Jun-99): }
floss$
```

Annotations And Branches

By default, annotation always shows activity on the main trunk of development. Even when invoked from a branch working copy, it shows annotations for the trunk unless you specify otherwise. (This tendency to favor the trunk is either a bug or a feature, depending on your point of view.) You can force CVS to annotate a branch by passing the branch tag as an argument to **-r**. Here is an example from a working copy in which hello.c is on a branch named "Brancho_Gratuito," with at least one change committed on that branch:

```
floss$ cvs status hello.c
=============================================================================
File: hello.c           Status: Up-to-date

   Working revision:    1.10.2.2        Sun Jul 25 21:29:05 1999
   Repository revision: 1.10.2.2        /usr/local/newrepos/myproj/hello.c,v
   Sticky Tag:          Brancho_Gratuito (branch: 1.10.2)
   Sticky Date:         (none)
   Sticky Options:      (none)
```

```
floss$ cvs annotate hello.c
Annotations for hello.c
***************
1.1          (jrandom  20-Jun-99): #include <stdio.h>
1.1          (jrandom  20-Jun-99):
1.1          (jrandom  20-Jun-99): void
1.1          (jrandom  20-Jun-99): main ()
1.1          (jrandom  20-Jun-99): {
1.10         (jrandom  12-Jul-99):   /* test */
1.1          (jrandom  20-Jun-99):   printf ("Hello, world!\n");
1.3          (jrandom  21-Jun-99):   printf ("hmmm\n");
1.4          (jrandom  21-Jun-99):   printf ("double hmmm\n");
1.2          (jrandom  21-Jun-99):   printf ("Goodbye, world!\n");
1.1          (jrandom  20-Jun-99): }
floss$ cvs annotate -r Brancho_Gratuito hello.c
Annotations for hello.c
***************
1.1          (jrandom  20-Jun-99): #include <stdio.h>
1.1          (jrandom  20-Jun-99):
1.1          (jrandom  20-Jun-99): void
1.1          (jrandom  20-Jun-99): main ()
1.1          (jrandom  20-Jun-99): {
1.10         (jrandom  12-Jul-99):   /* test */
1.1          (jrandom  20-Jun-99):   printf ("Hello, world!\n");
1.10.2.2     (jrandom  25-Jul-99):   printf ("hmmmmm\n");
1.4          (jrandom  21-Jun-99):   printf ("double hmmm\n");
1.10.2.1     (jrandom  25-Jul-99):   printf ("added this line");
1.2          (jrandom  21-Jun-99):   printf ("Goodbye, world!\n");
1.1          (jrandom  20-Jun-99): }
floss$
```

You can also pass the branch number itself:

```
floss$ cvs annotate -r 1.10.2 hello.c
Annotations for hello.c
***************
1.1          (jrandom  20-Jun-99): #include <stdio.h>
1.1          (jrandom  20-Jun-99):
1.1          (jrandom  20-Jun-99): void
1.1          (jrandom  20-Jun-99): main ()
1.1          (jrandom  20-Jun-99): {
1.10         (jrandom  12-Jul-99):   /* test */
1.1          (jrandom  20-Jun-99):   printf ("Hello, world!\n");
1.10.2.2     (jrandom  25-Jul-99):   printf ("hmmmmm\n");
1.4          (jrandom  21-Jun-99):   printf ("double hmmm\n");
1.10.2.1     (jrandom  25-Jul-99):   printf ("added this line");
```

```
1.2           (jrandom  21-Jun-99):   printf ("Goodbye, world!\n");
1.1           (jrandom  20-Jun-99): }
floss$
```

or a full revision number from the branch:

```
floss$ cvs annotate -r 1.10.2.1 hello.c
Annotations for hello.c
***************
1.1           (jrandom  20-Jun-99): #include <stdio.h>
1.1           (jrandom  20-Jun-99):
1.1           (jrandom  20-Jun-99): void
1.1           (jrandom  20-Jun-99): main ()
1.1           (jrandom  20-Jun-99): {
1.10          (jrandom  12-Jul-99):   /* test */
1.1           (jrandom  20-Jun-99):   printf ("Hello, world!\n");
1.3           (jrandom  21-Jun-99):   printf ("hmmm\n");
1.4           (jrandom  21-Jun-99):   printf ("double hmmm\n");
1.10.2.1      (jrandom  25-Jul-99):   printf ("added this line");
1.2           (jrandom  21-Jun-99):   printf ("Goodbye, world!\n");
1.1           (jrandom  20-Jun-99): }
floss$
```

If you do this, remember that the numbers are only valid for that particular file. In general, it's probably better to use the branch name wherever possible.

Using Keyword Expansion

You may recall a brief mention of "keyword expansion" in Chapter 2. RCS keywords are special words, surrounded by dollar signs, that CVS looks for in text files and expands into revision-control information. For example, if a file contains

```
$Author$
```

then when updating the file to a given revision, CVS will expand it to the username of the person who committed that revision:

```
$Author: jrandom $
```

CVS is also sensitive to keywords in their expanded form, so that once expanded, they continue to be updated as appropriate.

Although keywords don't actually offer any information that's not available by other means, they give people a convenient way to see revision control facts embedded in the text of the file itself, rather than by invoking some arcane CVS operation.

Here are a few other commonly used keywords:

```
$Date$        ==>  date of last commit, expands to ==>
$Date: 1999/07/26 06:39:46 $


$Id$          ==>  filename, revision, date, and author; expands to ==>
$Id: hello.c,v 1.11 1999/07/26 06:39:46 jrandom Exp $


$Revision$    ==>  exactly what you think it is, expands to ==>
$Revision: 1.11 $


$Source$      ==> path to corresponding repository file, expands to ==>
$Source: /usr/local/newrepos/tossproj/hello.c,v $


$Log$         ==>  accumulating log messages for the file, expands to ==>
$Log: hello.c,v $
Revision 1.2  1999/07/26 06:47:52  jrandom
...and this is the second log message.

Revision 1.1  1999/07/26 06:39:46  jrandom
This is the first log message...
```

The **Log** keyword is the only one of these that expands to cover multiple lines, so its behavior is unique. Unlike the others, it does not replace the old expansion with the new one, but instead inserts the latest expansion, plus an additional blank line, right after the keyword (thereby pushing any previous expansions downward). Furthermore, any text between the beginning of the line and **$Log** is used as a prefix for the expansions (this is done to ensure that the log messages stay commented in program code). For example, if you put this into the file

```
// $Log$
```

it will expand to something like this on the first commit:

```
// $Log: hello.c,v $
// Revision 1.14  1999/07/26 07:03:20  jrandom
// this is the first log message...
//
```

this on the second:

```
// $Log: hello.c,v $
// Revision 1.15  1999/07/26 07:04:40  jrandom
// ...and this is the second log message...
//
```

```
// Revision 1.14  1999/07/26 07:03:20  jrandom
// this is the first log message...
//
```

and so on:

```
// $Log: hello.c,v $
// Revision 1.16  1999/07/26 07:05:34  jrandom
// ...and this is the third!
//
// Revision 1.15  1999/07/26 07:04:40  jrandom
// ...and this is the second log message...
//
// Revision 1.14  1999/07/26 07:03:20  jrandom
// this is the first log message...
//
```

You may not want to keep your entire log history in the file all the time; if you do, you can always remove the older sections when it starts to get too lengthy. It's certainly more convenient than running **cvs log**, and it may be worthwhile in projects where people must constantly read over the logs.

A more common technique may be to include **$Revision$** in a file and use it as the version number for the program. This can work if the project consists of essentially one file or undergoes frequent releases and has at least one file that is guaranteed to be modified between every release. You can even use an RCS keyword as a value in program code:

```
VERSION = "$Revision: 1.114 $";
```

CVS expands that keyword just like any other; it has no concept of the programming language's semantics and does not assume that the double quotes protect the string in any way.

A complete list of keywords (there are a few more, rather obscure ones) is given in Chapter 9.

Going Out On A Limb: How To Work With Branches And Survive

Branches are simultaneously one of the most important and most easily misused features of CVS. Isolating risky or disruptive changes onto a separate line of development until they stabilize can be immensely helpful. If not properly managed, however, branches can quickly propel a project into confusion and cascading chaos, as people lose track of what changes have been merged when.

To work successfully with branches, your development group should adhere to these principles:

♦ Minimize the number of branches active at any one time. The more branches under development at the same time, the more likely they are to conflict when merged into the trunk. In practical terms, the way to accomplish this is to merge as frequently as you can (whenever a branch is at a stable point) and to move development back onto the trunk as soon as feasible. By minimizing the amount of parallel development going on, everyone is better able to keep track of what's going on on each branch, and the possibility of conflicts on merge is reduced.

Note

This does not mean minimizing the absolute number of branches in the project, just the number being worked on at any given time.

♦ Minimize the complexity—that is, the depth—of your branching scheme. There are circumstances in which it's appropriate to have branches from branches, but they are very rare (you may get through your entire programming life without ever encountering one). Just because CVS makes it technically possible to have arbitrary levels of nested branching, and to merge from any branch to any other branch, doesn't mean you actually want to do these things. In most situations, it's best to have all your branches rooted at the trunk and to merge from branch to trunk and back out again.

♦ Use consistently named tags to mark all branch and merge events. Ideally, the meaning of each tag and its relationship to other branches and tags should be apparent from the tag name. (The point of this will become clearer as we go through the examples.)

With those principles in mind, let's take a look at a typical branch development scenario. We'll have jrandom on the trunk and qsmith on the branch, but note that there could just as well be multiple developers on the trunk and/or on the branch. Regular development along either line can involve any number of people; however, the tagging and merging are best done by one person on each side, as you'll see.

Merging Repeatedly Into The Trunk

Let's assume qsmith needs to do development on a branch for a while, to avoid destabilizing the trunk that he shares with jrandom. The first step is to create the branch. Notice how qsmith creates a regular (non-branch) tag at the branch point first, and then creates the branch:

```
paste$ pwd
/home/qsmith/myproj
paste$ cvs tag Root-of-Exotic_Greetings
cvs tag: Tagging .
T README.txt
T foo.gif
T hello.c
```

```
cvs tag: Tagging a-subdir
T a-subdir/whatever.c
cvs tag: Tagging a-subdir/subsubdir
T a-subdir/subsubdir/fish.c
cvs tag: Tagging b-subdir
T b-subdir/random.c
paste$ cvs tag -b Exotic_Greetings-branch
cvs tag: Tagging .
T README.txt
T foo.gif
T hello.c
cvs tag: Tagging a-subdir
T a-subdir/whatever.c
cvs tag: Tagging a-subdir/subsubdir
T a-subdir/subsubdir/fish.c
cvs tag: Tagging b-subdir
T b-subdir/random.c
paste$
```

The point of tagging the trunk first is that it may be necessary someday to retrieve the trunk as it was the moment the branch was created. If you ever need to do that, you'll have to have a way of referring to the trunk snapshot without referring to the branch itself. Obviously, you can't use the branch tag because that would retrieve the branch, not the revisions in the trunk that form the root of the branch. The only way to do it is to make a regular tag at the same revisions the branch sprouts from. (Some people stick to this rule so faithfully that I considered listing it as "Branching Principle Number 4: Always create a non-branch tag at the branch point." However, many sites don't do it, and they generally seem to do okay, so it's really a matter of taste.) From here on, I will refer to this non-branch tag as the "branch point tag."

Notice also that a naming convention is being adhered to: The branch point tag begins with **Root-of-**, then the actual branch name, which uses underscores instead of hyphens to separate words. When the actual branch is created, its tag ends with the suffix **-branch** so that you can identify it as a branch tag just by looking at the tag name. (The branch point tag **Root-of-Exotic_Greetings** does not include the **-branch** because it is not a branch tag.) You don't have to use this particular naming convention, of course, but you should use some convention.

Of course, I'm being extra pedantic here. In smallish projects, where everyone knows who's doing what and confusion is easy to recover from, these conventions don't have to be used. Whether you use a branch point tag or have a strict naming convention for your tags depends on the complexity of the project and the branching scheme. (Also, don't forget that you can always go back later and update old tags to use new conventions by retrieving an old tagged version, adding the new tag, and then deleting the old tag.)

Now, qsmith is ready to start working on the branch:

```
paste$ cvs update -r Exotic_Greetings-branch
cvs update: Updating .
cvs update: Updating a-subdir
cvs update: Updating a-subdir/subsubdir
cvs update: Updating b-subdir
paste$
```

He makes some changes to a couple of files and commits them on the branch:

```
paste$ emacs README.txt a-subdir/whatever.c b-subdir/random.c
...
paste$ cvs ci -m "print greeting backwards, etc"
cvs commit: Examining .
cvs commit: Examining a-subdir
cvs commit: Examining a-subdir/subsubdir
cvs commit: Examining b-subdir
Checking in README.txt;
/usr/local/newrepos/myproj/README.txt,v  <--  README.txt
new revision: 1.14.2.1; previous revision: 1.14
done
Checking in a-subdir/whatever.c;
/usr/local/newrepos/myproj/a-subdir/whatever.c,v  <--  whatever.c
new revision: 1.3.2.1; previous revision: 1.3
done
Checking in b-subdir/random.c;
/usr/local/newrepos/myproj/b-subdir/random.c,v  <--  random.c
new revision: 1.1.1.1.2.1; previous revision: 1.1.1.1
done
paste$
```

Meanwhile, jrandom is continuing to work on the trunk. She modifies two of the three files that qsmith touched. Just for kicks, we'll have her make changes that conflict with qsmith's work:

```
floss$ emacs README.txt whatever.c
  ...
floss$ cvs ci -m "some very stable changes indeed"
cvs commit: Examining .
cvs commit: Examining a-subdir
cvs commit: Examining a-subdir/subsubdir
cvs commit: Examining b-subdir
Checking in README.txt;
/usr/local/newrepos/myproj/README.txt,v  <--  README.txt
new revision: 1.15; previous revision: 1.14
```

```
done
Checking in a-subdir/whatever.c;
/usr/local/newrepos/myproj/a-subdir/whatever.c,v  <--  whatever.c
new revision: 1.4; previous revision: 1.3
done
floss$
```

The conflict is not apparent yet, of course, because neither developer has tried to merge branch and trunk. Now, jrandom does the merge:

```
floss$ cvs update -j Exotic_Greetings-branch
cvs update: Updating .
RCS file: /usr/local/newrepos/myproj/README.txt,v
retrieving revision 1.14
retrieving revision 1.14.2.1
Merging differences between 1.14 and 1.14.2.1 into README.txt
rcsmerge: warning: conflicts during merge
cvs update: Updating a-subdir
RCS file: /usr/local/newrepos/myproj/a-subdir/whatever.c,v
retrieving revision 1.3
retrieving revision 1.3.2.1
Merging differences between 1.3 and 1.3.2.1 into whatever.c
rcsmerge: warning: conflicts during merge
cvs update: Updating a-subdir/subsubdir
cvs update: Updating b-subdir
RCS file: /usr/local/newrepos/myproj/b-subdir/random.c,v
retrieving revision 1.1.1.1
retrieving revision 1.1.1.1.2.1
Merging differences between 1.1.1.1 and 1.1.1.1.2.1 into random.c
floss$ cvs update
cvs update: Updating .
C README.txt
cvs update: Updating a-subdir
C a-subdir/whatever.c
cvs update: Updating a-subdir/subsubdir
cvs update: Updating b-subdir
M b-subdir/random.c
floss$
```

Two of the files conflict. No big deal; with her usual savoir-faire, jrandom resolves the conflicts, commits, and tags the trunk as successfully merged:

```
floss$ emacs README.txt a-subdir/whatever.c
  ...
floss$ cvs ci -m "merged from Exotic_Greetings-branch (conflicts resolved)"
cvs commit: Examining .
```

```
cvs commit: Examining a-subdir
cvs commit: Examining a-subdir/subsubdir
cvs commit: Examining b-subdir
Checking in README.txt;
/usr/local/newrepos/myproj/README.txt,v  <--  README.txt
new revision: 1.16; previous revision: 1.15
done
Checking in a-subdir/whatever.c;
/usr/local/newrepos/myproj/a-subdir/whatever.c,v  <--  whatever.c
new revision: 1.5; previous revision: 1.4
done
Checking in b-subdir/random.c;
/usr/local/newrepos/myproj/b-subdir/random.c,v  <--  random.c
new revision: 1.2; previous revision: 1.1
done
floss$ cvs tag merged-Exotic_Greetings
cvs tag: Tagging .
T README.txt
T foo.gif
T hello.c
cvs tag: Tagging a-subdir
T a-subdir/whatever.c
cvs tag: Tagging a-subdir/subsubdir
T a-subdir/subsubdir/fish.c
cvs tag: Tagging b-subdir
T b-subdir/random.c
floss$
```

Meanwhile, qsmith needn't wait for the merge to finish before continuing development, as long as he makes a tag for the batch of changes from which jrandom merged (later, jrandom will need to know this tag name; in general, branches depend on frequent and thorough developer communications):

```
paste$ cvs tag Exotic_Greetings-1
cvs tag: Tagging .
T README.txt
T foo.gif
T hello.c
cvs tag: Tagging a-subdir
T a-subdir/whatever.c
cvs tag: Tagging a-subdir/subsubdir
T a-subdir/subsubdir/fish.c
cvs tag: Tagging b-subdir
T b-subdir/random.c
paste$ emacs a-subdir/whatever.c
  ...
```

```
paste$ cvs ci -m "print a randomly capitalized greeting"
cvs commit: Examining .
cvs commit: Examining a-subdir
cvs commit: Examining a-subdir/subsubdir
cvs commit: Examining b-subdir
Checking in a-subdir/whatever.c;
/usr/local/newrepos/myproj/a-subdir/whatever.c,v  <--  whatever.c
new revision: 1.3.2.2; previous revision: 1.3.2.1
done
paste$
```

And of course, qsmith should tag those changes once he's done:

```
paste$ cvs -q tag Exotic_Greetings-2
T README.txt
T foo.gif
T hello.c
T a-subdir/whatever.c
T a-subdir/subsubdir/fish.c
T b-subdir/random.c
paste$
```

While all this is going on, jrandom makes a change in a different file, one that qsmith hasn't touched in his new batch of edits:

```
floss$ emacs README.txt
 ...
floss$ cvs ci -m "Mention new Exotic Greeting features" README.txt
Checking in README.txt;
/usr/local/newrepos/myproj/README.txt,v  <--  README.txt
new revision: 1.17; previous revision: 1.16
done
floss$
```

At this point, qsmith has committed a new change on the branch, and jrandom has committed a nonconflicting change in a different file on the trunk. Watch what happens when jrandom tries to merge from the branch again:

```
floss$ cvs -q update -j Exotic_Greetings-branch
RCS file: /usr/local/newrepos/myproj/README.txt,v
retrieving revision 1.14
retrieving revision 1.14.2.1
Merging differences between 1.14 and 1.14.2.1 into README.txt
rcsmerge: warning: conflicts during merge
RCS file: /usr/local/newrepos/myproj/a-subdir/whatever.c,v
retrieving revision 1.3
```

```
retrieving revision 1.3.2.2
Merging differences between 1.3 and 1.3.2.2 into whatever.c
rcsmerge: warning: conflicts during merge
RCS file: /usr/local/newrepos/myproj/b-subdir/random.c,v
retrieving revision 1.1
retrieving revision 1.1.1.1.2.1
Merging differences between 1.1 and 1.1.1.1.2.1 into random.c
floss$ cvs -q update
C README.txt
C a-subdir/whatever.c
floss$
```

There are conflicts! Is that what you expected?

The problem lies in the semantics of merging. Back in Chapter 2, I explained that when you run

```
floss$ cvs update -j BRANCH
```

in a working copy, CVS merges into the working copy the differences between **BRANCH**'s root and its tip. The trouble with that behavior, in this situation, is that most of those changes had already been incorporated into the trunk the first time that jrandom did a merge. When CVS tried to merge them in again (over themselves, as it were), it naturally registered a conflict.

What jrandom really wanted to do was merge into her working copy the changes between the branch's *most recent* merge and its current tip. You can do this by using two **-j** flags to update, as you may recall from Chapter 2, as long as you know what revision to specify with each flag. Fortunately, qsmith made a tag at exactly the last merge point (hurrah for planning ahead!), so this will be no problem. First, let's have jrandom restore her working copy to a clean state, from which she can redo the merge:

```
floss$ rm README.txt a-subdir/whatever.c
floss$ cvs -q update
cvs update: warning: README.txt was lost
U README.txt
cvs update: warning: a-subdir/whatever.c was lost
U a-subdir/whatever.c
floss$
```

Now she's ready to do the merge, this time using qsmith's conveniently placed tag:

```
floss$ cvs -q update -j Exotic_Greetings-1 -j Exotic_Greetings-branch
RCS file: /usr/local/newrepos/myproj/a-subdir/whatever.c,v
retrieving revision 1.3.2.1
retrieving revision 1.3.2.2
Merging differences between 1.3.2.1 and 1.3.2.2 into whatever.c
```

```
floss$ cvs -q update
M a-subdir/whatever.c
floss$
```

Much better. The change from qsmith has been incorporated into whatever.c; jrandom can now commit and tag:

```
floss$ cvs -q ci -m "merged again from Exotic_Greetings (1)"
Checking in a-subdir/whatever.c;
/usr/local/newrepos/myproj/a-subdir/whatever.c,v  <--  whatever.c
new revision: 1.6; previous revision: 1.5
done
floss$ cvs -q tag merged-Exotic_Greetings-1
T README.txt
T foo.gif
T hello.c
T a-subdir/whatever.c
T a-subdir/subsubdir/fish.c
T b-subdir/random.c
floss$
```

Even if qsmith had forgotten to tag at the merge point, all hope would not be lost. If jrandom knew approximately when qsmith's first batch of changes had been committed, she could try filtering by date:

```
floss$ cvs update -j Exotic_Greetings-branch:3pm -j Exotic_Greetings_branch
```

Although useful as a last resort, filtering by date is less than ideal because it selects the changes based on people's recollections rather than dependable developer designations. If qsmith's first mergeable set of changes had happened over several commits instead of in one commit, jrandom may mistakenly choose a date or time that would catch some of the changes, but not all of them.

> **Tip**
>
> *There's no reason why each taggable point in qsmith's changes needs to be sent to the repository in a single commit—it just happens to have worked out that way in these examples. In real life, qsmith may make several commits between tags. He can work on the branch in isolation, as he pleases. The point of the tags is to record successive points on the branch where he considers the changes to be mergeable into the trunk. As long as jrandom always merges using two -j flags and is careful to use qsmith's merge tags in the right order and only once each, the trunk should never experience the double-merge problem. Conflicts may occur, but they will be the unavoidable kind that requires human resolution—situations in which both branch and trunk made changes to the same area of code.*

The Dovetail Approach: Merging In And Out Of The Trunk

Merging repeatedly from branch to trunk is good for the people on the trunk, because they see all of their own changes and all the changes from the branch. However, the developer on the branch never gets to incorporate any of the work being done on the trunk.

To allow that, the branch developer needs to add an extra step every now and then (meaning whenever he feels like merging in recent trunk changes and dealing with the inevitable conflicts):

```
paste$ cvs update -j HEAD
```

The special reserved tag **HEAD** means the tip of the trunk. The preceding command merges in all of the trunk changes between the root of the current branch (**Exotic_Greetings-branch**) and the current highest revisions of each file on the trunk. Of course, qsmith should tag again after doing this, so that the trunk developers can avoid accidentally merging in their own changes when they're trying to get qsmith's.

The branch developer can likewise use the trunk's merge tags as boundaries, allowing the branch to merge exactly those trunk changes between the last merge and the trunk's current state (the same way the trunk does merges). For example, supposing jrandom had made some changes to hello.c after merging from the branch:

```
floss$ emacs hello.c
  ...
floss$ cvs ci -m "clarify algorithm" hello.c
Checking in hello.c;
/usr/local/newrepos/myproj/hello.c,v  <-- hello.c
new revision: 1.22; previous revision: 1.21
done
floss$
```

Then, qsmith can merge those changes into his branch, commit, and, of course, tag:

```
paste$ cvs -q update -j merged-Exotic_Greetings-1 -j HEAD
RCS file: /usr/local/newrepos/myproj/hello.c,v
retrieving revision 1.21
retrieving revision 1.22
Merging differences between 1.21 and 1.22 into hello.c
paste$ cvs -q update
M hello.c
paste$ cvs -q ci -m "merged trunk, from merged-Exotic_Greetings-1 to HEAD"
Checking in hello.c;
/usr/local/newrepos/myproj/hello.c,v  <-- hello.c
new revision: 1.21.2.1; previous revision: 1.21
done
```

```
paste$ cvs -q tag merged-merged-Exotic_Greetings-1
T README.txt
T foo.gif
T hello.c
T a-subdir/whatever.c
T a-subdir/subsubdir/fish.c
T b-subdir/random.c
paste$
```

Notice that jrandom did not bother to tag after committing the changes to hello.c, but qsmith did. The principle at work here is that although you don't need to tag after every little change, you should always tag after a merge or after committing your line of development up to a mergeable state. That way, other people—perhaps on other branches—have a reference point against which to base their own merges.

The Flying Fish Approach: A Simpler Way To Do It

There is a simpler, albeit slightly limiting, variant of the preceding. In it, the branch developers freeze while the trunk merges, and then the trunk developers create an entirely new branch, which replaces the old one. The branch developers move onto that branch and continue working. The cycle continues until there is no more need for branch development. It goes something like this (in shorthand—we'll assume jrandom@floss has the trunk and qsmith@paste has the branch, as usual):

```
floss$ cvs tag -b BRANCH-1
paste$ cvs checkout -r BRANCH-1 myproj
```

Trunk and branch both start working; eventually, the developers confer and decide it's time to merge the branch into the trunk:

```
paste$ cvs ci -m "committing all uncommitted changes"
floss$ cvs update -j BRANCH-1
```

All the changes from the branch merge in; the branch developers stop working while the trunk developers resolve any conflicts, commit, tag, and create a new branch:

```
floss$ cvs ci -m "merged from BRANCH-1"
floss$ cvs tag merged-from-BRANCH-1
floss$ cvs tag -b BRANCH-2
```

Now the branch developers switch their working copies over to the new branch; they know they won't lose any uncommitted changes by doing so, because they were up-to-date when the merge happened, and the new branch is coming out of a trunk that has incorporated the changes from the old branch:

```
paste$ cvs update -r BRANCH-2
```

And the cycle continues in that way, indefinitely; just substitute **BRANCH-2** for **BRANCH-1** and **BRANCH-3** for **BRANCH-2**.

I call this the "Flying Fish" technique, because the branch is constantly emerging from the trunk, traveling a short distance, then rejoining it. The advantages of this approach are that it's simple (the trunk always merges in all the changes from a given branch) and the branch developers never need to resolve conflicts (they're simply handed a new, clean branch on which to work each time). The disadvantage, of course, is that the branch people must sit idle while the trunk is undergoing merge (which can take an arbitrary amount of time, depending on how many conflicts need to be resolved). Another minor disadvantage is that it results in many little, unused branches laying around instead of many unused non-branch tags. However, if having millions of tiny, obsolete branches doesn't bother you, and you anticipate fairly trouble-free merges, Flying Fish may be the easiest way to go in terms of mental bookkeeping.

Whichever way you do it, you should try to keep the separations as short as possible. If the branch and the trunk go too long without merging, they could easily begin to suffer not just from textual drift, but semantic drift as well. Changes that conflict textually are the easiest ones to resolve. Changes that conflict conceptually, but not textually, often prove hardest to find and fix. The isolation of a branch, so freeing to the developers, is dangerous precisely because it shields each side from the effects of others' changes...for a time. When you use branches, communication becomes more vital than ever: Everyone needs to make extra sure to review each others' plans and code to ensure that they're all staying on the same track.

Branches And Keyword Expansion: Natural Enemies

If your files contain RCS keywords that expand differently on branch and trunk, you're almost guaranteed to get spurious conflicts on every merge. Even if nothing else changed, the keywords are overlapping, and their expansions won't match. For example, if README.txt contains this on the trunk

```
$Revision: 1.14 $
```

and this on the branch

```
$Revision: 1.14.2.1 $
```

then when the merge is performed, you'll get the following conflict:

```
floss$ cvs update -j Exotic_Greetings-branch
RCS file: /usr/local/newrepos/myproj/README.txt,v
retrieving revision 1.14
retrieving revision 1.14.2.1
```

```
Merging differences between 1.14 and 1.14.2.1 into README.txt
rcsmerge: warning: conflicts during merge
floss$ cat README.txt
  ...
<<<<<<< README.txt
key $Revision: 1.14 $
=======
key $Revision: 1.14.2.1 $
>>>>>>> 1.14.2.1
  ...
floss$
```

To avoid this, you can temporarily disable expansion by passing the **-kk** option (I don't know what it stands for; "kill keywords," maybe?) when you do the merge:

```
floss$ cvs update -kk -j Exotic_Greetings-branch
RCS file: /usr/local/newrepos/myproj/README.txt,v
retrieving revision 1.14
retrieving revision 1.14.2.1
Merging differences between 1.14 and 1.14.2.1 into README.txt
floss$ cat README.txt
  ...
$Revision$
  ...
floss$
```

There is one thing to be careful of, however: If you use **-kk**, it overrides whatever other keyword expansion mode you may have set for that file. Specifically, this is a problem for binary files, which are normally **-kb** (which suppresses all keyword expansion and line-end conversion). So if you have to merge binary files in from a branch, don't use **-kk**. Just deal with the conflicts by hand instead.

Tracking Third-Party Sources: Vendor Branches

Sometimes a site will make local changes to a piece of software received from an outside source. If the outside source does not incorporate the local changes (and there might be many legitimate reasons why it can't), the site has to maintain its changes in each received upgrade of the software.

CVS can help with this task, via a feature known as "vendor branches." In fact, vendor branches are the explanation behind the puzzling (until now) final two arguments to **cvs import**: the **vendor tag** and **release tag** that I glossed over in Chapter 2.

Here's how it works. The initial import is just like any other initial import of a CVS project (except that you'll want to choose the vendor tag and release tag with a little care):

```
floss$ pwd
/home/jrandom/theirproj-1.0
floss$ cvs import -m "Import of TheirProj 1.0" theirproj Them THEIRPROJ_1_0
N theirproj/INSTALL
N theirproj/README
N theirproj/src/main.c
N theirproj/src/parse.c
N theirproj/src/digest.c
N theirproj/doc/random.c
N theirproj/doc/manual.txt

No conflicts created by this import

floss$
```

Then you check out a working copy somewhere, make your local modifications, and **commit**:

```
floss$ cvs -q co theirproj
U theirproj/INSTALL
U theirproj/README
U theirproj/doc/manual.txt
U theirproj/doc/random.c
U theirproj/src/digest.c
U theirproj/src/main.c
U theirproj/src/parse.c
floss$ cd theirproj
floss$ emacs src/main.c src/digest.c
  ...
floss$ cvs -q update
M src/digest.c
M src/main.c
floss$ cvs -q ci -m "changed digestion algorithm; added comment to main"
Checking in src/digest.c;
/usr/local/newrepos/theirproj/src/digest.c,v  <-- digest.c
new revision: 1.2; previous revision: 1.1
done
Checking in src/main.c;
/usr/local/newrepos/theirproj/src/main.c,v  <-- main.c
new revision: 1.2; previous revision: 1.1
done
floss$
```

A year later, the next version of the software arrives from Them, Inc., and you must incorporate your local changes into it. Their changes and yours overlap slightly. They've added one new file, modified a couple of files that you didn't touch, but also modified two files that you modified.

First you must do another **import**, this time from the new sources. Almost everything is the same as it was in the initial import—you're importing to the same project in the repository, and on the same vendor branch. The only thing different is the release tag:

```
floss$ pwd
/home/jrandom/theirproj-2.0
floss$ cvs -q import -m "Import of TheirProj 2.0" theirproj Them THEIRPROJ_2_0
U theirproj/INSTALL
N theirproj/TODO
U theirproj/README
cvs import: Importing /usr/local/newrepos/theirproj/src
C theirproj/src/main.c
U theirproj/src/parse.c
C theirproj/src/digest.c
cvs import: Importing /usr/local/newrepos/theirproj/doc
U theirproj/doc/random.c
U theirproj/doc/manual.txt

2 conflicts created by this import.
Use the following command to help the merge:

        cvs checkout -jThem:yesterday -jThem theirproj

floss$
```

My goodness—we've never seen CVS try to be so helpful. It's actually telling us what command to run to merge the changes. And it's almost right, too! Actually, the command as given works (assuming that you adjust **yesterday** to be any time interval that definitely includes the first import but not the second), but I mildly prefer to do it by release tag instead:

```
floss$ cvs checkout -j THEIRPROJ_1_0 -j THEIRPROJ_2_0 theirproj
cvs checkout: Updating theirproj
U theirproj/INSTALL
U theirproj/README
U theirproj/TODO
cvs checkout: Updating theirproj/doc
U theirproj/doc/manual.txt
U theirproj/doc/random.c
cvs checkout: Updating theirproj/src
U theirproj/src/digest.c
RCS file: /usr/local/newrepos/theirproj/src/digest.c,v
retrieving revision 1.1.1.1
```

```
retrieving revision 1.1.1.2
Merging differences between 1.1.1.1 and 1.1.1.2 into digest.c
rcsmerge: warning: conflicts during merge
U theirproj/src/main.c
RCS file: /usr/local/newrepos/theirproj/src/main.c,v
retrieving revision 1.1.1.1
retrieving revision 1.1.1.2
Merging differences between 1.1.1.1 and 1.1.1.2 into main.c
U theirproj/src/parse.c
floss$
```

Notice how the **import** told us that there were two conflicts, but the **merge** only seems to claim one conflict. It seems that CVS's idea of a conflict is a little different when importing than at other times. Basically, **import** reports a conflict if both you and the vendor modified a file between the last import and this one. However, when it comes time to merge, **update** sticks with the usual definition of "conflict"—overlapping changes. Changes that don't overlap are merged in the usual way, and the file is simply marked as modified.

A quick **diff** verifies that only one of the files actually has conflict markers:

```
floss$ cvs -q update
C src/digest.c
M src/main.c
floss$ cvs diff -c
Index: src/digest.c
===================================================================
RCS file: /usr/local/newrepos/theirproj/src/digest.c,v
retrieving revision 1.2
diff -c -r1.2 digest.c
*** src/digest.c        1999/07/26 08:02:18      1.2
-- src/digest.c         1999/07/26 08:16:15
***************
*** 3,7 ****
-- 3,11 ----
 void
 digest ()
 {
+ <<<<<<< digest.c
   printf ("gurgle, slorp\n");
+ =======
+   printf ("mild gurgle\n");
+ >>>>>>> 1.1.1.2
 }
Index: src/main.c
===================================================================
RCS file: /usr/local/newrepos/theirproj/src/main.c,v
```

```
retrieving revision 1.2
diff -c -r1.2 main.c
*** src/main.c  1999/07/26 08:02:18     1.2
-- src/main.c 1999/07/26 08:16:15
***************
*** 7,9 ****
-- 7,11 ----
  {
    printf ("Goodbye, world!\n");
  }
+
+ /* I, the vendor, added this comment for no good reason. */
floss$
```

From here, it's just a matter of resolving the conflicts as with any other merge:

```
floss$ emacs  src/digest.c  src/main.c
  ...
floss$ cvs -q update
M src/digest.c
M src/main.c
floss$ cvs diff src/digest.c
cvs diff src/digest.c
Index: src/digest.c
===================================================================
RCS file: /usr/local/newrepos/theirproj/src/digest.c,v
retrieving revision 1.2
diff -r1.2 digest.c
6c6
<   printf ("gurgle, slorp\n");
--
>   printf ("mild gurgle, slorp\n");
floss$
```

Then commit the changes

```
floss$ cvs -q ci -m "Resolved conflicts with import of 2.0"
Checking in src/digest.c;
/usr/local/newrepos/theirproj/src/digest.c,v  <--  digest.c
new revision: 1.3; previous revision: 1.2
done
Checking in src/main.c;
/usr/local/newrepos/theirproj/src/main.c,v  <--  main.c
new revision: 1.3; previous revision: 1.2
done
floss$
```

and wait for the next release from the vendor. (Of course, you'll also want to test that your local modifications still work!)

That's All, Folks! Welcome To Guru-Hood

If you read and understood (and better yet, experimented with) everything in this chapter, you may rest assured that there are no big surprises left for you in CVS—at least until someone adds a major new feature to CVS, which does happen with some frequency. Everything you need to know to use CVS on a major project has been presented.

Before that goes to your head, let me reiterate the suggestion, first made in Chapter 4, that you subscribe to the **info-cvs@gnu.org** mailing list. Despite having the impoverished signal-to-noise ratio common to most Internet mailing lists, the bits of signal that do come through are almost always worth the wait. I was subscribed during the entire time I wrote this chapter (indeed, for all previous chapters as well), and you would be amazed to know how many important details I learned about CVS's behavior from reading other people's posts. If you're going to be using CVS seriously, and especially if you're the CVS administrator for a group of developers, you can benefit a lot from the shared knowledge of all the other serious users out there.

Chapter 7
Building, Testing, And Releasing

Why Release?

In previous chapters, I've said that free software projects are in a state of continuous release—that the official, numbered versions occasionally announced by the developers are nothing more than snapshots of particular moments in a project's lifetime. Although that's accurate from a developer's point of view, users don't tend to think of the process in this way. Compiling and installing from unstable development sources can be quite a hassle, and most people are understandably reluctant to deal with it. Instead, they'll get the software by downloading one of the "officially blessed" releases. They probably won't ever even look at the code, let alone monitor changes on a daily basis. Mainly, they want to get the software up and running right away and not worry about it until the next release comes out (at which point they can decide whether to upgrade or wait).

Because the overwhelming majority of users just want a product that works, developers now realize that the periodic releases need to be stable and relatively unthreatening. Unfortunately, this runs counter to what most developers want. In a developer's ideal world, every single user would update and reinstall the very latest software version every morning, use it all day long, and report every bug they find. Stability is not the point—finding the bugs is the point. The user base would, in effect, function as a continuously-running test harness, exercising all aspects of the software and reporting in detail on all failures and unexpected behaviors. In a user's ideal world, by contrast, the developers would organize legions of testers to try out every new version extensively before release, finding and fixing as many bugs as possible so that the release always ships with no known bugs (a goal that developers would also like to achieve, in the long run).

In other words, everybody wants the bugs to be found, but hardly anyone wants to find them. Bug discovery can be painful for the discoverer—maybe you first noticed the bug when it caused a valuable file to disappear unexpectedly or a sensitive email to be sent to the wrong recipient. The developers, on the other hand, welcome the news of your tragedy, because it allows them to fix a latent problem in the code. In a sense, they want you to encounter bugs, and the more the better. They'll probably even thank you in the log message for the bug fix (small consolation, though, for your missing file or insulted boss).

This tension between developer needs and user needs is not entirely resolvable. Users expect formal releases to be safe and as bug-free as possible. Developers have compromised to a degree, often imposing a feature freeze and a period of intense testing right before a major release. This accommodates users who don't want to deal with unstable software and, perhaps equally importantly, imposes a healthy discipline on developers, who otherwise may have no pressure to create stable software. Nevertheless, developers often regard the release process as an annoyance—a distraction from coding and improving the software.

Meanwhile, users have also had to make some adjustments: Instead of receiving sympathy when they encounter a bug, they're expected to file bug reports, which involves extra time in addition to the time lost by the bug itself. Users are also expected to understand that no release is completely bug-free and that developers rely on them to be the "testers of last resort."

This chapter concentrates on the developer side of this process, although there are glimpses of the users' point of view as well. Because this material is directed toward people managing software projects, you may want to skip it entirely if you're just using CVS to manage text documents. It is assumed that you are familiar with the jargon of software development, the concepts of configuration and build scripts, and the Unix **make** program.

The release procedures described here are most appropriate for medium- to large-sized projects, although you may choose to apply some of the techniques to releases of smaller programs as well. In general, the more complex your project and the more users depend on it, the stricter your release procedures should be.

Starting The Release Process

A new release of software does not happen overnight. It is the culmination of a long process, usually starting with a discussion among the developers about whether it's time for a new version. There are two primary motivations behind most releases:

♦ Many bugs have been fixed since the last release.

♦ Significant new features have been added.

A third reason, sometimes openly acknowledged and sometimes not, is publicity. If it's been a long time since the last release, people begin to wonder whether the software is still under active development. A release is a newsworthy event, a way of reminding the world that work on the software is continuing as usual. Publicity is, I suppose, an understandable motivation, but you shouldn't let it be the sole—or even the main—reason behind a release. If you start doing releases for attention, you just cause "release inflation." The perceived value of each new version decreases, and people start taking all of your releases less seriously. For best results, stick with substantive reasons such as bug fixes and new features.

Once a consensus has been reached that it's time for a release, the developers need to decide on a release manager to guide the process. The release manager's job is not just a matter of packaging up the software, placing it on the appropriate download sites, and making an announcement. The manager must first coordinate testing, possibly enforce a code freeze (by carefully reviewing, and occasionally reverting, changes to the source code during the period leading up to the release), and in general be responsible for seeing that the new version is stable. Often the release manager and the maintainer are the same person, but not always. The maintainer may simply not want the hassle of managing the release or may recognize that an independent third party's judgement is needed to distinguish between unnecessary, destabilizing changes and legitimate prerelease bug fixes.

Avoiding The "Code Cram" Effect

If the release manager is not the regular maintainer, the maintainer should very publicly confer a hefty amount of decision-making authority on the release manager for the duration of the release process. The manager must spend a lot of time saying "no," because when contributing developers realize that a new release is imminent, they tend to rush to finish up their current works-in-progress for inclusion in the next release. This, of course, is exactly what the release manager doesn't want. Hastily completed changes, checked in at the last minute with insufficient time for testing, are practically guaranteed to produce bugs that will be discovered by users after the release. (In fact, often the very best time to put a new feature or other significant change into the code is immediately *after* a release. It can then be tested for the maximum possible amount of time before the next release.)

Naturally, it's very hard to persuade developers to hold off. If they have a change 90 percent ready, they'll be tempted to finish the last 10 percent quickly and commit. They know that if the new code gets into the release, it will have many more testers than otherwise. However, users don't want to function as early testers and are unpleasantly surprised to encounter bugs that should have been caught before the release went out.

Unfortunately, the release manager can't simply refuse all code changes. The whole point of the release preparation process is to weed out as many bugs as possible, and therefore code changes can't be entirely avoided. The manager must exercise judgement about which ones should be permitted and which ones should wait until the release has gone out. Balancing the priorities of improvement versus stability can be tricky, and I can't really offer any firm guidelines about how to do it—it really depends on the nature of the software and of the proposed changes. In general, a change should probably be permitted if it fixes a known bug, is small, and seems unlikely to cause any dangerous new problems ("dangerous" in the sense of potentially doing damage to a user's data). However, if there is doubt, conservatism should rule. If a change destabilizes an area of the code known to be currently stable and it's difficult for the release manager to tell at first glance whether the change has any problems, it's probably best deferred until after the release.

Freezing

The release manager's decisions will be best received if they appear to be part of a unified and consistent policy, rather than as whims or case-by-case judgements. The policy most often used is called a "freeze" (because it cools down the code to a very slow rate of change for a while). Until now, I've been using the phrase "code freeze" as a generic name for all freezes; however, "freezes" can mean different things to different people. I'll try to summarize the uses I've heard and what people mean by them. However, keep in mind that it's all one basic idea: a period of time in which unnecessary changes are discouraged.

♦ *Feature freeze*—No significant new functionality is added to the program, but bug fixes are permitted. Minor improvements are allowed as long as they are isolated and (theoretically) cannot destabilize other code. A "minor improvement" means a trivial change that doesn't involve new code paths or dependencies (for example, changing an error message or adding a **-help** option).

♦ *Code freeze*—No changes are to be made to the code except those absolutely necessary to fix known bugs. Even these may be deferred if the bug is minor and the best available fix involves changes that could have repercussions elsewhere.

Many people use "code freeze" synonymously with "feature freeze," however, and the difference between them is fuzzy enough that I sometimes prefer to use these alternate terms instead:

♦ *Soft freeze*—This is similar to a feature freeze, but the decisive factor for permitting changes is how complex and destabilizing the changes are, rather than whether they implement a new feature or fix a bug. This essentially means, "Don't do anything big." The release manager has to review each submission carefully and ask, "Will the program be more or less likely to cause someone a problem if this change is allowed?" The answer is largely a matter of opinion and subjective judgement, but the decision should be biased in favor of the safe, conservative course until the release is done.

♦ *Hard freeze*—All code changes are discouraged. Only those that fix known bugs are permitted. Even with bug fixes, the release manager may elect to hold off if the bug in question is old and familiar to users, if its fix is complex, or if it is likely to have unexpected consequences. A hard freeze usually follows a soft freeze and is the last freeze before the actual release. If a bug is found, the code is thawed back to a soft freeze temporarily for the fix, then hard frozen again so it can go through a complete testing cycle without any changes.

Development Vs. Stable Branches

Freeze policies are only guidelines, of course. Release managers are constantly called on to violate their own policy by making exceptions for special cases. However, if you make too many exceptions, you'll have to come up with justifications for all the cases where the exception wasn't made.

One technique for sidestepping (at least partially) decisions about what to allow is to split the code into two branches: one for ongoing development and one for the stable release. Exactly when and where they split, and which one is on the main trunk, is up to the release manager. I recommend splitting off the release as a branch and leaving development on the trunk, so that developers can continue to work as they always have. As bugs are fixed on the release branch, the fixes should be merged back into the trunk (so those bugs will be absent from all future releases, too) and the release branch tagged as described in Chapter 6. When the release is made, the tip of that branch can be packaged and shipped as the new version. All activity on the branch will cease once any remaining changes have been merged into the trunk. When it's time for the next release, a new branch can be made, and the cycle starts again.

Having separate release and development branches does not obviate the need for a release manager, but it does mean that the draconian freeze policies need only apply on the release branch. Eager developers have a place to commit their changes without disturbing the code that's about to be released, instead of being asked to wait until the release is over before committing their changes.

The Two-Lane Approach

Some projects—most famously the Linux kernel—have taken this split approach to an extreme. They have a permanent stable branch and a permanent development branch. (Note that the Linux kernel is not using CVS to do this; I'm not sure what mechanism they use to merge changes from one branch to the other.) When they decide it's time to make a new stable release, the development branch goes into a freeze—I think the Linux folks call it a "feature freeze." When everything's been debugged, they take the frozen development branch, release it as the new stable branch, and start a new development branch immediately, even though the next release may be months or years away.

The important thing is that both branches are always available for downloading and installation by anyone at any time, whether or not there's a freeze or release planned. You choose which one to get based on your preferences: If you want safety, you go with the stable version; if you want to help test new features (or perhaps you need some of the new features for some reason), you get the development version. The kernel team advertises loudly and clearly that the development kernels are less safe and that using them is riskier than sticking with the stable ones. Nevertheless, many people do use the unstable kernels, and the developers get a constant supply of free testers to find bugs for them.

This approach can work for any project sufficiently large that some users will try out the development branch, but it obviously involves some bureaucratic overhead. Life is always simpler when you minimize the number of branches active at any one time. With two permanent, parallel code lines, every change has to be considered in terms of which branch it's most appropriate for. If a change goes onto the stable branch, a cross-branch operation may be required to make sure it gets into the development code as well. I wouldn't recommend this approach unless the benefits of having extra testers outweigh the hassles of dealing with branch management.

Stability And Version Numbers

The Linux kernel also started a tradition that has since spread to other projects: They use even version numbers to refer to stable releases and odd numbers for experimental ones. (Actually, I'm not sure this tradition started with Linux, but Linux was one of the earliest high-profile projects to do it.) The convention only applies to the minor version number—that is, the portion after the decimal point: Kernel 2.2 is stable, and 2.3 is unstable. Kernel 2.4, which should be out about the same time as this book, is the stable release derived from the 2.3 development branch and will be the root of a new 2.5 development version.

If you're going to use the two-lane approach of always having development and stable versions available, it's a good idea to follow this version number convention. Although the convention is not yet completely universal, more people have come to expect it, and many users may interpret your version numbers according to it, whether that was your intention or not. You should state somewhere (on the project home page and in the documentation) that you're following the convention, so those who don't assume it's universal will know what to think, too.

Testing

In a perfect world, thousands of devoted testers would try out each release until no bugs remain. In the real world, testing is far too often a thankless task that developers usually end up doing themselves (and without time to be very thorough). However, having a team of dedicated people testing the code before the release greatly increases the odds of shipping stable software.

Getting and keeping this team is not easy. Testing is not, for most people, an inherently attractive task. It has none of the glory of code development, and it can be risky if you are testing with live data. However, if you can persuade people to do it, you'll be very glad. A good testing team will uncover problems you never even suspected.

Recruiting And Retaining Testers

To recruit testers, you should first post announcements on the appropriate mailing lists and newsgroups. Stress that the release process has already started and that you're planning to have the new version out by a certain date—people always respond more positively to tasks that have a definite goal and lifespan. Once you've collected some volunteers, here are some tips to help them understand their role, and even come back next time:

♦ *Make it easy for your volunteers to download and install the test releases.* This means making the releases conveniently accessible both via CVS and via nightly downloadable "snapshots." The snapshots should be packaged just as the final release will be, so that your team can test the installation process as well as the actual software application. (See the section "Building, Installing, And Packaging" later in this chapter.)

♦ *Organize the testing.* If the program is particularly complex, you'll want to assign people to test particular areas or subsystems. Keep the assignment list posted in a public place so everyone knows who's accountable for what. Whether people are assigned particular responsibilities or not, you should regularly query them individually on their progress. (If you haven't heard from them for a while, it may mean they've found no bugs, or it may mean that they haven't actually tried the code yet.) If people feel that their efforts, or lack of same, are being noticed, they'll devote more time. But if you just throw the code onto a download site and don't give the testing team any deadlines or expectations, they'll probably make testing the last item in their priority queue.

♦ *Be responsive.* Every bug report from a tester should be answered right away, even if it's only to say that the bug has already been found and fixed. If testers are sending in vague or unreproducible reports, you may need to train them on what should be included in bug reports. Nonprogrammers often don't realize that the core of most good bug reports is the "reproduction recipe," which gives the developers a reliable way to make the bug happen on demand.

♦ *Remember to thank your testing team, by name, in a prominent place.* For example, the top-level README file in the CVS source distribution contains a list of testers. Many other software distributions contain equally prominent acknowledgements. Also, when writing the log message for a bug fix, you should mention the discoverer's name. That may seem unimportant, but people really appreciate it and often contribute more when their work is noticed. Recording their contribution in the permanent history of the code is a great way to give recognition.

Automated Testing

Depending on what your program does, it may be possible to automate some of the testing. Any user-interaction code must still be tested by humans—they actually have to type at the keyboard, click the mouse, and so on, to test the program's responses to those actions. However, any circumstance where the code takes discrete inputs and produces predictable output can, in theory, be tested automatically.

The exact implementation of automated testing is, of course, totally dependent on the program, so we won't go into detail about it here. To see a particularly complicated (to be charitable) example of an automated test suite, take a look at the Bourne shell script src/sanity.sh in the CVS distribution. If you do decide to implement automated testing, you should probably set the test script to run nightly on a fresh version of the sources, especially during periods of release preparation, and possibly even have it email the results to all of the developers and testers.

Although useful, automated testing can never be a complete substitute for human testing. Many so-called "bugs" turn out to be deficiencies in the program's documentation or nonintuitive behaviors that surprise the tester. An automated test suite would not detect these because the program's developers won't make the same sorts of "mistakes" that an outside tester would, even when the design of the software encourages the mistakes. More generally, the problem with automated testing is that the developers—who usually write the test suite—are far too familiar with the intended use of each feature to think of unexpected and creative ways in which it may be misused.

Thus, test suites tend to be very good at confirming that what worked yesterday still works today, but bad at finding problems no one ever considered. Historically, the CVS test suite (the one with which I'm most familiar) has caught some bugs during release preparation, but not all. In one recent case, the test suite utterly failed to notice a major bug before the release went out. Or rather, the developers never anticipated the bug and so did not include code in the test suite to look for it.

Building, Installing, And Packaging

The compilation, installation, and packaging of source code are tasks performed with such regularity that, in the free software world, certain standard automated methods have evolved to handle them. By adhering to these standards, you can make life much easier for other developers and testers, who expect everything to work in the conventional way.

The standard revolves around the Unix program **make** and, to a lesser degree, around GNU **autoconf**. For years, the **make** program has been the standard method of compiling from source code in Unix. The **autoconf** program is a more recent system, introduced by the Free Software Foundation, for dealing with portability issues across Unix variants. Unfortunately, documenting these two systems is quite beyond the scope of this book, but I'll give very brief introductions. You can read more about the GNU implementation of **make** at **http://www.gnu. org/software/make/make.html**; its online manual is available at **http://www.gnu.org/manual/ make/**. Information about **autoconf** may be found at **http://www.gnu.org/software/autoconf/ autoconf.html** and its manual at **http://www.gnu.org/manual/autoconf/**. I'll assume that you're acquainted with tar and GNU zip.

Let's start by looking at how most free software is compiled and installed these days. You unpack the package as follows:

```
floss$ zcat somesoft-1.2.tar.gz | tar xvf -
...
floss$ ls
somesoft-1.2.tar.gz    somesoft-1.2/
```

Go into the top level of its source tree and configure it:

```
floss$ cd somesoft-1.2
floss$ ./configure
...
```

Compile it:

```
floss$ make
...
```

And install it (note that this step must often be done as the superuser):

```
floss# make install
...
```

Let's examine those steps in (almost) reverse order. Typing

```
floss# make
```

at the command prompt invokes the **make** program, which in turn looks for a Makefile file in the current directory. The Makefile specifies how the program is to be compiled. It usually also contains specifications on how to install the program once it's compiled, uninstall it, and clean up the source tree after compilation, among other things. Running

```
floss# make install
```

tells **make** to find a rule (that is, a specification) named "install" in the Makefile, and do whatever the rule says to do—in this case, copy the newly built executables to the appropriate system location. (Actually, if binaries haven't yet been built, **make install** first goes through the steps that a plain **make** invocation would have gone through and then installs the compiled software. Some people prefer the two-step process, however, just in case anything goes wrong during the compilation.)

The previous command

```
floss$ ./configure
```

ran a script named "configure," located in the top level of the source tree. That script reads in a meta-Makefile, named "Makefile.in," performs various textual substitutions in a platform-dependent way, and writes out the result as "Makefile" (without the .in suffix). Once you have the Makefile, of course, you can run **make** to compile the program.

However, that's not the whole story. The configure script itself was originally produced, by the program's distributors, from a file named "configure.in" (which defines various parameters that tell configure what to look for), and the command to do that is **autoconf**:

```
floss$ ls configure.in
configure.in
floss$ ls configure
configure: no such file or directory
floss$ autoconf
floss$ ls configure
configure
floss$
```

In summary, **autoconf** is a system for producing a portable configure script that can be run on any platform to produce a *nonportable* Makefile. This Makefile can compile the software only on the platform where configure was run. (This is a bit simplified, but it will do for our purposes.)

It is sometimes difficult to understand which of these files should be stored in the project repository and which should be generated locally, as needed. Obviously, the configure.in file should be in the repository, because it is not derived from anything higher up. However, should the configure script (which is derived from configure.in) be kept in the repository?

Your first instinct may be that it should not. Because the configure script can be generated on demand from configure.in by running **autoconf**, you may think it could only cause confusion to store it in the repository as well. However, if it is not distributed, anyone who wants to run configure (that is, anyone who wants to compile the program) must have **autoconf** installed on their system. Although not uncommon, **autoconf** is not as common as, say, the Bourne shell and the **make** program are.

Therefore, it's probably better to keep both configure.in and configure under revision control. You simply must make sure that whenever a change is made to configure.in, configure is regenerated and checked in as well. Changes to configure.in are fairly rare, so this works out okay in practice.

Meanwhile, the configure script itself does not depend on the presence of **autoconf**—it only needs the Bourne shell and various standard Unix utilities, which every version of Unix has. Therefore, anyone can run configure to generate a Makefile, given Makefile.in. So, although it's vital that Makefile.in be kept under revision control, because it cannot be derived from anything else, it's not necessary to store Makefile as well. In fact, because the Makefile is platform-dependent, storing it is not a good idea.

You may not need to autoconfiscate your program (yes, that's the official GNU word for incorporating a package into the **autoconf** system) at all if it's small and fairly simple in terms of its portability requirements. However, as your program grows in complexity, you will find that an increasing proportion of the code is devoted to dealing with portability issues, and you will begin to think, "There's got to be a better way." Unfortunately, there isn't a better way, but there is GNU **autoconf**. Although **autoconf** may seem daunting at first, it is the standard way to deal with portability problems these days. (To be perfectly fair, **autoconf** is probably as simple as it can be, given the inherent messiness of the problem it's trying to solve.)

If you don't use **autoconf**, it's fine to just have a Makefile with hardcoded rules for compiling and installing the program (you can instruct users to edit the Makefile if they don't like the defaults). Most people will just type

```
floss$ make install
```

and not worry about it. Your testers will be grateful that you're following the standard, so they don't have to remember any unusual commands to install the software.

I've even seen some projects include a dummy configure script in their distributions that outputs something like this when run:

```
floss$ configure
No need to run configure, just type 'make install'
floss$
```

However, most people know to go directly to the **make** step if they see no configure script.

Let CVS Help You With Packaging

Automating the build and install process is useful for general users, but developers (and often testers) will also want an automated way to package the software for release. Although there is only one "real" release, there will probably be many test releases leading up to it, and it's important to have a consistent procedure for producing them.

If you've set things up in CVS in a reasonable way, it should be possible to configure, build, and install directly from a working copy. The only trick is to turn that working copy into a compressed tar file suitable for distribution. The contents of that tar file will be the same as the working copy tree, but without the administrative CVS subdirectories. You could just write a script to remove all those directories, but that would ruin your working copy. Anyway, CVS provides a command to check out a project as a simple tree (not as a working copy, so it will have no CVS subdirectories).

The command is **cvs export**, and it's similar to **checkout**, except that it demands a tag name or date. The following shows how to create a tag and then export based on that tag (because some of these commands take place outside a working copy, we'll assume that the **CVSROOT** environment variable is set):

```
floss$ cvs -q tag Release_1_0
T README.txt
T foo.gif
```

```
T hello.c
T a-subdir/whatever.c
T a-subdir/subsubdir/fish.c
T b-subdir/random.c
floss$ cd ..
floss$ cvs -q export -r Release_1_0 -d myproj-1.0 myproj
U myproj-1.0/README.txt
U myproj-1.0/foo.gif
U myproj-1.0/hello.c
U myproj-1.0/a-subdir/whatever.c
U myproj-1.0/a-subdir/subsubdir/fish.c
U myproj-1.0/b-subdir/random.c
floss$
```

The **-d myproj-1.0** makes the exported copy go into a directory with a different name than the working copy (you don't want to destroy the working copy, because there's probably still work to be done there). Once you have the myproj-1.0 directory, it's a simple matter to package it up:

```
floss$ tar cvf myproj-1.0.tar myproj-1.0
myproj-1.0/
myproj-1.0/README.txt
myproj-1.0/foo.gif
myproj-1.0/hello.c
myproj-1.0/a-subdir/
myproj-1.0/a-subdir/whatever.c
myproj-1.0/a-subdir/subsubdir/
myproj-1.0/a-subdir/subsubdir/fish.c
myproj-1.0/b-subdir/
myproj-1.0/b-subdir/random.c
floss$ gzip myproj-1.0.tar
floss$ ls -l myproj-1.0.tar.gz
-rw-r--r--   1 jrandom  users          1611 Aug  9 02:43 myproj-1.0.tar.gz
floss$
```

It's easy to come up with scripts or Makefile rules to automate this process. A typical method is to start the process by invoking

```
floss$ make dist
```

which goes through the preceding steps and deposits the package myproj-1.0.tar.gz in the top level of the working copy, presumably for removal to an appropriate publicly accessible location. (By the way, although I chose not to in the example, you can run **export** inside a working copy, as long as the exported directory won't overwrite any subdirectories of the working tree.)

During the prerelease testing phase, there's no need to create (or delete) lots of spurious tags just to placate **export**. If you've frozen the trunk and just want to export its tip for each prerelease, you should just pass **export** a date—specifically, the special date **now**:

```
floss$ cvs -q export -D now -d myproj-1.0-beta myproj
U myproj-1.0-beta/README.txt
U myproj-1.0-beta/foo.gif
U myproj-1.0-beta/hello.c
U myproj-1.0-beta/a-subdir/whatever.c
U myproj-1.0-beta/a-subdir/subsubdir/fish.c
U myproj-1.0-beta/b-subdir/random.c
floss$
```

I have found, however, that using **now** can sometimes miss very recent changes in the repository, due to slight clock differences between the repository machine and the working copy machine. So to be perfectly safe, you may want to pass **tomorrow** instead

```
floss$ cvs -q export -D tomorrow -d myproj-1.0-beta myproj
...
```

counterintuitive as that may seem!

I won't describe the details of scripting the packaging process—There's More Than One Way To Do It (as the Perl motto says). As long as the end result is a file with a name like myproj-1.0.tar.gz, which unpacks into a directory named myproj-1.0/ you will be adhering to a widely recognized standard, and people will know what to do without having to look at your README file.

Releasing

If you've done all the preparation work right, releasing is a simple matter of putting the new version online for downloading and announcing it in the appropriate forums. If the program is a popular one, you should make sure that the primary download server is able to handle the load or that mirror sites are available if it can't.

Sometimes a prerelease—also known as a "beta" release—is done when the program appears to be approaching stability but still has a few kinks to be worked out. Beta releases are usually considered safe but not necessarily stable (as opposed to earlier "alpha" releases, which by convention are neither safe nor stable, and are meant only for the hardiest testers and early adopters). It is normal for beta releases to be distributed with the word "beta" somewhere in the version number, as in "myproj-1.0-beta." The fact that they have already been through a testing cycle makes them palatable to the general public, some percentage of whom will usually download the beta version and start using it. Once bug reports from the beta have slowed down to a trickle, it's normal to give it an official blessing and remove the "beta" from the name.

Telling The World What Changed

Most free software packages contain a file named NEWS at the top level, summarizing the changes from the previous release. Normally, the NEWS file is kept up to date continuously as new features are added, so there should be no need to edit it when the release process starts. Nevertheless, sometimes people forget to mention their changes there, so it's a good idea to look it over before the release to see if anything important is missing.

The most recent portion of the NEWS file (the portion covering changes in the new release) is usually pasted into the release announcement that gets posted to mailing lists and newsgroups; that way people know before they download what improvements to expect. The format of NEWS files seems fairly standardized by now (see the one in the CVS distribution for a good example).

Recording The Release In CVS: Tags And Revision Numbers

You will definitely want to tag the CVS tree with some tag name, such as "Release_1_0," when the release is finally ready. This is so you can refer back to the released revisions later on, for example, when trying to reproduce bugs reported in the released version. Having a tag also gives people a way to retrieve or **diff** against a stable version of the software from their CVS working copies.

If you've incremented the major version number of the software, you might consider incrementing the major revision numbers of all the files in the project. Until now, all of the revision numbers we've used have been of the form "1.X." CVS provides a way to change the "1," but only in an upward direction (it is assumed that version numbers never move backwards):

```
floss$ pwd
/home/jrandom/myproj
floss$ cvs commit -m "upping major version number" -r 2.0
  ...
```

This will add a new Revision 2.0 to each file, and the contents of the new revision will be the same as those of the file's current highest revision (if any files in the working copy are not at the highest repository revision, the **commit** will complain and abort). Also, this command only works if all the files in the project are currently below Revision 2.0 (but that's probably the case, since the project has never crossed Release 2.0 before).

Running a **commit** with the **-r** flag does have the unexpected consequence of setting a sticky tag "2.0" on everything in the working copy, making further commits impossible. Afterward, you'll have to run **cvs update -A** or check out a new working copy if you want to continue working on the project.

Incrementing the revision numbers this way is entirely optional. There's no actual need for any relationship between the program's version number and the revision numbers of its files. It's just a convenience for reminding developers on which major version they're working at any given time.

Finding Out More

The best source for current release practices is to participate in, or observe, someone else's release. In this chapter, I've tried to cover the process in some detail, but of course there's no substitute for the real thing. If you are a developer on other projects, watch carefully how they handle their releases and make notes on what works and what doesn't. If you're managing your own release for the first time, just remember these main goals:

♦ During the release preparation period, avoid unnecessary changes to the code.

♦ Pamper your testers.

♦ Fix all the bugs you can find.

♦ Once the software is released, make it easy for people to find out what's new and get the software.

If everything you do is directed toward these goals, your release will go smoothly.

Chapter 8
Tips And Troubleshooting

When Things Go Wrong

I've said in earlier chapters that CVS is not "black box" software. Black boxes don't let you peek inside; they don't give you internal access so that you can fix (or break) things. The premise is that the black box usually doesn't need to be fixed. Most of the time, the software should work perfectly, so users don't need internal access. But when black boxes do fail, they tend to fail completely. Any problem at all is a showstopper, because there aren't many options for repair.

CVS is more like a perfectly transparent box—except without the box. Its moving parts are exposed directly to the environment, not hermetically sealed off, and bits of that environment (unexpected file permissions, interrupted commands, competing processes, whatever) can sometimes get inside the mechanism and gum up the gears. But even though CVS does not always work perfectly, it rarely fails completely, either. It has the advantage of graceful degradation; the degree to which it doesn't work is usually proportional to the number and severity of problems in its environment. If you know enough about what CVS is trying to do—and how it's trying to do it—you'll know what to do when things go wrong.

Although I can't list all of the problems that you might encounter, I've included some of the more common ones here. This chapter is divided into two sections: The first describes those parts of the environment to which CVS is most sensitive (mainly repository permissions and the working copy administrative area), and the second describes some of the most frequently encountered problems and their solutions. By seeing how to handle these common situations, you will get a feeling for how to approach any unexpected problem in CVS.

The Usual Suspects

As a CVS administrator (read "field doctor"), you will find that 90 percent of your users' problems are caused by inconsistent working copies, and the other 90 percent by incorrect repository permissions. Therefore, before looking at any specific situations, I'll give a quick overview of the working copy administrative area and review a few important things about repository permissions.

The Working Copy Administrative Area

You've already seen the basics of working copy structure in Chapter 2; in this section, we'll go into a bit more detail. Most of the details concern the files in the CVS/ administrative subdirectories. You already know about Entries, Root, and Repository, but the CVS/ subdirectory can also contain other files, depending on the circumstances. I'll describe those other files here, partly so they don't surprise you when you encounter them, and partly so you can fix them if they ever cause trouble.

CVS/Entries.Log

Sometimes, a file named "CVS/Entries.Log" will mysteriously appear. The sole purpose of this file is to temporarily cache minor changes to CVS/Entries, until some operation significant enough to be worth rewriting the entire Entries file comes along. CVS has no ability to edit the Entries file in place; it must read the entire file in and write it back out to make any change. To avoid this effort, CVS sometimes records small changes in Entries.Log, until the next time it needs to rewrite Entries.

The format of Entries.Log is like Entries, except for an extra letter at the beginning of each line. "A" means that the line is to be added to the main Entries file, and "R" means it is to be removed.

For the most part, you can ignore Entries.Log; it's rare that a human has to understand the information it contains. However, if you're reading over an Entries file to debug some problem in a working copy, you should also examine Entries.Log.

CVS/Entries.Backup

The CVS/Entries.Backup file is where CVS actually writes out a new Entries file, before renaming it to "Entries" (similar to the way it writes to temporary RCS files in the repository and then moves them to their proper name when they're complete). Because it becomes Entries when it's complete, you'll rarely see an Entries.Backup file; if you do see one, it probably means CVS got interrupted in the middle of some operation.

CVS/Entries.Static

If the CVS/Entries.Static file exists, it means that the entire directory has not been fetched from the repository. (When CVS knows a working directory is in an incomplete state, it will not bring additional files into that directory.)

The Entries.Static file is present during checkouts and updates and removed immediately when the operation is complete. If you see Entries.Static, it means that CVS was interrupted, and its presence prevents CVS from creating any new files in the working copy. (Often, running **cvs update -d** solves the problem and removes Entries.Static.)

Note

*The absence of Entries.Static does not necessarily imply that the working copy contains all of the project's files. Whenever a new directory is created in the project's repository, and someone updates their working copy without passing the **-d** flag to **update**, the new directory will not be created in the working copy. Locally, CVS is unaware that there is a new directory in the repository, so it goes ahead and removes the Entries.Static file when the update is complete, even though the new directory is not present in the working copy.*

CVS/Tag

If the CVS/Tag file is present, it names a tag associated, in some sense, with the directory. I say "in some sense" because, as you know, CVS does not actually keep any revision history for directories and, strictly speaking, cannot attach tags to them. Tags are attached to regular files only or, more accurately, to particular revisions in regular files.

However, if every file in a directory is on a particular tag, CVS likes to think of the entire directory as being on the tag, too. For example, if you were to check out a working copy on a particular branch:

```
floss$ cvs co -r Bugfix_Branch_1
```

and then add a file inside it, you'd want the new file's initial revision to be on that branch, too. For similar reasons, CVS also needs to know if the directory has a nonbranch sticky tag or date set on it.

Tag files contain one line. The first character on the line is a single-letter code telling what kind of tag it is, and the rest of the line is the tag's name. Currently, CVS uses only these three single-letter codes:

♦ *T*—A branch tag

♦ *N*—A nonbranch (regular) tag

♦ *D*—A sticky date, which occurs if a command such as

```
floss$ cvs checkout -D 1999-05-15 myproj
```

or

```
floss$ cvs update -D 1999-05-15 myproj
```

is run.

(If you see some other single-letter code, it just means that CVS has added a new tag type since this chapter was written.)

You should not remove the Tag file manually; instead, use **cvs update -A**.

Rarities

There are a few other files you may occasionally find in a CVS/ subdirectory:

♦ CVS/Checkin.prog, CVS/Update.prog

♦ CVS/Notify, CVS/Notify.tmp

♦ CVS/Base/, CVS/Baserev, CVS/Baserev.tmp

♦ CVS/Template

These files are usually not the cause of problems, so I'm just listing them (see Chapter 9 for their full descriptions).

Portability And Future Extension

As features are added to CVS, new files (not listed here) may appear in working copy administrative areas. As new files are added, they'll probably be documented in the Cederqvist manual, in the node "Working Directory Storage." You can also start looking in src/cvs.h in the source distribution, if you prefer to learn from code.

Finally, note that all CVS/* files—present and future—use whatever line-ending convention is appropriate for the working copy's local system (for example, LF for Unix or CRLF for Windows). This means that if you transport a working copy from one kind of machine to the other, CVS won't be able to handle it (but then, you'd have other problems, because the revision-controlled files themselves would have the wrong line-end conventions for their new location).

Repository Permissions

CVS does not require any particular repository permission scheme—it can handle a wide variety of permission arrangements. However, to avoid getting confusing behaviors, you should make sure your repository setup meets at least the following criteria:

♦ If a user wants any kind of access at all—even read-only access—to a given subdirectory of the repository, she usually needs file system-level write permission to that subdirectory. This is necessary because CVS creates temporary lock files in the repository to ensure data consistency. Even read-only operations (such as **checkout** or **update**) create locks, to signal that they need the data to stay in one state until they're done.

As noted in Chapter 4, you can get around this writeability requirement by setting the **LockDir** parameter in CVSROOT/config, like this:

```
LockDir=/usr/local/cvslocks
```

Of course, then you would need to make sure the directory /usr/local/cvslocks is writeable by all CVS users. Either way, most CVS operations, including read-only ones, are going to require a writeable directory somewhere. By default, that directory is the project's repository; if you're very security conscious, you can change it to be somewhere else.

◆ Make sure the CVSROOT/history file is world-writeable (if it exists at all). If the history file exists, most CVS operations attempt to append a record to it; if the attempt fails, the operation exits with an error.

Unfortunately (and inexplicably), the history file is not born world-writeable when you create a new repository with **cvs init**. At least with the current version of CVS, you should explicitly change its permissions after you create a new repository (or just remove it, if you want to disable history logging entirely).

Note

This problem may go away—I just now submitted a patch to the CVS maintainers that makes the history file world-writeable when you initialize a new repository. So perhaps if you get a more recent version of CVS than the one available now (September 1999), it won't be a problem for you.

◆ For security purposes, you almost certainly want to make sure that most CVS users do not have Unix-level write access to the CVSROOT directory in the repository. If someone has checkin access to CVSROOT, they can edit commitinfo, loginfo, or any of the other trigger files to invoke a program of their choice—they could even commit a new program if the one they want isn't on the system already. Therefore, you should assume that anyone who has commit access to CVSROOT is able to run arbitrary commands on the system.

Common Problems And How To Solve Them

The rest of this chapter is organized into a series of questions and answers, similar to an Internet FAQ (Frequently Asked Questions) document. These are all based on actual CVS experiences. But before we look at individual cases, let's take a moment to consider CVS troubleshooting from a more general point of view.

The first step in solving a CVS problem is usually to determine whether it's a working copy or repository problem. The best technique for doing that, not surprisingly, is to see if the problem occurs in working copies other than the one where it was first noticed. If it does, it's likely a repository issue; otherwise, it's probably just a local issue.

Working copy problems tend to be encountered more frequently, not because working copies are somehow less reliable than repositories, but because each repository usually has many working copies. Although most working copy knots can be untied with enough patience, you may occasionally find it more time-efficient simply to delete the working copy and check it out again.

Of course, if checking out again takes too long, or there is considerable uncommitted state in the working copy that you don't want to lose, or if you just want to know what's wrong, it's worth digging around to find the cause of the problem. When you start digging around, one of the first places to look is in the CVS/ subdirectories. Check the file contents and the file permissions. Very occasionally, the permissions can mysteriously become read-only or even unreadable. (I suspect this is caused by users accidentally mistyping Unix commands rather than any mistake on CVS's part.)

Repository problems are almost always caused by incorrect file and directory permissions. If you suspect a problem may be due to bad repository permissions, first find out the effective repository user ID of the person who's having the trouble. For all local and most remote users, this is either their regular username or the username they specified when they checked out their working copy. If they're using the pserver method with user-aliasing (see the section "The Password-Authenticating Server And Anonymous Access" in Chapter 4), the effective user ID is the one on the right in the CVSROOT/passwd file. Failure to discover this early on can cause you to waste a lot of time debugging the wrong thing.

And now, without further ado...

Some Real Life Problems, With Solutions

All of these situations are ones I've encountered in my real-life adventures as a CVS trouble-shooter (plus a couple of items that are not really problems, just questions that I've heard asked so often that they may as well be answered here). The list is meant to be fairly comprehensive, and it may repeat material you've seen in earlier chapters.

The situations are listed according to how frequently they seem to arise, with the most common ones first.

I Keep Getting Messages About Waiting For Locks. What's Going On?

If you see a message like this

```
cvs update: [22:58:26] waiting for qsmith's lock in /usr/local/newrepos/myproj
```

it means you're trying to access a subdirectory of the repository that is locked by some other CVS process at the moment. A process is being run in that directory so it may not be in a consistent state for other CVS processes to use.

However, if the **wait** message persists for a long time, it probably means that a CVS process failed to clean up after itself, for whatever reason. It can happen when CVS dies suddenly and unexpectedly, say, due to a power failure on the repository machine.

The solution is to remove the lock files by hand from the repository subdirectory in question. Go into that part of the repository and look for files named "#cvs.lock" or that begin with "#cvs.wfl" or "#cvs.rfl". Compare the file's timestamps with the start times of any currently running CVS processes. If the files could not possibly have been created by any of those processes, it's safe to delete them. The waiting CVS processes eventually notice when the lock files are gone—this should take about 30 seconds—and allow the requested operation to proceed.

See the node "Locks" in the Cederqvist manual for more details.

CVS Claims A File Is Failing Up-To-Date Check. What Do I Do?

Don't panic—it just means that the file has changed in the repository since the last time you checked it out or updated it.

Run **cvs update** on the file to merge in the changes from the repository. If the received changes conflict with your local changes, edit the file to resolve the conflict. Then try your **commit** again—it will succeed, barring the possibility that someone committed yet another revision while you were busy merging the last changes.

I Can't Seem To Get The Pserver Access Method To Work.

The most common, less obvious cause of this problem is that you forgot to list the repository using an – –allow-root option in your inetd configuration file.

Recall this example /etc/inetd.conf line from Chapter 4:

```
cvspserver stream tcp nowait root /usr/local/bin/cvs cvs \
        --allow-root=/usr/local/newrepos pserver
```

(In the actual file, this is all one long line, with no backslash.)

The – –allow-root=/usr/local/newrepos portion is a security measure, to make sure that people can't use CVS to get pserver access to repositories that are not supposed to be served remotely. Any repository intended to be accessible via pserver must be mentioned in an – –allow-root. You can have as many different – –allow-root options as you need for all of your system's repositories (or anyway, as many as you want until you bump up against your inetd's argument limit).

See Chapter 4 for more details on setting up the password-authenticating server.

The Pserver Access Method STILL Isn't Working!

Okay, if the problem is not a missing – –allow-root, here are a few other possibilities:

♦ The user has no entry in the CVSROOT/passwd file, and the CVSROOT/config file has **SystemAuth=no** so CVS will not fall back on the system password file (or **SystemAuth=yes**, but the system password file has no entry for this user either).

- The user has an entry in the CVSROOT/passwd file, but there is no user by that name on the system, and the CVSROOT/passwd entry does not map the user to any valid system username.

- The password is wrong (but CVS is usually pretty good about informing the user of this, so that's probably not the answer).

- Everything is set up correctly with the passwd files and in /etc/inetd.conf, but you forgot an entry like this in /etc/services:

```
cvspserver       2401/tcp
```

so inetd is not even listening on that port to pass connections off to CVS.

My Commits Seem To Happen In Pieces, Not Atomically.

That's because CVS commits happen in pieces, not atomically. More specifically, CVS operations happen directory by directory. When you do a **commit** (or an **update**, or anything else, for that matter) spanning multiple directories, CVS locks each corresponding repository directory in turn while it performs the operation for that directory.

For small- to medium-sized projects, this is rarely a problem—CVS manages to do its thing in each directory so quickly that you never notice the nonatomicity. Unfortunately, in large projects, scenarios like the following can occur (imagine this taking place in a project with at least two deep, many-filed subdirectories, A and B):

1. User qsmith starts a **commit**, involving files from both subdirectories. CVS commits the files in B first (perhaps because qsmith specified the directories on the command line in that order).

2. User jrandom starts a **cvs update**. The update, for whatever reason, starts with working copy directory A (CVS makes no guarantees about the order in which it processes directories or files, if left to its own devices). Note that there is no locking contention, because qsmith is not active in A yet.

3. Then, qsmith's **commit** finishes B, moves on to A, and finishes A.

4. Finally, jrandom's **update** moves on to B and finishes it.

Clearly, when this is all over, jrandom's working copy reflects qsmith's changes to B but not A. Even though qsmith intended the changes to be committed as a single unit, it didn't happen that way. Now jrandom's working copy is in a state that qsmith never anticipated.

The solution, of course, is for jrandom to do another **cvs update** to fetch the uncaught changes from qsmith's commit. However, that assumes that jrandom has some way of finding out in the first place that he only got part of qsmith's changes.

There's no easy answer to this quandary. You simply have to hope that the inconsistent state of the working copy will somehow become apparent (maybe the software won't build, or jrandom and qsmith will have a conversation that's confusing until they realize what must have happened).

CVS's failure to provide "atomic" transaction guarantees is widely considered a bug. The only reason that locks are not made at the top level of the repository is that this would result in intolerably frequent lock contentions for large projects with many developers. Therefore, CVS has chosen the lesser of two evils, reducing the contention frequency but allowing the possibility of interleaved reads and writes. Someday, someone may modify CVS (say, speeding up repository operations) so that it doesn't have to choose between two evils; until then, we're stuck with nonatomic actions.

For more information, see the node "Concurrency" in the Cederqvist manual.

CVS Keeps Changing The Permissions Of My Files. Why Does It Do That?

In general, CVS doesn't do a very good job of preserving permissions on files. When you import a project and then check it out, there is no guarantee that the file permissions in the new working copy will be the same as when the project was imported. More likely, the working copy files will be created with the same standard permissions that you normally get on newly created files.

However, there is at least one exception. If you want to store executable shell scripts in the project, you can keep them executable in all working copies by making the corresponding repository file executable:

```
floss$ ls -l /usr/local/newrepos/someproj
total 6
-r--r--r--   1 jrandom  users          630 Aug 17 01:10 README.txt,v
-r-xr-xr-x   1 jrandom  users         1041 Aug 17 01:10 scrub.pl,v*
-r--r--r--   1 jrandom  users          750 Aug 17 01:10 hello.c,v
```

Notice that although the file is executable, it is still read-only, as all repository files should be (remember that CVS works by making a temporary copy of the RCS file, doing everything in the copy, and then replacing the original with the copy when ready).

When you import or add an executable file, CVS preserves the executable bits, so if the permissions were correct from the start, you have nothing to worry about. However, if you accidentally add the file before making it executable, you must go into the repository and manually set the RCS file to be executable.

Note

The repository permissions always dominate. If the file is nonexecutable in the repository, but executable in the working copy, the working copy file will also be nonexecutable after you do an update. Having your files' permissions silently change can be extremely frustrating. If this happens, first check the repository and see if you can solve it by setting the appropriate permissions on the corresponding RCS files.

A feature called "PreservePermissions" has recently been added to CVS that may alleviate some of these problems. However, using this feature can cause other unexpected results (which is why I'm not recommending it unconditionally here). Make sure you read the nodes "config" and "Special Files" in the Cederqvist before putting **PreservePermissions=yes** in CVSROOT/config.

CVS On Windows Complains It Can't Find My .cvspass File. Why?

For pserver connections, CVS on the client side tries to find the .cvspass file in your home directory. Windows machines don't have a natural "home" directory, so CVS consults the environment variable %HOME%. However, you have to be very careful about how you set **HOME**. This will work:

```
set HOME=C:
```

This will not:

```
set HOME=C:\
```

That final backslash is enough to confuse CVS, and it will be unable to open C:\.cvspass.

So, the quick and permanent solution is to put

```
set HOME=C:
```

into your autoexec.bat and reboot. CVS pserver should work fine after that.

My Working Copy Is On Several Different Branches. Help!

You mean different subdirectories of your working copy somehow got on different branches? You probably ran updates with the **-r** flag, but from places other than the top level of the working copy.

No big deal. If you want to return to the trunk, just run this

```
cvs update -r HEAD
```

or this

```
cvs update -A
```

from the top directory. Or, if you want to put the whole working copy on one of the branches, do this:

```
cvs update -r Branch_Name
```

There's nothing necessarily wrong with having one or two subdirectories of your working copy on a different branch than the rest of it, if you need to do some temporary work on that branch just in those locations. However, it's usually a good idea to switch them back when you're done—life is much less confusing when your whole working copy is on the same line of development.

When I Do An Export -D, It Sometimes Seems To Miss Recent Commits!

This is due to a clock difference between the repository and local machines. You can solve it by resetting one or both of the clocks, or specifying a different date as the argument to **-D**. It's perfectly acceptable to specify a date in the future (such as **-D tomorrow**), if that's what it takes to compensate for the time difference.

I Can't Export -r, Something About "val-tags." What's Going On?

See the next question.

Tag Operations Fail, Something About "val-tags." What's Going On?

If you see an error like this:

```
cvs [export aborted]: cannot write /usr/local/myproj/CVSROOT/val-tags: \
   Operation not permitted
```

it means the user CVS is running as does not have permission to write to the CVSROOT/val-tags file. This file stores valid tag names, to give CVS a fast way to determine what tags are valid. Unfortunately, CVS sometimes modifies this file even for operations that are read-only with respect to the repository, such as checking out a project.

This is a bug in CVS and may be fixed by the time you read this. Until then, the solution is either to make val-tags world-writeable or, failing that, to remove it or change its ownership to the user running the CVS operation. (You'd think just changing the permissions would be enough, but on several occasions I've had to change the ownership, too.)

I'm Having Problems With Sticky Tags; I Just Want To Get Rid Of Them.

Various CVS operations cause the working copy to have a "sticky tag," meaning a single tag that corresponds to each revision for each file (in the case of a branch, the sticky tag is applied to any new files added in the working copy). You get a sticky tagged working area whenever you check out or update by tag or date, for example:

```
floss$ cvs update -r Tag_Name
```

or

```
floss$ cvs checkout -D "1999-08-16"
```

If a date or a nonbranch tag name is used, the working copy will be a frozen snapshot of that moment in the project's history—so naturally you will not be able to commit any changes from it.

To remove a sticky tag, run **update** with the **-A** flag

```
floss$ cvs update -A
```

which clears all the sticky tags and updates each file to its most recent trunk revision.

CVS Checkout/Update Exits With Error, Saying It Cannot Expand Modules.

This is just a case of a bad error message in CVS; probably someone will get around to fixing it sooner or later, but meanwhile it may bite you.

The error message looks something like this:

```
floss$ cvs co -d bwf-misc user-space/bwf/writings/misc
cvs server: cannot find module 'user-space/bwf/writings/misc' - ignored
cvs [checkout aborted]: cannot expand modules
```

CVS appears to be saying that there's something wrong with the CVSROOT/modules file. However, what's really going on is a permission problem in the repository. The directory I'm trying to check out isn't readable, or one of its parents isn't readable. In this case, it was a parent:

```
floss$ ls -ld /usr/local/cvs/user-space/bwf

drwx------  19 bwf      users      1024 Aug 17 01:24 bwf/
```

Don't let that egregiously wrong error message fool you—this is a repository permission problem.

I Can't Seem To Turn Off Watches!

You probably did

```
floss$ cvs watch remove
```

on all the files, but forgot to also do:

```
floss$ cvs watch off
```

A hint for diagnosing watch problems: Sometimes it can be immensely clarifying to just go into the repository and examine the CVS/fileattr files directly. See Chapter 4 for more information about them.

My Binary Files Are Messed Up.

Did you remember to use **-kb** when you added them? If not, CVS may have performed line-end conversion or RCS keyword substitution on them. The easiest solution is usually to mark them as binary

```
floss$ cvs admin -kb foo.gif
```

and then commit a fixed version of the file. CVS will not corrupt the new commit or any of the commits thereafter, because it now knows the file is binary.

CVS Isn't Doing Line-End Conversion Correctly.

If you're running the CVS client on a non-Unix platform and are not getting the line-end conventions that you want in some working copy files, it's usually because they were accidentally added with **-kb** when they shouldn't have been. This can be fixed in the repository with, believe it or not, the command:

```
floss$ cvs admin -kkv FILE
```

The **-kkv** means to do normal keyword substitution and implies normal line-end conversions as well. (Internally, CVS is a bit confused about the difference between keyword substitution and line-end conversion. This confusion is reflected in the way the **-k** options can control both parameters.)

Unfortunately, that **admin** command only fixes the file in the repository—your working copy still thinks the file is binary. You can hand edit the **CVS/Entries** line for that file, removing the **-kb**, but that won't solve the problem for any other working copies out there.

I Need To Remove A Subdirectory In My Project. How Do I Do It?

Well, you can't exactly remove the subdirectory, but you can remove all of the files in it (first remove them, then **cvs remove** them, and then **commit**). Once the directory is empty, people can have it automatically pruned out of their working copies by passing the **-P** flag to **update**.

Can I Copy .cvspass Files Or Portions Of Them?

Yes, you can. You can copy .cvspass files from machine to machine, and you can even copy individual lines from one .cvspass file to another. For high-latency servers, this may be faster than running **cvs login** from each working copy machine.

Remember that if you transport a .cvspass file between two machines with different line-ending conventions, it probably won't work (of course, you can probably do the line-end conversion manually without too much trouble).

I Just Committed Some Files With The Wrong Log Message.

You don't need to hand-edit anything in the repository to solve this. Just run **admin** with the **-m** flag. Remember to have no space between **-m** and its argument, and to quote the replacement log message as you would a normal one:

```
floss$ cvs admin -m1.17:"I take back what I said about the customer." hello.c
```

I Need To Move Files Around Without Losing Revision History.

In the repository, copy (don't move) the RCS files to the desired new location in the project. They must remain in their old locations as well.

Then, in a working copy, do:

```
floss$ rm oldfile1 oldfile2 ...
floss$ cvs remove oldfile1 oldfile2 ...
floss$ cvs commit -m "removed from here" oldfile1 oldfile2 ...
```

When people do updates after that, CVS correctly removes the old files and brings the new files into the working copies just as though they had been added to the repository in the usual way (except that they'll be at unusually high revision numbers for supposedly new files).

How Can I Get A List Of All Tags In A Project?

Currently, there is no convenient way to do this in CVS. The lack is sorely felt by all users, and I believe work is under way to make this feature available. By the time you read this, a **cvs tags** command or something similar may be available.

Until then, there are workarounds. You can run **cvs log -h** and read the sections of the output following the header **symbolic names:**. Or, if you happen to be on the repository machine, you can just look at the beginnings of some of the RCS files directly in the repository. All of the tags (branches and nonbranches) are listed in the **symbols** field:

```
floss$ head /usr/local/newrepos/hello.c,v
head        2.0;
access;
symbols
    Release_1_0:1.22
    Exotic_Greetings-2:1.21
    merged-Exotic_Greetings-1:1.21
    Exotic_Greetings-1:1.21
    merged-Exotic_Greetings:1.21
    Exotic_Greetings-branch:1.21.0.2
    Root-of-Exotic_Greetings:1.21
    start:1.1.1.1
    jrandom:1.1.1;
locks; strict;
comment     @ * @;
```

How Can I Get A List Of All Projects In A Repository?

As with getting a list of tags, this is not implemented in the most current version of CVS, but it's highly likely that it will be implemented soon. I imagine the command will be called **cvs list** with a short form of **cvs ls**, and it probably will both parse the modules file and list the repository subdirectories.

In the meantime, examining the CVSROOT/modules file (either directly or by running **cvs checkout -c**) is probably your best bet. However, if no one has explicitly made a module for a particular project, it won't show up there.

Some Commands Fail Remotely But Not Locally. How Should I Debug?

Sometimes there's a problem in the communication between the client and the server. If so, it's a bug in CVS, but how would you go about tracking down such a thing?

CVS gives you a way to watch the protocol between the client and server. Before you run the command on the local (working copy) machine, set the environment variable **CVS_ CLIENT_LOG**. Here's how in Bourne shell syntax:

```
floss$ CVS_CLIENT_LOG=clog; export CVS_CLIENT_LOG
```

Once that variable is set, CVS will record all communications between client and server in two files whose names are based on the variable's value:

```
floss$ ls
CVS/          README.txt    a-subdir/    b-subdir/    foo.gif      hello.c
floss$ cvs update
? clog.in
? clog.out
cvs server: Updating .
cvs server: Updating a-subdir
cvs server: Updating a-subdir/subsubdir
cvs server: Updating b-subdir
floss$ ls
CVS/              a-subdir/    clog.in      foo.gif
README.txt        b-subdir/    clog.out     hello.c
floss$
```

The clog.in file contains everything that the client sent into the server, and clog.out contains everything the server sent back out to the client. Here are the contents of clog.out, to give you a sense of what the protocol looks like:

```
Valid-requests Root Valid-responses valid-requests Repository         \
Directory Max-dotdot Static-directory Sticky Checkin-prog Update-prog \
Entry Kopt Checkin-time Modified Is-modified UseUnchanged Unchanged   \
Notify Questionable Case Argument Argumentx Global_option Gzip-stream \
wrapper-sendme-rcsOptions Set expand-modules ci co update diff log add \
```

```
remove update-patches gzip-file-contents status rdiff tag rtag import   \
admin export history release watch-on watch-off watch-add watch-remove   \
watchers editors init annotate noop
ok
M ? clog.in
M ? clog.out
E cvs server: Updating .
E cvs server: Updating a-subdir
E cvs server: Updating a-subdir/subsubdir
E cvs server: Updating b-subdir
ok
```

The clog.in file is even more complex, because it has to send revision numbers and other per-file information to the server.

There isn't space here to document the client/server protocol, but you can read the "cvsclient" information pages that were distributed with CVS for a complete description. You may be able to figure out a good deal of it just from reading the raw protocol itself. Although you probably won't find yourself using client logging until you've eliminated all of the other possible causes of a problem, it is an invaluable tool for finding out what's really going on between the client and server.

I Don't See My Problem Covered In This Chapter.

Email an accurate and complete description of your problem to **info-cvs@gnu.org**, the CVS discussion list. Its members are located in many different time zones, and I've usually gotten a response within an hour or two of sending a question. Please join the list by sending email to **info-cvs-request@gnu.org**, so you can help answer questions, too.

I Think I've Discovered A Bug In CVS. What Do I Do?

CVS is far from perfect—if you've already tried reading the manual and posting a question on the mailing list, and you still think you're looking at a bug, then you probably are.

Send as complete a description of the bug as you can to **bug-cvs@gnu.org** (you can also subscribe to that list; just use **bug-cvs-request** instead). Be sure to include the version number of CVS (both client and server versions, if applicable), and a recipe for reproducing the bug.

If you have written a patch to fix the bug, include it and mention on the subject line of your message that you have a patch. The maintainers will be very grateful.

(Further details about these procedures are outlined in the node "BUGS" in the Cederqvist manual and the file HACKING in the source distribution.)

I've Implemented A New Feature In CVS. To Whom Do I Send It?

Same as with a bug: Send the patch to **bug-cvs@gnu.org**. Make sure you've read over the HACKING file first, though.

Things Change

The troubleshooting techniques and known bugs described in this chapter are accurate as of (approximately) CVS Version 1.10.7. Things move fast in the CVS world, however. While I was writing the last few chapters, the unofficial mantle of CVS maintainership passed from Cyclic Software to SourceGear, Inc (**www.sourcegear.com**), which purchased Cyclic. SourceGear has publicly announced its intention to take an active role in CVS maintainership and has received Cyclic's approval, which is more or less enough to make it the "lead maintainer" of CVS as of right now. (The **www.cyclic.com** address will continue to work, however, so all of the URLs given previously in this book should remain valid.)

SourceGear is, at this very moment, busy organizing and cleaning up various patches that have been floating around, with the intention of incorporating many of them into CVS. Some of these patches will probably fix bugs listed previously, and others may afford new troubleshooting tools to CVS users.

The best way to stay up to date with what's going on is to read the NEWS file in your CVS distribution, watch the mailing lists, and look for changes to the Cederqvist manual and the online version of some of the chapters of this book.

## Chapter 9

Complete CVS Reference

Organization And Conventions

This chapter is a complete reference to CVS commands, repository administrative files, keyword substitution, run control files, working copy files, and environment variables—everything in CVS as of CVS version 1.10.7 (more accurately, as of August 20, 1999).

The commands are the most important part of any CVS reference, so we'll start there.

Commands

This section is organized alphabetically to make it easy for you to look up a particular command or option. The following conventions are used:

♦ Arguments to commands and options are in all-capitalized letters and are italicized in the synopsis that begins each explanation.

♦ Optional items appear between square brackets: [ ].

♦ If you must choose one from a set, the choices are separated by bars, like this: "x | y | z."

♦ Plurals or ellipses indicate multiples, usually separated by whitespace. For example, *FILES* means one or more files, but [*FILES*] means zero or more files. The entry [&*MOD*...] means an ampersand followed immediately by a module name, then whitespace, then maybe another ampersand-module, and so on, zero or more times. (The ellipsis is used because a plural would have left it unclear whether the ampersand is needed only the first time or once for each module.)

When a plural is parenthesized, as in *FILE(S)*, it means that although technically there can be two or more files, usually there is only one.

♦ *REV* is often used to stand for a revision argument. This is usually either a revision number or a tag name. There are very few places in CVS where you can use one but not the other, and those places are noted in the text.

General Patterns In CVS Commands

CVS commands follow this form:

```
cvs [GLOBAL_OPTIONS] COMMAND [OPTIONS] [FILES]
```

The second set of options is sometimes called "command options." Because there are so many of them, though, I'll just call them "options" in most places to save space.

Many commands are meant to be run within a working copy and, therefore, may be invoked without file arguments. These commands default to all of the files in the current directory and below. So when I refer to the "file" or "files" in the text, I'm talking about the files on which CVS is acting. Depending on how you invoked CVS, these files may or may not have been explicitly mentioned on the command line.

Date Formats

Many options take a date argument. CVS accepts a wide variety of date formats—too many to list here. When in doubt, stick with the standard ISO 8601 format:

```
1999-08-23
```

This means "23 August 1999" (in fact, "23 August 1999" is a perfectly valid date specifier too, as long as you remember to enclose it in double quotes). If you need a time of day as well, you can do this:

```
"1999-08-23 21:20:30 CDT"
```

You can even use certain common English constructs, such as "now," "yesterday," and "12 days ago." In general, you can safely experiment with date formats; if CVS understands your format at all, it most likely will understand it in the way you intended. If it doesn't understand, it will exit with an error immediately.

Global Options

Here are all the global options to CVS.

--allow-root=REPOSITORY

The alphabetically first global option is one that is virtually never used on the command line. The – **–allow-root** option is used with the **pserver** command to allow authenticated access to the named repository (which is a repository top level, such as /usr/local/newrepos, not a project subdirectory such as /usr/local/newrepos/myproj).

This global option is virtually never used on the command line. Normally, the only place you'd ever use it is in /etc/inetd.conf files (see Chapter 4), which is also about the only place the **pserver** command is used.

Every repository to be accessed via **cvs pserver** on a given host needs a corresponding – –**allow-root** option in /etc/inetd.conf. This is a security device, meant to ensure that people can't use a CVS pserver to gain access to private repositories.

(See also the node "Password Authentication Server" in the Cederqvist manual.)

-a

This authenticates all communications with the server. This option has no effect unless you're connecting via the GSSAPI server (gserver). GSSAPI connections are not covered in this book, because they're still somewhat rarely used (although that may change). (See the nodes "Global Options" and "GSSAPI Authenticated" in the Cederqvist manual for more information.)

-b (Obsolete)

This option formerly specified the directory where the RCS binaries could be found. CVS now implements the RCS functions internally, so this option has no effect (it is kept only for backward compatibility).

-d REPOSITORY

This specifies the repository, which might be an absolute pathname or a more complex expression involving a connection method, username and host, and path. If it is an expression specifying a connection method, the general syntax is:

`:METHOD:USER@HOSTNAME:PATH_TO_REPOSITORY`

Here are examples using each of the connection methods:

- **:ext:jrandom@floss.red-bean.com:/usr/local/newrepos**—Connects using rsh, ssh, or some other external connection program. If the **CVS_RSH** environment variable is unset, this defaults to "rsh"; otherwise, it uses the value of that variable.

- **:server:jrandom@floss.red-bean.com:/usr/local/newrepos**—Like **:ext:**, but uses CVS's internal implementation of rsh. (This may not be available on all platforms.)

- **:pserver:jrandom@floss.red-bean.com:/usr/local/newrepos**—Connects using the password authenticating server (see "The Password-Authenticating Server" in Chapter 4; see also the **login** command.)

- **:kserver:jrandom@floss.red-bean.com:/usr/local/newrepos**—Connects using Kerberos authentication.

- **:gserver:jrandom@floss.red-bean.com:/usr/local/newrepos**—Connects using GSSAPI authentication.

- **:fork:jrandom@floss.red-bean.com:/usr/local/newrepos**—Connects to a local repository, but using the client/server network protocol instead of directly accessing the repository files. This is useful for testing or debugging remote CVS behaviors from your local machine.

- **:local:jrandom@floss.red-bean.com:/usr/local/newrepos**—Accesses a local repository directly, as though only the absolute path to the repository had been given.

-e EDITOR

Invokes **EDITOR** for your commit message, if the commit message was not specified on the command line with the **-m** option. Normally, if you don't give a message with **-m**, CVS invokes the editor based on the **CVSEDITOR**, **VISUAL**, or **EDITOR**, which it checks in that order. Failing that, it invokes the popular Unix editor vi.

If you pass both the **-e** global option and the **-m** option to **commit**, the **-e** is ignored in favor of the commit message given on the command line (that way it's safe to use **-e** in a .cvsrc file).

-f

This global option suppresses reading of the .cvsrc file.

--help [COMMAND] -H [COMMAND]

These two options are synonymous. If no **COMMAND** is specified, a basic usage message is printed to the standard output. If **COMMAND** is specified, a usage message for that command is printed.

--help-options

Prints out a list of all global options to CVS, with brief explanations.

--help-synonyms

Prints out a list of CVS commands and their short forms ("up" for "update," and so on).

-l

Suppresses logging of this command in the CVSROOT/history file in the repository. The command is still executed normally, but no record of it is made in the history file.

-n

Doesn't change any files in the working copy or in the repository. In other words, the command is executed as a "dry run"—CVS goes through most of the steps of the command but stops short of actually running it.

This is useful when you want to see what the command would have done had you actually run it. One common scenario is when you want to see what files in your working directory have been modified, but not do a full update (which would bring down changes from the repository). By running **cvs -n update**, you can see a summary of what's been done locally, without changing your working copy.

-q

This tells CVS to be moderately quiet by suppressing the printing of unimportant informational messages. What is considered "important" depends on the command. For example, in updates, the messages that CVS normally prints on entering each subdirectory of the working copy are suppressed, but the one-line status messages for modified or updated files are still printed.

-Q

This tells CVS to be very quiet, by suppressing all output except what is absolutely necessary to complete the command. Commands whose sole purpose is to produce some output (such as **diff** or **annotate**), of course, still give that output. However, commands that could have an effect independent of any messages that they may print (such as **update** or **commit**) print nothing.

-r

Causes new working files to be created read-only (the same effect as setting the **CVSREAD** environment variable).

If you pass this option, checkouts and updates make the files in your working copy read-only (assuming your operating system permits it). Frankly, I'm not sure why one would ever want to use this option.

-s VARIABLE=VALUE

This sets an internal CVS variable named **VARIABLE** to **VALUE**.

On the repository side, the CVSROOT/*info trigger files can expand such variables to values that were assigned in the **-s** option. For example, if CVSROOT/loginfo contains a line like this

```
myproj   /usr/local/bin/foo.pl ${=FISH}
```

and someone runs a **commit** from a myproj working copy like this

```
floss$ cvs -s FISH=carp commit -m "fixed the bait bug"
```

the foo.pl script is invoked with **carp** as an argument. Note the funky syntax, though: The dollar sign, equal sign, and curly braces are all necessary—if any of them are missing, the expansion will not take place (at least not as intended). Variable names may contain alpha-numerics and underscores only. Although it is not required that they consist entirely of capital letters, most people do seem to follow that convention.

You can use the **-s** flag as many times as you like in a single command. However, if the trigger script refers to variables that aren't set in a particular invocation of CVS, the command still succeeds, but none of the variables are expanded, and the user sees a warning. For example, if loginfo has this

```
myproj  /usr/local/bin/foo.pl  ${=FISH}  ${=BIRD}
```

but the same command as before is run

```
floss$ cvs -s FISH=carp commit -m "fixed the bait bug"
```

the person running the command sees a warning something like this (placed last in the output)

```
loginfo:31: no such user variable ${=BIRD}
```

and the foo.pl script is invoked with no arguments. But if this command were run

```
floss$ cvs -s FISH=carp -s BIRD=vulture commit -m "fixed the bait bug"
```

there would be no warning, and both **${=FISH}** and **${=BIRD}** in loginfo would be correctly expanded. In either case, the commit itself would still succeed.

Note

*Although these examples all use **commit**, variable expansion can be done with any CVS command that can be noticed in a CVSROOT/ trigger file—which is why the **-s** option is global.*

(See the section "Repository Administrative Files" later in this chapter for more details about variable expansion in trigger files.)

-T DIR

Stores any temporary files in **DIR** instead of wherever CVS normally puts them (specifically, this overrides the value of the **TMPDIR** environment variable, if any exists). **DIR** should be an absolute path.

This option is useful when you don't have write permission (and, therefore, CVS doesn't either) to the usual temporary locations.

-t

Traces the execution of a CVS command. This causes CVS to print messages showing the steps that it's going through to complete a command. You may find it particularly useful in conjunction with **-n** to preview the effects of an unfamiliar command before running it for real. It can also be handy when you're trying to discover why a command failed.

-v --version

Causes CVS to print out its version and copyright information and then exit with no error.

-w

Causes new working files to be created read-write (overrides any setting of the **CVSREAD** environment variable). Because files are created read-write by default anyway, this option is rarely used.

If both **-r** and **-w** are passed, **-w** dominates.

-x

Encrypts all communications with the server. This option has no effect unless you're connecting via the GSSAPI server (gserver). GSSAPI connections are not covered in this book, because they're still somewhat rarely used (although that may change). (See the nodes "Global Options" and "GSSAPI Authenticated" in the Cederqvist manual for more information.)

-z GZIPLEVEL

Sets the compression level on communications with the server. The argument *GZIPLEVEL* must be a number from 1 to 9. Level 1 is minimal compression (very fast, but doesn't compress much); Level 9 is highest compression (uses a lot of CPU time, but sure does squeeze the data). Level 9 is only useful on very slow network connections. Most people find levels between 3 and 5 to be most beneficial.

A space between **-z** and its argument is optional.

List Of Commands

Following is a list of all the CVS commands.

add [OPTIONS] FILES

- *Alternate names*—**ad**, **new**
- *Requires*—Working copy, repository
- *Changes*—Working copy

Adds a new file or files to an existing project. Although the repository is contacted for confirmation, the file does not actually appear in it until a subsequent **commit** is performed. (See also "remove" and "import.")

Options:

♦ **-kKEYWORD_SUBSTITUTION_MODE**—Specifies that the file is to be stored with the given RCS keyword substitution mode. There is no space between the **-k** and its argument. (See the section "Keyword Substitution" later in this chapter for a list of valid modes and examples.)

♦ **-m MESSAGE**—Records **MESSAGE** as the creation message, or description, for the file. This is different from a per-revision log message—each file has only one description. Descriptions are optional.

Note

*As of version 1.10.7, there is a bug in CVS whereby the description is lost if you add a file via client/server CVS. The rest of the **add** process seems to work fine, however, if that's any comfort.*

admin [OPTIONS] [FILES]

♦ *Alternate names*—**adm, rcs**

♦ *Requires*—Working copy, repository

♦ *Changes*—Repository

This command is an interface to various administrative tasks—specifically, tasks applicable to individual RCS files in the repository, such as changing a file's keyword substitution mode or changing a log message after it's been committed.

Although **admin** behaves recursively if no files are given as arguments, you normally will want to name files explicitly. It's very rare for a single **admin** command to be meaningful when applied to all files in a project, or even in a directory. Accordingly, when the following explanations refer to the "file," they mean the file or (rarely) files passed as arguments to the **admin** command.

Note

*If there is a system group named "cvsadmin" on the repository machine, only members of that group can run **admin** (with the exception of the **cvs admin -k** command, which is always permitted). Thus you can disallow **admin** for all users by setting the group to have no users.*

Options:

♦ **-AOLDFILE**—(Obsolete) Appends the RCS access list of **OLDFILE** to the access list of the file that is the argument to **admin**. CVS ignores RCS access lists, so this option is useless.

♦ **-a USER1 [,USER2...]**—(Obsolete) Appends the users in the comma-separated list to the access list of the file. Like **-A**, this option is useless in CVS.

♦ **-bREV**—Sets the revision of the file's default branch (usually the trunk) to **REV**. You won't normally need this option, because you can usually get the revisions you need via sticky tags, but you may use it to revert to a vendor's version if you're using vendor branches. There should be no space between the **-b** and its argument.

♦ **-cCOMMENT_PREFIX**—(Obsolete) Sets the comment leader of the file to **COMMENT_PREFIX**. The comment leader is not used by CVS or even by recent versions of RCS; therefore, this option is useless and is included only for backward-compatibility.

♦ **-eUSER1[,USER2...]**—(Obsolete) Removes the usernames appearing in the comma-separated list from the access list of the RCS file. Like **-a** and **-A**, this option is now useless in CVS.

♦ **-i** or **-I**—These two are so obsolete I'm not even going to tell you what they used to do. (See the Cederqvist manual if you're curious.)

♦ **-kMODE**—Sets the file's default keyword substitution mode to **MODE**. This option behaves like the **-k** option to add, only it gives you a way to change a file's mode after it's been added. (See the section "Keyword Substitution" later in this chapter for valid modes.) There should be no space between **-k** and its argument.

♦ **-L**—Sets locking to "strict." (See **-l**.)

♦ **-l[REV]**—Locks the file's revision to **REV**. If **REV** is omitted, it locks the latest revision on the default branch (usually the trunk). If **REV** is a branch, it locks the latest revision on that branch.

The intent of this option is to give you a way to do "reserved checkouts," where only one user can be editing the file at a time. I'm not sure how useful this really is, but if you want to try it, you should probably do so in conjunction with the rcslock.pl script in the CVS source distribution's contrib/ directory. See comments in that file for further information. Among other things, those comments indicate that the locking must be set to "strict." (See **-L**.) There is no space between **-l** and its argument.

♦ **-mREV:MESSAGE**—Changes the log message for revision **REV** to **MESSAGE**. Very handy—along with **-k**, this is probably the most frequently used **admin** option. There are no spaces between option and arguments or around the colon between the two arguments. Of course, **MESSAGE** may contain spaces within itself (in which case, remember to surround it with quotes so the shell knows it's all one thing).

♦ **-NNAME[:[REV]]**—Just like **-n**, except it forces the override of any existing assignment of the symbolic name **NAME**, instead of exiting with error.

♦ **-nNAME[:[REV]]**—This is a generic interface to assigning, renaming, and deleting tags. There is no reason, as far as I can see, to prefer it to the **tag** command and the various options available there (**-d**, **-r**, **-b**, **-f**, and so on). I recommend using the **tag** command instead. The **NAME** and optional **REV** can be combined in the following ways:

♦ If only the **NAME** argument is given, the symbolic name (tag) named **NAME** is deleted.

♦ If **NAME:** is given but no **REV**, **NAME** is assigned to the latest revision on the default branch (usually the trunk).

♦ If **NAME:REV** is given, **NAME** is assigned to that revision. **REV** can be a symbolic name itself, in which case it is translated to a revision number first (can be a branch number).

♦ If **REV** is a branch number and is followed by a period ("."), **NAME** is attached to the highest revision on that branch. If **REV** is just $, **NAME** is attached to revision numbers found in keyword strings in the working files.

In all cases where a **NAME** is assigned, CVS exits with an error if there is already a tag named **NAME** in the file (but see **-N**). There are no spaces between **-n** and its arguments.

♦ **-oRANGE**—Deletes the revisions specified by RANGE (also known as "outdating," hence the **-o**). Range can be specified in one of the following ways:

♦ **REV1::REV2**—Collapses all intermediate revisions between **REV1** and **REV2**, so that the revision history goes directly from **REV1** to **REV2**. After this, any revisions between the two no longer exist, and there will be a noncontiguous jump in the revision number sequence.

♦ **::REV**—Collapses all revisions between the beginning of **REV**'s branch (which may be the beginning of the trunk) and **REV**, noninclusively of course. **REV** is then the first revision on that line.

♦ **REV::**—Collapses all revisions between **REV** and the end of its branch (which may be the trunk). **REV** is then the last revision on that line.

♦ **REV**—Deletes the revision **REV** (**-o1.8** would be equivalent to **-o1.7::1.9**).

♦ **REV1:REV2**—Deletes the revisions from **REV1** to **REV2**, inclusive. They must be on the same branch. After this, you cannot retrieve **REV1**, **REV2**, or any of the revisions in between.

♦ **:REV**—Deletes revisions from the beginning of the branch (or trunk) to **REV**, inclusive. (See the preceding warning.)

♦ **REV:**—Deletes revisions from **REV** to the end of its branch (or trunk), inclusive. (See the preceding warning.)

> **Note**
>
> *None of the revisions being deleted may have branches or locks. If any of the revisions have symbolic names attached, you have to delete them first with **tag -d** or **admin -n**. (Actually, right now CVS only protects against deleting symbolically named revisions if you're using one of the **::** syntaxes, but the single-colon syntaxes may soon change to this behavior as well.)*

Instead of using this option to undo a bad commit, you should commit a new revision that undoes the bad change. There are no spaces between -o and its arguments.

♦ **-q**—Tells CVS to run quietly—don't print diagnostic messages (just like the global **-q** option).

♦ **-sSTATE[:REV]**—Sets the state attribute of revision **REV** to **STATE**. If **REV** is omitted, the latest revision on the default branch (usually the trunk) is used. If **REV** is a branch tag or number, the latest revision on that branch is used.

Any string of letters or numbers is acceptable for **STATE**; some commonly used states are **Exp** for experimental, **Stab** for stable, and **Rel** for released. (In fact, CVS sets the state to **Exp** when a file is created.) Note that CVS uses the state **dead** for its own purposes, so don't specify that one.

States are displayed in **cvs log** output, and in the **$Log** and **$State** RCS keywords in files. There is no space between **-s** and its arguments.

♦ **-t[DESCFILE]**—Replaces the description (creation message) for the file with the contents of **DESCFILE**, or reads from standard input if no **DESCFILE** is specified.

This useful option, unfortunately, does not currently work in client/server CVS. In addition, if you try it in client/server and omit **DESCFILE**, any existing description for the file is wiped out and replaced with the empty string. If you need to rewrite a file's description, either do so using only local CVS on the same machine as the repository or **-t-STRING**. There is no space between **-t** and its argument. **DESCFILE** may not begin with a hyphen ("-"). (See **-t-STRING**.)

♦ **-t-STRING**—Like **-t**, except that **STRING** is taken directly as the new description. **STRING** may contain spaces, in which case you should surround it with quotes. Unlike the other syntax for **-t**, this works in client/server as well as locally.

♦ **-U**—Sets locking to nonstrict. (See **-l** and **-L** options, discussed earlier.)

♦ **-u[REV]**—Unlocks revision **REV**. (See **-l**.) If **REV** is omitted, CVS unlocks the latest lock held by the caller. If **REV** is a branch, CVS unlocks the latest revision on that branch. If someone other than the owner of a lock breaks the lock, a mail message is sent to the original locker. The content for this message is solicited on standard input from the person breaking the lock. There is no space between **-u** and its argument.

♦ **-VRCS_VERSION_NUMBER**—(Obsolete) This used to be a way to tell CVS to produce RCS files acceptable to previous versions of RCS. Now the RCS format used by CVS is drifting away from the RCS format used by RCS, so this option is useless. Specifying it results in an error.

♦ **-xSUFFIX**—(Obsolete)—Theoretically, this gives you a way to specify the suffix for RCS file names. However, CVS and related tools all depend on that suffix being the default (,v), so this option does nothing.

annotate [OPTIONS] [FILES]

- ◆ *Alternate name*—**ann**
- ◆ *Requires*—Working copy, repository
- ◆ *Changes*—Nothing

Shows information on who last modified each line of each file and when. Each line of output corresponds to one line of the file. From left to right, the line displays the revision number of the last modification of that line, a parenthetical expression containing the user and date of the modification, a colon, and the contents of the line in the file.

For example, if a file looks like this

```
this is a test file
it only has too lines
I mean "two"
```

the annotations for that file could look like this

```
1.1         (jrandom  22-Aug-99): this is a test file
1.1         (jrandom  22-Aug-99): it only has too lines
1.2         (jrandom  22-Aug-99): I mean "two"
```

from which you would know that the first two lines were in the initial revision, and the last line was added or modified (also by jrandom) in Revision 1.2.

Options:

- ◆ **-D DATE**—Shows the annotations as of the latest revision no later than **DATE**.
- ◆ **-f**—Forces use of the head revision if the specified tag or date is not found. You can use this in combination with **-D** or **-r** to ensure that there is some output from the **annotate** command, even if only to show Revision 1.1 of the file.
- ◆ **-l**—Local. Runs in the current working directory only. Does not descend into subdirectories.
- ◆ **-R**—Recursive. Descends into subdirectories (the default). The point of the **-R** option is to override any **-l** option set in a .cvsrc file.
- ◆ **-r REV**—Shows annotations as of revision **REV** (can be a revision number or a tag).

checkout [OPTIONS] PROJECT(S)

- ◆ *Alternate names*—**co**, **get**
- ◆ *Requires*—Repository
- ◆ *Changes*—Current directory

Checks out a module from the repository into a working copy. The working copy is created if it doesn't exist already and updated if it does. (See also "update.")

Options:

♦ **-A**—Resets any sticky tags, sticky dates, or sticky **-k** (RCS keyword substitution mode) options. This is like the **-A** option to **update** and is probably more often used there than with **checkout**.

♦ **-c**—Doesn't check anything out; just prints the CVSROOT/modules file, sorted, on standard output. This is a good way to get an overview of what projects are in a repository. However, a project without an entry in modules does not appear (this situation is quite normal because the name of the project's top-level directory in the repository functions as the project's "default" module name).

♦ **-D DATE**—Checks out the latest revisions no later than **DATE**. This option is sticky, so you won't be able to commit from the working copy without resetting the sticky date. (See **-A**.) This option also implies **-P**, described later.

♦ **-d DIR**—Creates the working copy in a directory named **DIR**, instead of creating a directory with the same name as the checked-out module. If you check out only a portion of a project and the portion is located somewhere beneath the project's top level, the locally empty intermediate directories are omitted. You can use **-N** to suppress this directory-collapsing behavior.

♦ **-f**—Forces checkout of the head revision if the specified tag or date is not found. Most often used in combination with **-D** or **-r** to ensure that something always gets checked out.

♦ **-j REV[:DATE] -j REV1[:DATE] -j REV2[:DATE]**—Joins (merges) two lines of development. This is just like the **-j** option to **update**, where it is more commonly used. (See "update" for details.)

♦ **-k MODE**—Substitutes RCS keywords according to **MODE** (which can override the default modes for the files). (See the section "Keyword Substitution" later in this chapter for valid modes.) The mode chosen will be sticky—future updates of the working copy will keep that mode.

♦ **-l**—Local. Checks out the top-level directory of the project only. Does not process subdirectories.

♦ **-N**—Suppresses collapsing of empty directories with **-d** option. (See **-d**.)

♦ **-n**—Doesn't run any checkout program that was specified with **-o** in CVSROOT/modules. (See the section "Repository Administrative Files" later in this chapter for more on this.)

♦ **-P**—Prunes empty directories from the working copy (like the **-P** option to **update**).

- **-p**—Checks files out to standard output, not into files (like the **-p** option to **update**).

- **-R**—Checks out subdirectories as well (the default). (See also the **-f** option.)

- **-r TAG**—Checks out the project as of revision **TAG** (it would make almost no sense to specify a numeric revision for **TAG**, although CVS lets you). This option is sticky and implies **-P**.

- **-s**—Like **-c**, but shows the status of each module and sorts by status. (See "CVSROOT/ modules" in the section "Repository Administrative Files" for more information.)

commit [OPTIONS] [FILES]

- *Alternate names*—**ci**, **com**

- *Requires*—Working copy, repository

- *Changes*—Repository (and working copy administrative area)

Commits changes from a working copy to the repository.

Options:

- **-F MSGFILE**—Uses the contents of **MSGFILE** for the log message instead of invoking an editor. This option cannot be combined with **-m**.

- **-f**—Forces commit of a new revision even if no changes have been made to the files. **commit** does not recurse with this option (it implies **-l**). You can force it to recurse with **-R**.

> **Note**
>
> *This meaning of -f is at odds with its usual meaning ("force to head revision") in CVS commands.*

- **-l**—Local. Commits changes from the current directory only. Doesn't descend into subdirectories.

- **-m MESSAGE**—Uses **MESSAGE** as the log message instead of invoking an editor. Cannot be used with **-F**.

- **-n**—Does not run any module program. (See the section "Repository Administrative Files" in this chapter for information about module programs.)

- **-R**—Commits changes from subdirectories as well as from the current directory (the default). This option is used only to counteract the effect of a **-l** in .cvsrc.

- **-r REV**—Commits to revision **REV**, which must be either a branch or a revision on the trunk that is higher than any existing revision. Commits to a branch always go on the tip of the branch (extending it); you cannot commit to a specific revision on a branch. Use of this option sets the new revision as a sticky tag on the file. This can be cleared with **update -A**.

The **-r REV** option implies **-f** as well. A new revision is committed even if there are no changes to commit.

diff [OPTIONS] [FILES]

♦ *Alternate names*—**di**, **dif**

♦ *Requires*—Working copy, repository

♦ *Changes*—Nothing

Shows the difference between two revisions (in Unix **diff** format). When invoked with no options, CVS **diff**s the repository base revisions against the (possibly uncommitted) contents of the working copy. The "base" revisions are the latest revisions of this working copy retrieved from the repository; note that there could be even later revisions in the repository, if someone else committed changes but this working copy hasn't been updated yet. (See also "rdiff.")

Options:

♦ **-D DATE**—Diffs against the latest revisions no later than **DATE**. Behaves like **-r REV**, except uses dates rather than revisions (See **-r** for details.)

♦ **-k MODE**—Expands RCS keywords in the diffs according to **MODE**. (See the section "Keyword Substitution" in this chapter for possible modes.)

♦ **-l**—Local. If no files were specified as arguments, this option diffs files in the current directory, but does not descend into subdirectories.

♦ **-R**—Recursive. This option is the opposite of **-l**. This is the default behavior, so the only reason to specify **-R** is to counteract a **-l** in a .cvsrc file.

♦ **-r REV** or **-r REV1 -r REV2**—Diffs against (or between) the specified revisions. With one **-r** option, this diffs revision **REV** against your working copy of that file (so when multiple files are being diffed, **REV** is almost always a tag). With two **-r** options, it diffs **REV1** against **REV2** for each file (and the working copy is, therefore, irrelevant). The two revisions can be in any order—**REV1** does not have to be an earlier revision than **REV2**. The output reflects the direction of change. With no **-r** options, it shows the difference between the working file and the revision on which it is based.

Diff Compatibility Options

In addition to the preceding options, **cvs diff** also shares a number of options with the GNU version of the standard command-line **diff** program. Following is a complete list of these options, along with an explanation of a few of the most commonly used ones. (See the GNU diff documentation for the others.)

```
-0 -1 -2 -3 -4 -5 -6 -7 -8 -9
   --binary
   --brief
   --changed-group-format=ARG
   -c
     -C NLINES
     --context[=LINES]
   -e --ed
   -t --expand-tabs
   -f --forward-ed
   --horizon-lines=ARG
   --ifdef=ARG
   -w --ignore-all-space
   -B --ignore-blank-lines
   -i --ignore-case
   -I REGEXP
       --ignore-matching-lines=REGEXP
   -h
   -b --ignore-space-change
   -T --initial-tab
   -L LABEL
      --label=LABEL
   --left-column
   -d --minimal
   -N --new-file
   --new-line-format=ARG
   --old-line-format=ARG
   --paginate
   -n --rcs
   -s --report-identical-files
   -p
   --show-c-function
   -y --side-by-side
   -F REGEXP
   --show-function-line=REGEXP
   -H --speed-large-files
   --suppress-common-lines
   -a --text
   --unchanged-group-format=ARG
   -u
     -U NLINES
     --unified[=LINES]
   -V ARG
   -W COLUMNS
      --width=COLUMNS
```

Following are the GNU **diff** options most frequently used with **cvs diff**.

- ◆ **-B**—Ignores differences that are merely the insertion or deletion of blank lines (lines containing nothing but whitespace characters).

- ◆ **-b**—Ignores differences in the amount of whitespace. This option treats all whitespace sequences as being equal and ignores whitespace at line end. More technically, this option collapses each whitespace sequence in the input to a single space and removes any trailing whitespace from each line, before taking the diff. (See also **-w**.)

- ◆ **-c**—Shows output in context diff format, defaulting to three lines of context per difference (for the sake of the **patch** program, which requires at least two lines of context).

- ◆ **-C NUM** —**context=NUM**—Like **-c**, but with **NUM** lines of context.

- ◆ **-i**—Compares case insensitively. Treats upper- and lowercase versions of a letter as the same.

- ◆ **-u**—Shows output in unified **diff** format.

- ◆ **-w**—Ignores all whitespace differences, even when one side of the input has whitespace where the other has none. Essentially a stronger version of **-b**.

edit [OPTIONS] [FILES]

- ◆ *Alternate names*—None
- ◆ *Requires*—Working copy, repository
- ◆ *Changes*—Permissions in working copy, watchlist in repository

Signals that you are about to begin editing a watched file or files. Also adds you as a temporary watcher to the file's watch list (you'll be removed when you do **cvs unedit**). (See also "watch," "watchers," "unedit," and "editors.")

Options:

- ◆ **-a ACTIONS**—Specifies for which actions you want to be a temporary watcher. **ACTIONS** should be either **edit**, **unedit**, **commit**, **all**, or **none**. (If you don't use **-a**, the temporary watch will be for **all** actions.)

- ◆ **-l**—Local. Signals editing for files in the current working directory only.

- ◆ **-R**—Recursive (this is the default). Opposite of **b**; you would only need to pass **-R** to counteract a **-l** in a .cvsrc file.

editors [OPTIONS] [FILES]

- ◆ *Alternate names*—None
- ◆ *Requires*—Working copy, repository
- ◆ *Changes*—Nothing

Shows who is currently editing a watched file. (See also "watch," "watchers," "edit," and "unedit.")

Options:

- ◆ -l—Local. Views editors for files in current directory only.

- ◆ -R—Recursive. Views editors for files in this directory and its subdirectories (the default). You may need to pass -R to counteract a -l in a .cvsrc file, though.

export [OPTIONS] PROJECT(S)

- ◆ *Alternate names*—**exp, ex**

- ◆ *Requires*—Repository

- ◆ *Changes*—Current directory

Exports files from the repository to create a project tree that is not a working copy (has no CVS/ administrative subdirectories). Useful mainly for packaging distributions.

Options:

- ◆ **-D DATE**—Exports the latest revisions no later than **DATE**.

- ◆ **-d DIR**—Exports into **DIR** (otherwise, defaults to the module name).

- ◆ **-f**—Forces use of head revisions, if a given tag or date would result in nothing being found (for use with **-D** or **-r**).

- ◆ **-k MODE**—Expands RCS keywords according to **MODE**. (See the section "Keyword Substitution" later in this chapter.)

- ◆ **-l**—Local. Exports only the top level of the project, no subdirectories.

- ◆ **-N**—Doesn't "collapse" empty intermediate directories. This option is like the **-N** option to **checkout**.

- ◆ **-n**—Does not run a module program as may be specified in CVSROOT/modules. (See "Repository Administrative Files" later in this chapter for more about this.)

- ◆ **-P**—Prunes empty directories (like the **-P** option to **checkout** or **update**).

- ◆ **-R**—Recursive. Exports all subdirectories of the project (the default). The only reason to specify **-R** is to counteract a **-l** in a .cvsrc file.

- ◆ **-r REV**—Exports revision **REV**. **REV** is almost certainly a tag name, not a numeric revision.

gserver

This is the GSSAPI (Generic Security Services API) server. This command is not normally run directly by users. Instead, it is started up on the server side when a user connects from a client with the **:gserver:** access method:

```
cvs -d :gserver:floss.red-bean.com:/usr/local/newrepos checkout myproj
```

Note
*GSSAPI provides, among other things, Kerberos Version 5; for Kerberos Version 4, use :**kserver:**.*

Setting up and using a GSSAPI library on your machines is beyond the scope of this book. (See the node "GSSAPI Authenticated" in the Cederqvist manual for some useful hints, however.)

Options: None.

history [OPTIONS] [FILENAME_SUBSTRING(S)]

♦ *Alternate names*—**hi**, **his**

♦ *Requires*—Repository, CVSROOT/history

♦ *Changes*—Nothing

Shows a history of activity in the repository. Specifically, this option shows records of checkouts, commits, rtags, updates, and releases. By default, the option shows checkouts (but see the **-x** option). This command won't work if there's no CVSROOT/history file in the repository.

The **history** command differs from other CVS commands in several ways. First, it must usually be given options to do anything useful (and some of those options mean different things for **history** than they do elsewhere in CVS). Second, instead of taking full file names as arguments, it takes one or more substrings to match against file names (all records matching at least one of those substrings are retrieved). Third, **history**'s output looks a lot like line noise until you learn to read it, so I'll explain the output format in a special section, after the options. (See also "log.")

Options:

♦ **-a**—Shows history for all users (otherwise, defaults to **self**).

♦ **-b STR**—Shows data back to record containing string **STR** in the module name, file name, or repository path.

♦ **-c**—Reports commits.

♦ **-D DATE**—Shows data since **DATE** (the usual CVS date formats are available).

♦ **-e**—Everything—reports on all record types.

♦ **-f FILE**—Reports the most recent event concerning **FILE**. You can specify this option multiple times. This is different from the usual meaning of **-f** in CVS commands: "Force to head revision as a last resort."

♦ **-l**—Shows the record representing the last (as in "most recent") event of each project. This is different from the usual meaning of **-l** in CVS commands: "Run locally, do not recurse."

- ♦ **-m MODULE**—This provides a full report about **MODULE** (a project name). You can specify this option multiple times.

- ♦ **-n MODULE**—Reports the most recent event about **MODULE**. For example, checking out the module is about the module itself, but modifying or updating a file inside the module is about that file, not about the module. You can specify this option multiple times. This is different from the usual meaning of **-n** in CVS commands: "Don't run a CVSROOT/modules program."

- ♦ **-o**—Shows checkout records (the default).

- ♦ **-p REPOS**—Shows data for a particular directory in the repository. You can specify this option multiple times. The meaning of this option differs from the usual meaning of **-p** in CVS commands: "Pipe the data to standard output instead of a file."

Note

This option appears to be at least partially broken as of summer 1999.

- ♦ **-r REV**—Shows records referring to revisions since the revision or tag named **REV** appears in individual RCS files. Each RCS file is searched for the revision or tag.

- ♦ **-T**—Reports on all tag events.

- ♦ **-t TAG**—Shows records since tag **TAG** was last added to the history file. This differs from the **-r** flag in that it reads only the CVSROOT/history file, not the RCS files, and is therefore much faster.

- ♦ **-u USER**—Shows events associated with **USER**. You can specify this option multiple times.

- ♦ **-w**—Shows records that are associated with the same working directory from which you are invoking history.

- ♦ **-X HISTORYFILE**—Uses **HISTORYFILE** instead of CVSROOT/history. This option is mainly for debugging and is not officially supported; nevertheless, you may find it useful (perhaps for generating human-readable reports from old history files you've kept around).

- ♦ **-x TYPES**—Reports on events specified in **TYPES**. Each type is represented by a single letter, from the set "TOEFWUCGMAR"; any number of letters can be combined. Here is what they mean:
  - ♦ **T**—Tag
  - ♦ **O**—Checkout
  - ♦ **E**—Export
  - ♦ **F**—Release
  - ♦ **W**—Update (newly obsolete file removed from working copy)
  - ♦ **U**—Update (file was checked out over user file)
  - ♦ **C**—Update (merge, with conflicts)
  - ♦ **G**—Update (merge, no conflicts)

- ◆ **M**—Commit (file was modified)
- ◆ **A**—Commit (file was added)
- ◆ **R**—Commit (file was removed)

The default, if no **-x** option is given, is to show checkouts (like **-x O**).

- ◆ **-z ZONE**—Displays times in output as for time zone **ZONE**. **ZONE** is an abbreviated time zone name, such as UTC, GMT, BST, CDT, CCT, and so on. A complete list of time zones is available in the TimezoneTable in the file lib/getdate.c in the CVS source distribution.

History Output

The output of the **history** command is a series of lines; each line represents one "history event" and starts with a single code letter indicating what type of event it is. For example:

```
floss$ cvs history -D yesterday -x TMO
M 08/21 20:19 +0000 jrandom 2.2                  baar       myproj == <remote>
M 08/22 04:18 +0000 jrandom 1.2                  README     myproj == <remote>
O 08/22 05:15 +0000 jrandom myproj =myproj= ~/src/*
M 08/22 05:33 +0000 jrandom 2.18                 README.txt myproj == ~/src/myproj
O 08/22 14:25 CDT jrandom myproj =myproj= ~/src/*
O 08/22 14:26 CDT jrandom [99.08.23.19.26.03] myproj =myproj= ~/src/*
O 08/22 14:28 CDT jrandom [Exotic_Greetings-branch] myproj =myproj= ~/src/*
```

The code letters are the same as for the **-x** option just described. Following the code letter is the date of the event (expressed in UTC/GMT time, unless the **-z** option is used), followed by the user responsible for the event.

After the user might be a revision number, tag, or date, but only if such is appropriate for the event (date or tag will be in square brackets and formatted as shown in the preceding example). If you commit a file, it shows the new revision number; if you check out with **-D** or **-r**, the sticky date or tag is shown in square brackets. For a plain checkout, nothing extra is shown.

Next comes the name of the file in question, or module name if the event is about a module. If the former, the next two things are the module/project name and the location of the working copy in the user's home directory. If the latter, the next two things are the name of the module's checked-out working copy (between two equal signs), followed by its location in the user's home directory. (The name of the checked-out working copy may differ from the module name if the **-d** flag is used with checkout.)

import [OPTIONS] REPOSITORY VENDOR_TAG RELEASE_TAG(S)

- ◆ *Alternate names*—**im**, **imp**
- ◆ *Requires*—Repository, current directory (the source directory)
- ◆ *Changes*—Repository

Imports new sources into the repository, either creating a new project or creating a new vendor revision on a vendor branch of an existing project. (See Chapter 6 for a basic explanation of vendor branches in **import**, which will help you to understand the following.)

It's normal to use **import** to add many files or directories at once or to create a new project. To add single files, you should use **add**.

Options:

♦ **-b BRANCH**—Imports to vendor branch **BRANCH**. (**BRANCH** is an actual branch number, not a tag.) This is rarely used but can be helpful if you get sources for the same project from different vendors. A normal **import** command assumes that the sources are to be imported on the default vendor branch, which is "1.1.1." Because it is the default, you normally don't bother to specify it with **-b**:

```
floss$ cvs import -m "importing from vendor 1" theirproj THEM1 THEM1-0
```

To import to a vendor branch other than the default, you must specify a different branch number explicitly:

```
floss$ cvs import -b 1.1.3 -m "from vendor 2" theirproj THEM2 THEM2-0
```

The 1.1.3 branch can absorb future imports and be merged like any other vendor branch. However, you must make sure any future imports that specify **-b 1.1.3** also use the same vendor tag (**THEM2**). CVS does not check to make sure that the vendor branch matches the vendor tag. However, if they mismatch, odd and unpredictable things will happen.

Note
Vendor branches are odd-numbered, the opposite of regular branches.

♦ **-d**—Takes the file's modification time as the time of import instead of using the current time. This does not work with client/server CVS.

♦ **-I NAME**—Gives file names that should be ignored in the import. You can use this option multiple times in one import. Wildcard patterns are supported: ***.foo** means ignore everything ending in ".foo." (See "CVSROOT/cvsignore" in "Repository Administration Files" for details about wildcards.)

The following file and directory names are ignored by default:

♦ .

♦ ..

♦ .#*

♦ #*

♦ ,*

♦ _$*

- *~
- *$
- *.a
- *.bak
- *.BAK
- *.elc
- *.exe
- *.ln
- *.o
- *.obj
- *.olb
- *.old
- *.orig
- *.rej
- *.so
- *.Z
- .del-*
- .make.state
- .nse_depinfo
- core
- CVS
- CVS.adm
- cvslog.*
- RCS
- RCSLOG
- SCCS
- tags
- TAGS

You can suppress the ignoring of those file name patterns, as well as any specified in .cvsignore, CVSROOT/cvsignore, and the **CVSIGNORE** environment variable, by using **-I !**. That is,

```
floss$ cvs import -I ! -m "importing the universe" proj VENDOR VENDOR_0
```

imports all files in the current directory tree, even those that would otherwise be ignored.

Using a **-I !** clears whatever ignore list has been created to that point, so any **-I** options that came before it would be nullified, but any that come after will still count. Thus,

```
floss$ cvs import -I ! -I README.txt -m "some msg" theirproj THEM THEM_0
```

is not the same as

```
floss$ cvs import -I README.txt -I ! -m "some msg" theirproj THEM THEM_0
```

The former ignores (fails to import) README.txt, whereas the latter imports it.

♦ **-k MODE**—Sets the default RCS keyword substitution mode for the imported files. (See "Keyword Substitution" later in this chapter for a list of valid modes.)

♦ **-m MESSAGE**—Records **MESSAGE** as the import log message.

♦ **-W SPEC**—Specifies filters based on file names that should be in effect for the **import**. You can use this option multiple times. (See "CVSROOT/cvswrappers" in "Repository Administration Files" for details about wrapper specs.)

init NEW_REPOSITORY

♦ *Alternate names*—None

♦ *Requires*—Location for new repository

♦ *Creates*—Repository

Creates a new repository (that is, a root repository in which many different projects are stored). You will almost always want to use the global **-d** option with this, as in

```
floss$ cvs -d /usr/local/yet_another_repository init
```

because even if you have a **CVSROOT** environment variable set, it's probably pointing to an existing repository, which would be useless and possibly dangerous in the context of this command. (See Chapter 4 for additional steps that you should take after initializing a new repository.)

Options: None.

kserver

This is the Kerberos server. (If you have Kerberos libraries Version 4 or below—Version 5 just uses GSSAPI, see "gserver.") This command is not normally run directly by users but is instead started up on the server side when a user connects from a client with the **:kserver:** access method:

```
cvs -d :kserver:floss.red-bean.com:/usr/local/newrepos checkout myproj
```

Setting up and using Kerberos on your machine is beyond the scope of this book. (However, see the node "Kerberos Authenticated" in the Cederqvist manual for some useful hints.)

Options: None.

log [OPTIONS] [FILES]

- *Alternate names*—**lo**, **rlog**
- *Requires*—Working copy, repository
- *Changes*—Nothing

Shows log messages for a project, or for files within a project. The output of **log** is not quite in the same style as the output of other CVS commands, because **log** is based on an older RCS program (**rlog**). Its output format gives a header, containing various pieces of non-revision-specific information about the file, followed by the log messages (arranged by revision). Each revision shows not merely the revision number and log message, but also the author and date of the change and the number of lines added or deleted. All times are printed in UTC (GMT), not local time.

Because **log** output is per file, a single commit involving multiple files may not immediately appear as a conceptually atomic change. However, if you read all of the log messages and dates carefully, you may be able to reconstruct what happened. (For information about a tool that can reformat multifile log output into a much more readable form, see "cvs2cl.pl: Generate GNU-Style ChangeLogs From CVS Logs" in Chapter 10 for details.) (See also "history.")

Options:

As you read over the following filtering options, it may not be completely clear how they behave when combined. A precise description of **log**'s behavior is that it takes the intersection of the revisions selected by **-d**, **-s**, and **-w**, intersected with the union of those selected by **-b** and **-r**.

- **-b**—Prints log information about the default branch only (usually the highest branch on the trunk). This is usually done to avoid printing the log messages for side branches of development.
- **-dDATES**—Prints log information for only those revisions that match the date or date range given in **DATES**, a semicolon-separated list. Dates can be given in any of the usual date formats (see "Date Formats" earlier in this section) and can be combined into ranges as follows:
  - **DATE1<DATE2**—Selects revisions created between **DATE1** and **DATE2**. If **DATE1** is after **DATE2**, use ">" instead; otherwise, no log messages are retrieved.
  - **<DATE DATE>**—All revisions from **DATE** or earlier.
  - **>DATE DATE<**—All revisions from **DATE** or later.

♦ **DATE**—Just selects the most recent single revision from **DATE** or earlier. You may use "<=" and ">=" instead of "<" and ">" to indicate an inclusive range (otherwise, ranges are exclusive). Multiple ranges should be separated with semicolons, for example

```
floss$ cvs log -d"1999-06-01<1999-07-01;1999-08-01<1999-09-01"
```

selects log messages for revisions committed in June or August of 1999 (skipping July). There can be no space between **-d** and its arguments.

♦ **-h**—Prints only the header information for each file, which includes the file name, working directory, head revision, default branch, access list, locks, symbolic names (tags), and the file's default keyword substitution mode. No log messages are printed.

♦ **-l**—Local. Runs only on files in the current working directory.

♦ **-N**—Omits the list of symbolic names (tags) from the header. This can be helpful when your project has a lot of tags but you're only interested in seeing the log messages.

♦ **-R**—Prints the name of the RCS file in the repository.

Note

*This is different from the usual meaning of **-R**: "recursive." There's no way to override a **-l** for this command, so don't put **log -l** in your .cvsrc.*

♦ **-rREVS**—Shows log information for the revisions specified in **REVS**, a comma-separated list. **REVS** can contain both revision numbers and tags. Ranges can be specified like this:

   ♦ **REV1:REV2**—Revisions from **REV1** to **REV2** (they must be on the same branch).

   ♦ **:REV**—Revisions from the start of **REV**'s branch up to and including **REV**.

   ♦ **REV:**—Revisions from **REV** to the end of **REV**'s branch.

   ♦ **BRANCH**—All revisions on that branch, from root to tip.

   ♦ **BRANCH1:BRANCH2**—A range of branches—all revisions on all the branches in that range.

   ♦ **BRANCH.**—The latest (tip) revision on **BRANCH**.

Finally, a lone **-r**, with no argument, means select the latest revision on the default branch (normally the trunk). There can be no space between **-r** and its argument.

Note

*If the argument to **-r** is a list, it is comma-separated, not semicolon-separated like **-d**.*

♦ **-sSTATES**—Selects revisions whose state attribute matches one of the states given in **STATES**, a comma-separated list. There can be no space between **-s** and its argument.

> **Note**
>
> *If the argument to **-s** is a list, it is comma-separated, not semicolon-separated like **-d**.*

♦ **-t**—Like **-h**, but also includes the file's description (its creation message).

♦ **-wUSERS**—Selects revisions committed by users whose usernames appear in the comma-separated list **USERS**. A lone **-w** with no **USERS** means to take the username of the person running **cvs log**.

Remember that when user aliasing is in effect (see the section "The Password-Authenticating Server" in Chapter 4), CVS records the CVS username, not the system username, with each commit. There can be no space between **-w** and its argument.

> **Note**
>
> *If the argument to **-w** is a list, it is comma-separated, not semicolon-separated like **-d**.*

login

♦ *Alternate names*—**logon**, **lgn**

♦ *Requires*—Repository

♦ *Changes*—~/.cvspass file

Contacts a CVS server and confirms authentication information for a particular repository. This command does not affect either the working copy or the repository; it just confirms a password (for use with the **:pserver:** access method) with a repository and stores the password for later use in the .cvspass file in your home directory. Future commands accessing the same repository with the same username will not require you to rerun **login**, because the client-side CVS will just consult the .cvspass file for the password.

If you use this command, you should specify a repository using the **pserver** access method, like this

```
floss$ cvs -d :pserver:jrandom@floss.red-bean.com:/usr/local/newrepos
```

or by setting the CVSROOT environment variable.

If the password changes on the server side, you have to rerun **login**.

Options: None.

logout

♦ *Alternative names*—None

♦ *Requires*—~/.cvspass file

♦ *Changes*—~/.cvspass file

The opposite of **login**—removes the password for this repository from .cvspass.

Options: None.

pserver
- ◆ *Alternative names*—None
- ◆ *Requires*—Repository
- ◆ Changes—Nothing

This is the password-authenticating server. This command is not normally run directly by users but is started up from /etc/inetd.conf on the server side when a user connects from a client with the **:pserver:** access method. (See also "login," "logout," and ".cvspass" in the "Run Control Files" section in this chapter. See Chapter 4 for details on setting up a password-authenticating CVS server.)

Options: None.

rdiff [OPTIONS] PROJECTS
- ◆ *Alternate names*—**patch**, **pa**
- ◆ *Requires*—Repository
- ◆ *Changes*—Nothing

Like the **diff** command, except it operates directly in the repository and, therefore, requires no working copy. This command is meant for obtaining the differences between one release and another of your project, in a format suitable as input to the **patch** program (perhaps so you can distribute patch files to users who want to upgrade).

The operation of the **patch** program is beyond the scope of this book. However, note that if the patch file contains diffs for files in subdirectories, you may need to use the **-p** option to **patch** to get it to apply the differences correctly. (See the **patch** documentation for more about this.) (See also "diff.")

Options:
- ◆ **-c**—Prints output in context diff format (the default).
- ◆ **-D DATE** or **-D DATE1 -D DATE2**—With one date, this shows the differences between the files as of **DATE** and the head revisions. With two dates, it shows the differences between the dates.
- ◆ **-f**—Forces the use of head revision if no matching revision is found for the **-D** or **-r** flag (otherwise, **rdiff** would just ignore the file).
- ◆ **-l**—Local. Won't descend into subdirectories.
- ◆ **-R**—Recursive. Descends into subdirectories (the default). You only specify this option to counteract a **-l** in your .cvsrc.

- ◆ **-r REV -r REV1 -r REV2**—With one revision, this shows the differences between revision **REV** of the files and the head revisions. With two, it shows the differences between the revisions.

- ◆ **-s**—Displays a summary of differences. This shows which files have been added, modified, or removed, without showing changes in their content. The output looks like this:

```
floss$ cvs -Q rdiff -s -D 1999-08-20 myproj
File myproj/Random.txt is new; current revision 1.4
File myproj/README.txt changed from revision 2.1 to 2.20
File myproj/baar is new; current revision 2.3
```

- ◆ **-t**—Shows the diff between the top two revisions of each file. This is a handy shortcut for determining the most recent changes to a project. This option is incompatible with **-D** and **-r**.

- ◆ **-u**—Prints output in unidiff format. Older versions of **patch** can't handle unidiff format; therefore, don't use **-u** if you're trying to generate a distributable patch file—use **-c** instead.

- ◆ **-V** (Obsolete)—CVS reports an error if you try to use this option now. I've included it here only in case you see some old script trying to use it.

release [OPTIONS] DIRECTORY

- ◆ *Alternate names*—**re**, **rel**

- ◆ *Requires*—Working copy

- ◆ *Changes*—Working copy, CVSROOT/history

Cancels a checkout (indicates that a working copy is no longer in use). Unlike most CVS commands that operate on a working copy, this one is not invoked from within the working copy but from directly above it (in its parent directory). You either have to set your CVSROOT environment variable or use the **-d** global option, as CVS will not be able to find out the repository from the working copy.

Using **release** is never necessary. Because CVS doesn't normally do locking, you can just remove your working copy.

However, if you have uncommitted changes in your working copy or you want your cessation of work to be noted in the CVSROOT/history file (see the **history** command), you should use **release**. CVS first checks for any uncommitted changes; if there are any, it warns you and prompts for continuation. Once the working copy is actually released, that fact is recorded in the repository's CVSROOT/history file.

Options:

- ◆ **-d**—Deletes the working copy if the release succeeds. Without **-d**, the working copy remains on disk after the release.

> **Note**
>
> *If you created any new directories inside your working copy but did not add them to the repository, they are deleted along with the rest of the working copy, if you specified the -d flag.*

remove [OPTIONS] [FILES]

◆ *Alternate names*—**rm, delete**

◆ *Requires*—Working copy

◆ *Changes*—Working copy

Removes a file from a project. Normally, the file itself is removed from disk when you invoke this command (but see **-f**). Although this command operates recursively by default, it is common to explicitly name the files being removed. Note the odd implication of the previous sentence: Usually, you run **cvs remove** on files that don't exist anymore in your working copy.

Although the repository is contacted for confirmation, the file is not actually removed until a subsequent **commit** is performed. Even then, the RCS file is not really removed from the repository; if it is removed from the trunk, it is just moved into an Attic/ subdirectory, where it is still available to exist on branches. If it is removed from a branch, its location is not changed, but a new revision with state **dead** is added on the branch. (See also "add.")

Options:

◆ **-f**—Force. Deletes the file from disk before removing it from CVS. This meaning differs from the usual meaning of **-f** in CVS commands: "Force to head revision."

◆ **-l**—Local. Runs only in current working directory.

◆ **-R**—Recursive. Descends into subdirectories (the default). This option exists only to counteract a **-l** in .cvsrc.

rtag [OPTIONS] TAG PROJECT(S)

◆ *Alternate names*—**rt, rfreeze**

◆ *Requires*—Repository

◆ *Changes*—Repository

Tags a module directly in the repository (requires no working copy). You probably need to have your CVSROOT environment variable set or use the **-d** global option for this to work. (See also "tag.")

Options:

◆ **-a**—Clears the tag from any removed files, because removed files stay in the repository for historical purposes but are not considered part of the live project anymore. Although it's illegal to tag files with a tag name that's already in use, there should be no interference if the name is only used in removed files (which, from the current point of view of the project, don't exist anymore).

♦ **-b**—Creates a new branch, with branch name **TAG**.

♦ **-D DATE**—Tags the latest revisions no later than **DATE**.

♦ **-d**—Deletes the tag. No record is made of this change—the tag simply disappears. CVS does not keep a change history for tags.

♦ **-F**—Forces reassignment of the tag name, if it happens to exist already for some other revision in the file.

♦ **-f**—Forces to head revision if a given tag or date is not found. (See **-r** and **-D**.)

♦ **-l**—Local. Runs in the current directory only.

♦ **-n**—Won't execute a tag program from CVSROOT/modules. (See the section "Repository Administrative Files" later in this chapter for details about such programs.)

♦ **-R**—Recursive. Descends into subdirectories (the default). The **-R** option exists only to counteract a **-l** in .cvsrc.

♦ **-r REV**—Tags revision **REV** (which may itself be a tag name).

server

Starts up a CVS server. This command is never invoked by users (unless they're trying to debug the client/server protocol), so forget I even mentioned it.

Options: None.

status [OPTIONS] [FILES]

♦ *Alternate names*—**st, stat**

♦ *Requires*—Working copy

♦ *Changes*—Nothing

Shows the status of files in the working copy.

Options:

♦ **-l**—Local. Runs in the current directory only.

♦ **-R**—Recursive. Descends into subdirectories (the default). The **-R** option exists only to counteract a **-l** in .cvsrc.

♦ **-v**—Shows tag information for the file.

tag [OPTIONS] TAG [FILES]

♦ *Alternate names*—**ta, freeze**

♦ *Requires*—Working copy, repository

♦ *Changes*—Repository

Attaches a name to a particular revision or collection of revisions for a project. Often called "taking a snapshot" of the project. This command is also used to create branches in CVS. (See the **-b** option—see also "rtag.")

Options:

♦ **-b**—Creates a branch named **TAG**.

♦ **-c**—Checks that the working copy has no uncommitted changes. If it does, the command exits with a warning, and no tag is made.

♦ **-D DATE**—Tags the latest revisions no later than **DATE**.

♦ **-d**—Deletes the tag. No record is made of this change; the tag simply disappears. CVS does not keep a change history for tags.

♦ **-F**—Forces reassignment of the tag name, if it happens to exist already for some other revision in the file.

♦ **-f**—Forces to head revision if a given tag or date is not found. (See **-r** and **-D**.)

♦ **-l**—Local. Runs in the current directory only.

♦ **-R**—Recursive. Descends into subdirectories (the default). The **-R** option exists only to counteract a **-l** in .cvsrc.

♦ **-r REV**—Tags revision **REV** (which may itself be a tag name).

unedit [OPTIONS] [FILES]

♦ *Alternative names*—None

♦ *Requires*—Working copy, repository

♦ *Changes*—edit/watch lists in the repository

Signals to watchers that you are done editing a file. (See also "watch," "watchers," "edit," and "editors.")

Options:

♦ **-l**—Local. Signals editing for files in the current working directory only.

♦ **-R**—Recursive (opposite of **-l**). Recursive is the default; the only reason to pass **-R** is to counteract a **-l** in your .cvsrc file.

update [OPTIONS] [FILES]

♦ *Alternate names*—**up**, **upd**

♦ *Requires*—Working copy, repository

♦ *Changes*—Working copy

Merges changes from the repository into your working copy. As a side effect, it indicates which files in your working copy are modified (but if the **-Q** global option is passed, these indications won't be printed). (See also "checkout.")

Options:

♦ **-A**—Clears any sticky tags, sticky dates, or sticky RCS keyword expansion modes. This may result in the contents of files changing, if the trunk-head revisions are different from the former sticky revisions. (Think of **-A** as being like a fresh checkout of the project trunk.)

♦ **-D DATE**—Updates to the most recent revisions no later than **DATE**. This option is sticky and implies **-P**. If the working copy has a sticky date, commits are not possible.

♦ **-d**—Retrieves absent directories—that is, directories that exist in the repository but not yet in the working copy. Such directories may have been created in the repository after the working copy was checked out. Without this option, **update** only operates on the directories present in the working copy; new files are brought down from the repository, but new directories are not. (See also **-P**.)

♦ **-f**—Forces to head revision if no matching revision is found with the **-D** or **-r** flags.

♦ **-I NAME**—Like the **-I** option of **import**.

♦ **-j REV[:DATE]** or **-j REV1[:DATE] -j REV2[:DATE]**—Joins, or merges, two lines of development. Ignoring the optional **DATE** arguments for the moment (we'll get to them later), here's how **-j** works: If only one **-j** is given, it takes all changes from the common ancestor to **REV** and merges them into the working copy. The "common ancestor" is the latest revision that is ancestral to both the revisions in the working directory and to **REV**. If two **-j** options are given, it merges the changes from **REV1** to **REV2** into the working copy.

The special tags **HEAD** and **BASE** may be used as arguments to **-j**; they mean the most recent revision in the repository, and the revision on which the current working copy file is based, respectively.

As for the optional **DATE** arguments, if **REV** is a branch, it is normally taken to mean the latest revision on that branch, but you can restrict it to the latest revision no later than **DATE**. The date should be separated from the revision by a colon, with no spaces, for instance:

```
floss$ cvs update -j ABranch:1999-07-01 -j ABranch:1999-08-01
```

In this example, different dates on the same branch are used, so the effect is to take the changes on that branch from July to August and merge them into the working copy. However, note that there is no requirement that the branch be the same in both **-j** options.

♦ **-k MODE**—Does RCS keyword substitution according to **MODE**. (See the section "Keyword Substitution" later in this chapter.) The mode remains sticky on the working copy, so it will affect future updates (but see **-A**).

♦ **-l**—Local. Updates the current directory only.

♦ **-P**—Prunes empty directories. Any CVS-controlled directory that contains no files at the end of the update are removed from the working copy. (See also **-d**.)

- **-p**—Sends file contents to standard output instead of to the files. Used mainly for reverting to a previous revision without producing sticky tags in the working copy. For example:

```
floss$ cvs update -p -r 1.3 README.txt > README.txt
```

Now README.txt in the working copy has the contents of its past Revision 1.3, just as if you had hand-edited it into that state.

- **-R**—Recursive. Descends into subdirectories to update (the default). The only reason you'd specify it is to counteract a **-l** in .cvsrc.

- **-r REV**—Updates (or downdates, or crossdates) to revision **REV**. When updating a whole working copy, **REV** is most often a tag (regular or branch). However, when updating an individual file, it is just as likely to be a revision number as a tag.

  This option is sticky. If the files are switched to a nonbranch tag or sticky revision, they cannot be committed until the stickiness is removed. (See **-A**.) If **REV** was a branch tag, however, commits are possible. They'll simply commit new revisions on that branch.

- **-WSPEC**—Specifies wrapper-style filters to use during the update. You can use this option multiple times. (See "CVSROOT/cvswrappers" in "Repository Administration Files" in this chapter for details about wrapper specs.) There is no space between **-W** and its argument.

watch on|off|add|remove [OPTIONS] [FILES]

- *Alternate names*—None
- *Requires*—Working copy, repository
- *Changes*—Watch list in repository

Sets a watch on one or more files. Unlike most CVS commands, **watch** requires a further subcommand to do something useful. (See also "watchers," "edit," "editors," and "unedit," and "CVSROOT/users" in the "Repository Administrative Files" section in this chapter.)

Subcommands:

- **on**—Declares that the files are being watched. This means that they are created read-only on checkout, and users should do **cvs edit** to make them read-write (and notify any watchers that the file is now being edited). Turning on a watch does not add you to the watch list for any files. (See "watch add" and "watch remove" for that.)

- **off**—Opposite of **watch on**. Declares that the files are no longer being watched.

- **add**—Adds you to the list of watchers for this file. You are notified when someone commits or runs **cvs edit** or **cvs unedit** (but see the **-a** option).

- **remove**—Opposite of **watch add**. Removes you from the list of watchers for this file.

Options (for use with any **watch** subcommand). All three options have the same meanings as for **edit**:

- ◆ *-a ACTIONS*
- ◆ *-l*
- ◆ *-R*

watchers [OPTIONS] [FILES]

- ◆ *Alternate names*—None
- ◆ *Requires*—Working copy, repository
- ◆ *Changes*—Nothing

Shows who's watching what files.

Options—these options mean the same thing here as for **edit**:

- ◆ *-l*
- ◆ *-R*

Keyword Substitution (RCS Keywords)

CVS can perform certain textual substitutions in files, allowing you to keep some kinds of information automatically up to date in your files. All of the substitutions are triggered by a certain keyword pattern, surrounded by dollar signs. For example,

```
$Revision$
```

in a file expands to something like

```
$Revision: 1.5 $
```

and CVS continues to keep the revision string up to date as new revisions are committed.

Controlling Keyword Expansion

By default, CVS performs keyword expansion unless you tell it to stop. You can permanently suppress keyword expansion for a file with the **-k** option when you **add** the file to the project, or you can turn it off later by invoking **admin** with **-k**. The **-k** option offers several different modes of keyword control; usually you want mode **o** or **b**, for example:

```
floss$ cvs add -ko chapter-9.sgml
```

This command added chapter-9.sgml to the project with keyword expansion turned off. It sets the file's default keyword expansion mode to **o**, which means no substitution. (Actually, the "o" stands for "old," meaning to substitute the string with its old value, which is the same as substituting it for itself, resulting in no change. I'm sure this logic made sense to somebody at the time.)

Each file's default keyword mode is stored in the repository. However, each working copy can also have its own local keyword substitution mode—accomplished with the **-k** options to **checkout** or **update**. You can also have a mode in effect for the duration of just one command, with the **-k** option to **diff**.

Here are all the possible modes, presented with the **-k** option prepended (as one would type at a command line). Any of these options can be used as either the default or local keyword substitution mode for a file:

♦ **-kkv**—Expands to keyword and value. This is the default keyword expansion mode, so you don't need to set it for new files. You might use it to change a file from another keyword mode, however.

♦ **-kkvl**—Like **-kkv**, but includes the locker's name if the revision is currently locked. (See the **-l** option to **admin** for more on this.)

♦ **-kk**—Won't expand values in keyword strings, just uses the keyword name. For example, with this option,

```
$Revision: 1.5 $
```

and

```
$Revision$
```

would both "expand" (okay, contract) to:

```
$Revision$
```

♦ **-ko**—Reuses the keyword string found in the file (hence "o" for "old"), as it was in the working file just before the commit.

♦ **-kb**—Like **-ko**, but also suppresses interplatform line-end conversions. The "b" stands for "binary"; it is the mode you should use for binary files.

♦ **-kv**—Substitutes the keyword with its value, for example

```
$Revision$
```

might become:

```
1.5
```

Of course, after that's happened once, future substitutions will not take place, so this option should be used with care.

List Of Keywords

These are all the dollar-sign-delimited keywords that CVS recognizes. Following is a list of the keyword, a brief description, and an example of its expanded form:

♦ **$Author$**—Author of the change:

```
$Author: jrandom $
```

♦ **$Date$**—The date and time of the change, in UTC (GMT):

```
$Date: 1999/08/23 18:21:13 $
```

♦ **$Header$**—Various pieces of information thought to be useful: full path to the RCS file in the repository, revision, date (in UTC), author, state, and locker. (Lockers are rare; although in the following example, qsmith has a lock.):

```
$Header: /usr/local/newrepos/myproj/hello.c,v 1.1 1999/06/01 03:21:13 \
        jrandom Exp qsmith $
```

♦ **Id**—Like **$Header$**, but without the full path to the RCS file:

```
$Id: hello.c,v 1.1 1999/06/01 03:21:13 jrandom Exp qsmith $
```

♦ **Log**—The log message of this revision, along with the revision number, date, and author. Unlike other keywords, the previous expansions are not replaced. Instead, they are pushed down, so that the newest expansion appears at the top of an ever-growing stack of **Log** messages:

```
$Log: hello.c,v $    Revision 1.12  1999/07/19 06:12:43  jrandom
        say hello in Aramaic
```

Any text preceding the **Log** keyword on the same line will be prepended to the downward expansions too; this is so that if you use it in a comment in a program source file, all of the expansion is commented, too.

♦ **$Locker$**—Name of the person who has a lock on this revision (usually no one):

```
$Locker: qsmith $
```

♦ **$Name$**—Name of the sticky tag:

```
$Name: release_1_14 $
```

- **$RCSfile$**—Name of the RCS file in the repository:

  ```
  $RCSfile: hello.c,v $
  ```

- **$Revision$**—Revision number:

  ```
  $Revision: 1.1 $
  ```

- **$Source$**—Full path to the RCS file in the repository:

  ```
  $Source: /usr/local/newrepos/myproj/hello.c,v $
  ```

- **$State$**—State of this revision:

  ```
  $State: Exp $
  ```

Repository Administrative Files

The repository's administrative files are stored in the CVSROOT subdirectory of the repository. These files control various aspects of CVS's behavior (in that repository only, of course).

Generally, the administrative files are kept under revision control just like any other file in the repository (the exceptions are noted). However, unlike other files, checked-out copies of the administrative files are stored in the repository right next to the corresponding RCS files. These checked-out copies actually govern CVS's behavior.

The normal way to modify the administrative files is to check out a working copy of the CVSROOT module, make your changes, and commit. CVS updates the checked-out copies in the repository automatically. (See "checkoutlist".) In an emergency, however, it is also possible to edit the checked-out copies in the repository directly.

You may also want to refer to the discussion of administrative files in Chapter 4, which includes examples.

Shared Syntax

In all of the administrative files, a "#" at the beginning of a line signifies a comment; that line is ignored by CVS. A backslash preceding a newline quotes the newline out of existence.

Some of the files (commitinfo, loginfo, taginfo, and rcsinfo) share more syntactic conventions as well. In these files, on the left of each line is a regular expression (which is matched against a file or directory name), and the rest of the line is a program, possibly with arguments, which is invoked if something is done to a file matching the regular expression. The program is run with its working directory set to the top of the repository.

In these files, there are two special regular expressions that may be used: **ALL** and **DE-FAULT**. **ALL** matches any file or directory, whether or not there is some other match for it, and **DEFAULT** matches only if nothing else matched.

Shared Variables

The info files also allow certain variables to be expanded at runtime. To expand a variable, precede it with a dollar sign (and put it in curly braces just to be safe). Here are the variables CVS knows about:

♦ **${CVSROOT}**—The top of the repository.

♦ **${RCSBIN}**—(Obsolete) Don't use this variable. It is only applicable in CVS Version 1.9.18 and older. Specifying it now may result in an error.

♦ **${CVSEDITOR} ${VISUAL} ${EDITOR}**—These all expand to the editor that CVS is using for a log message.

♦ **${USER}**—The user running CVS (on the server side).

User Variables

Users can set also set their own variables when they run any CVS command. (See the **-s** global option.) These variables can be accessed in the *info files by preceding them with an equal sign, as in **${=VAR}**.

List Of Repository Administrative Files

Following is a list of all the repository administrative files:

checkoutlist

This contains a list of files for which checked-out copies should be kept in the repository. Each line gives the file name and an error message for CVS to print if, for some reason, the file cannot be checked out in the repository:

```
FILENAME  ERROR_MESSAGE
```

Because CVS already knows to keep checked-out copies of the existing administrative files, they do not need to be listed in checkoutlist. Specifically, the following files never need entries in checkoutlist: loginfo, rcsinfo, editinfo, verifymsg, commitinfo, taginfo, ignore, checkoutlist, cvswrappers, notify, modules, readers, writers, and config.

commitinfo

Specifies programs to run at commit time, based on what's being committed. Each line consists of a regular expression followed by a command template:

```
REGULAR_EXPRESSION PROGRAM [ARGUMENTS]
```

The **PROGRAM** is passed additional arguments following any arguments you may have written into the template. These additional arguments are the full path to the repository, followed by the name of each file about to be committed. These files can be examined by **PROGRAM**; their contents are the same as those of the working copy files about to be committed. If **PROGRAM** exits with nonzero status, the **commit** fails; otherwise, it succeeds. (See also "Shared Syntax" earlier in this chapter.)

config
Controls various global (non-project-specific) repository parameters. The syntax of each line is

```
ParameterName=yes|no
```

except for the **LockDir** parameter, which takes an absolute pathname as argument.

The following parameters are supported:

♦ **RCSBIN (default: =no)**—(Obsolete) This option is silently accepted for backwards compatibility, but no longer has any effect.

♦ **SystemAuth (default: =no)**—If "yes," CVS pserver authentication tries the system user database—usually /etc/passwd—if a username is not found in CVSROOT/passwd. If "no," the user must exist in CVSROOT/passwd to gain access via the **:pserver:** method.

♦ **PreservePermissions (default: =no)**—If "yes," CVS tries to preserve permissions and other special file system information (such as device numbers and symbolic link targets) for files. You probably don't want to do this, as it does not necessarily behave as expected. (See the node "Special Files" in the Cederqvist manual for details.)

♦ **TopLevelAdmin (default: =no)**—If "yes," checkouts create a CVS/ subdirectory next to each working copy tree (in the parent directory of the working copy). This can be useful if you will be checking out many working copies from the same repository; on the other hand, setting it here affects everyone who uses this repository.

♦ **LockDir (unset by default)**—The argument after the equal sign is a path to a directory in which CVS can create lockfiles. If not set, lockfiles are created in the repository, in locations corresponding to each project's RCS files. This means that users of those projects must have file-system-level write access to those repository directories.

cvsignore
Ignores certain files when doing updates, imports, or releases. By default, CVS already ignores some kinds of files. (For a full list, see the **-I** option to **import**, earlier in this chapter.) You can add to this list by putting additional file names or wildcard patterns in the cvsignore file. Each line gives a file name or pattern, for example:

```
README.msdos
*.html
blah?.out
```

This causes CVS to ignore any file named "README.msdos," any file ending in ".html," and any file beginning with "blah" and ending with ".out." (Technically, you can name multiple files or patterns on each line, separated by whitespace, but it is more readable to keep them to one per line. The whitespace separation rule does, unfortunately, mean that there's no way to specify a space in a file name, except to use wildcards.)

A "!" anywhere in the list cancels all previous entries. (See "$CVSIGNORE" in the section "Environment Variables" in this chapter for a fuller discussion of ignore processing.)

cvswrappers

Specifies certain filtering behaviors based on file name. Each line has a file-globbing pattern (that is, a file name or file wildcards), followed by an option indicating the filter type and an argument for the option.

Options:

♦ **-m**—Specifies an update method. Possible arguments are **MERGE**, which means to merge changes into working files automatically, and **COPY**, which means don't try to automerge but present the user with both versions of the file and let them work it out. **MERGE** is the default, except for binary files (those whose keyword substitution mode is **-kb**). (See the "Keyword Substitution" section in this chapter.) Files marked as binary automatically use the **COPY** method, so there is no need to make a **-m COPY** wrapper for them.

♦ **-k**—Specifies a keyword substitution mode. All of the usual modes are possible. (See the "Keyword Substitution" section in this chapter for a complete list.)

Here is an example cvswrappers file:

```
*.blob    -m COPY
*.blink   -k o
```

This cvswrappers file says to not attempt merges on files ending in ".blob" and suppress keyword substitution for files ending in ".blink." (See also ".cvswrappers" in the "Working Copy Files" section in this chapter.)

editinfo

This file is obsolete. Very.

history

Stores an ever-accumulating history of activity in the repository, for use by the **cvs history** command. To disable this feature, simply remove the history file. If you don't remove the file, you should probably make it world-writeable to avoid permission problems later.

The contents of this file do not modify CVS's behavior in any way (except for the output of **cvs history**, of course).

loginfo

Specifies programs to run on the log message for each commit, based on what's being committed. Each line consists of a regular expression followed by a command template:

```
REGULAR_EXPRESSION PROGRAM [ARGUMENTS]
```

The **PROGRAM** is passed the log message on its standard input.

Several special codes are available for use in the arguments: %s expands to the names of the files being committed, %V expands to the old revisions from before the commit, and %v expands to the new revisions after the commit. When there are multiple files involved, each element of the expansion is separated from the others by whitespace. For example, in a **commit** involving two files, %s might expand into **hello.c README.txt**, and %v into **1.17 1.12**.

You may combine codes inside curly braces, in which case, each unit of expansion is internally separated by commas and externally separated from the other units by whitespace. Continuing the previous example, %{sv} expands into **hello.c,1.17 README.txt,1.12**.

If any % expansion is done at all, the expansion is prefixed by the full path of the repository. So that last expansion would actually be:

```
/usr/local/newrepos  hello.c,1.17  README.txt,1.12
```

If **PROGRAM** exits with nonzero status, the **commit** fails; otherwise, it succeeds. (See also the "Shared Syntax" section in this chapter.)

modules

This maps names to repository directories. The general syntax of each line is:

```
MODULE [OPTIONS] [&OTHERMODULE...] [DIR] [FILES]
```

DIR need not be a top-level project directory—it could be a subdirectory. If any **FILES** are specified, the module consists of only those files from the directory.

An ampersand followed by a module name means to include the expansion of that module's line in place.

Options:

♦ **-a**—This is an "alias" module, meaning it expands literally to everything after the **OPTIONS**. In this case, the usual **DIR/FILES** behavior is turned off, and everything after the **OPTIONS** is treated as other modules or repository directories.

If you use the **-a** option, you may exclude certain directories from other modules by putting them after an exclamation point (!). For example

```
top_proj -a !myproj/a-subdir !myproj/b-subdir myproj
```

means that checking out **top_proj** will get all of **myproj** except **a-subdir** and **b-subdir**.

♦ **-d NAME**—Names the working directory **NAME** instead of the module name.

♦ **-e PROGRAM**—Runs **PROGRAM** whenever files in this module are exported.

♦ **-i PROGRAM**—Runs **PROGRAM** whenever files in this module are committed. The program is given a single argument—the full pathname in the repository of the file in question. (See "commitinfo", "loginfo", and "verifymsg" for more sophisticated ways to run commit-triggered programs.)

♦ **-o PROGRAM**—Runs **PROGRAM** whenever files in this module are checked out. The program is given a single argument, the name of the module.

♦ **-s STATUS**—Declares a status for the module. When the modules file is printed (with **cvs checkout -s**), the modules are sorted by module status and then by name. This option has no other effects in CVS, so go wild. You can use it to sort anything—status, person responsible for the module, or the module's file language, for example.

♦ **-t PROGRAM**—Runs **PROGRAM** whenever files in this module are tagged with **cvs rtag**. The program is passed two arguments: the name of the module and the tag name. The program is not used for **tag**, only for **rtag**. I have no idea why this distinction is made. You may find the taginfo file more useful if you want to run programs at tag time.

♦ **-u PROGRAM**—Runs **PROGRAM** whenever a working copy of the module is updated from its top-level directory. The program is given a single argument, the full path to the module's repository.

notify

Controls how the notifications for watched files are performed. (You may want to read up on the **watch** and **edit** commands, or see the section "Watches" in Chapter 6.) Each line is of the usual form:

```
REGULAR_EXPRESSION  PROGRAM  [ARGUMENTS]
```

A **%s** in **ARGUMENTS** is expanded to the name of the user to be notified, and the rest of the information regarding the notification is passed to **PROGRAM** on standard input (usually this information is a brief message suitable for emailing to the user). (See the section "Shared Syntax" earlier in this chapter.)

As shipped with CVS, the notify file has one line

```
ALL mail %s -s "CVS notification"
```

which is often all you need.

passwd
Provides authentication information for the pserver access method. Each line is of the form:

```
USER:ENCRYPTED_PASSWORD[:SYSTEM_USER]
```

If no **SYSTEM_USER** is given, **USER** is taken as the system username.

rcsinfo
Specifies a form that should be filled out for log messages that are written with an interactive editor. Each line of **rcsinfo** looks like:

```
REGULAR_EXPRESSION   FILE_CONTAINING_TEMPLATE
```

This template is brought to remote working copies at checkout time, so if the template file or rcsinfo file changes after checkout, the remote copies won't know about it and will continue to use the old template. (See also the section "Shared Syntax" in this chapter.)

taginfo
Runs a program at tag time (usually done to check that the tag name matches some pattern). Each line is of the form:

```
REGULAR_EXPRESSION   PROGRAM
```

The program is handed a set group of arguments. In order, they are the tag name, the operation (see below), the repository, and then as many file name/revision-number pairs as there are files involved in the tag. The file/revision pairs are separated by whitespace, like the rest of the arguments.

The operation is one of **add**, **mov**, or **del** (**mov** means the **-F** option to tag was used).

If **PROGRAM** exits with nonzero status, the tag operation will not succeed. (See also the section "Shared Syntax" in this chapter.)

users
Maps usernames to email addresses. Each line looks like:

```
USERNAME:EMAIL_ADDRESS
```

This sends watch notifications to **EMAIL_ADDRESS** instead of to **USERNAME** at the repository machine. (All this really does is control the expansion of %s in the notify file.) If **EMAIL_ADDRESS** includes whitespace, make sure to surround it with quotes.

If user aliasing is being used in the passwd file, the username that will be matched is the CVS username (the one on the left), not the system username (the one on the right, if any).

val-tags

Caches valid tag names for speedier lookups. You should never need to edit this file, but you may need to change its permissions, or even ownership, if people are having trouble retrieving or creating tags.

verifymsg

Used in conjunction with **rcsinfo** to verify the format of log messages. Each line is of the form:

```
REGULAR_EXPRESSION   PROGRAM   [ARGUMENTS]
```

The full path to the current log message template (see "rcsinfo" earlier in this chapter) is appended after the last argument written in the verifymsg file. If **PROGRAM** exits with nonzero status, the **commit** fails.

Run Control Files

There are a few files on the client (working copy) side that affect CVS's behavior. In some cases, they are analogs of repository administrative files; in other cases, they control behaviors that are only appropriate for the client side.

.cvsrc

Specifies options that you want to be used automatically with every CVS command. The format of each line is

```
COMMAND   OPTIONS
```

where each **COMMAND** is an unabbreviated CVS command, such as **checkout** or **update** (but not **co** or **up**). The **OPTIONS** are those that you want to always be in effect when you run that command. Here is a common .cvsrc line:

```
update -d -P
```

To specify global options, simple use **cvs** as the **COMMAND**.

.cvsignore

Specifies additional ignore patterns. (See "cvsignore" in the "Repository Administrative Files" section in this chapter for the syntax.)

You can have a .cvsignore file in your home directory, which will apply every time you use CVS. You can also have directory-specific ones in each project directory of a working copy (these last only apply to the directory where the .cvsignore is located, and not to its subdirectories).

(See "$CVSIGNORE" in the section "Environment Variables" in this chapter, for a fuller discussion of ignore processing.)

.cvspass

Stores passwords for each repository accessed via the pserver method. Each line is of the form:

```
REPOSITORY   LIGHTLY_SCRAMBLED_PASSWORD
```

The password is essentially stored in cleartext—a very mild scrambling is done to prevent accidental compromises (such as the root user unintentionally looking inside the file). However, this scrambling will not deter any serious-minded person from gaining the password if they get access to the file.

The .cvspass file is portable. You can copy it from one machine to another and have all of your passwords at the new machine, without ever having run **cvs login** there. (See also the "login" and "logout" commands.)

.cvswrappers

This is a client side version of the cvswrappers file. (See the "Repository Administrative Files" section in this chapter.) There can be a .cvswrappers file in your home directory and in each directory of a working copy directory, just as with .cvsignore.

Working Copy Files

The CVS/ administrative subdirectories in each working copy contain some subset of the following files.

CVS/Base/ (directory)

If watches are on, **cvs edit** stores the original copy of the file in this directory. That way, **cvs unedit** can work even if it can't reach the server.

CVS/Baserev

Lists the revision for each file in **Base/**. Each line looks like this:

```
FILE/REVISION/EXPANSION
```

EXPANSION is currently ignored to allow for, well, future expansion.

CVS/Baserev.tmp

This is the temp file for the preceding. (See "CVS/Notify.tmp" or "CVS/Entries.Backup" later in this section for further explanation.)

CVS/Checkin.prog

Records the name of the program specified by the **-i** option in the modules file. (See the "Repository Administrative Files" section in this chapter.)

CVS/Entries

Stores the revisions for the files in this directory. Each line is of the form:

`[CODE_LETTER]/FILE/REVISION/DATE/[KEYWORD_MODE]/[STICKY_OPTION]`

If **CODE_LETTER** is present, it must be **D** for directory (anything else is silently ignored by CVS, to allow for future expansion), and the rest of the items on the line are absent.

This file is always present.

CVS/Entries.Backup

This is just a temp file. If you're writing some program to modify the Entries file, have it write the new contents to Entries.backup and then atomically rename it to "Entries".

CVS/Entries.Log

This is basically a patch file to be applied to Entries after Entries has been read (this is an efficiency hack, to avoid having to rewrite all of Entries for every little change). The format is the same as Entries, except that there is an additional mandatory code letter at the front of every line: An "**A**" means this line is to be added to what's in Entries; "**R**" means it's to be removed from what's in Entries. Any other letters should be silently ignored, to allow for future expansion.

CVS/Entries.Static

If this file exists, it means only part of the directory was fetched from the repository, and CVS will not create additional files in that directory. This condition can usually be cleared by using **update -d**.

CVS/Notify

Stores notifications that have not yet been sent to the server.

CVS/Notify.tmp

Temp file for Notify. The usual procedure for modifying Notify is to write out Notify.tmp and then rename it to "Notify".

CVS/Repository

The path to the project-specific subdirectory in the repository. This may be an absolute path, or it may be relative to the path given in **Root**.

This file is always present.

CVS/Root

This is the repository; that is, the value of the CVSROOT environment variable or the argument to the **-d** global option.

This file is always present.

CVS/Tag

If there is a sticky tag or date on this directory, it is recorded in the first line of the file. The first character is a single letter indicating the type of tag: "**T**," "**N**," or "**D**," for branch tag, nonbranch tag, or date respectively. The rest of the line is the tag or date itself.

CVS/Template

Contains a log message template as specified by the rcsinfo file. (See "Repository Administrative Files" earlier in this chapter.) It is relevant only for remote working copies; working copies on the same machine as the repository just read rcsinfo directly.

CVS/Update.prog

Records the name of the program specified by the **-u** option in the modules file. (See the "Repository Administrative Files" section in this chapter.)

Environment Variables

Following is a list of all of the environment variables that affect CVS.

$COMSPEC

This is used in OS/2 only; it specifies the name of the command interpreter. It defaults to "CMD.EXE."

$CVS_CLIENT_LOG

Used for debugging the client/server protocol. Set this variable to a file name before you start using CVS; all traffic to the server will be logged in filename.in, and everything from the server will be logged in filename.out.

$CVS_CLIENT_PORT

Used in Kerberos-authenticated client/server access.

$CVSEDITOR

Specifies the program to use to edit log messages for commits. This overrides **$EDITOR** and **$VISUAL**.

$CVSIGNORE

A whitespace-separated list of file names and wildcard patterns that CVS should ignore. (See also the **-I** option to the **import** command.)

This variable is appended last to the ignore list during a command. The list is built up in this order: CVSROOT/cvsignore, the .cvsignore file in your home directory, the $CVSIGNORE variable, a **-I** command option, and finally the contents of .cvsignore files in the working copy used as CVS works in each directory. A "!" as the ignore specification at any point nullifies the entire ignore list built up to that point.

$CVS_IGNORE_REMOTE_ROOT
Recently obsolete.

$CVS_PASSFILE
Tells CVS to use some file other than .cvspass in your home directory. (See ".cvspass" in the "Run Control Files" section in this chapter.)

$CVS_RCMD_PORT
Specifies the port number to contact the rcmd daemon on the server side. (This variable is currently ignored in Unix CVS clients.)

$CVSREAD
Makes working copy files read-only on checkout and update, if possible (the default is for them to be read-write). (See also the **-r** global option.)

$CVSROOT
This specifies the path to the repository. This is overridden with the **-d** global option and by the ambient repository for a given working copy. The path to the repository may be preceded by an access method, username, and host, according to the following syntax:

```
[[:METHOD:][[USER@]HOST]:]/REPOSITORY_PATH
```

See the **-d** global option, in the section "Global Options" near the beginning of this chapter, for a list of valid methods.

$CVS_RSH
Specifies an external program for connecting to the server when using the **:ext:** access method. Defaults to **rsh**, but **ssh** is a common replacement value.

$CVS_SERVER
Program to invoke for CVS on the server side. Defaults to **cvs**, of course.

$CVS_SERVER_SLEEP
Delays the start of the server child process by the specified number of seconds. This is used only for debugging, to allow time for a debugger to connect.

$CVSUMASK

Permissions for files and directories in the repository. (You probably don't want to set this; it doesn't work for client/server anyway.)

$CVSWRAPPERS

A whitespace-separated list of file names, wildcards, and arguments that CVS should use as wrappers. (See "cvswrappers" in the "Repository Administrative Files" section in this chapter for more information.)

$EDITOR

(See "$CVSEDITOR.")

$HOME $HOMEDRIVE $HOMEPATH

Where the .cvsrc, .cvspass, and other such files are found (under Unix, only **HOME** is used). In Windows NT, **HOMEDRIVE** and **HOMEPATH** might be set for you; in Windows 95, you may need to set them for yourself.

> **Note**
>
> *In Windows 95, you may also need to set **HOME**. Make sure not to give it a trailing backslash; use **set HOME=C:** or something similar.*

$PATH

Obsolete.

$TEMP $TMP $TMPDIR

Where temporary files go (the server uses **TMPDIR**; Windows NT uses **TMP**). Setting this on the client side will not affect the server. Setting this on either side will not affect where CVS stores temporary lock files. (See "config" in the "Repository Administrative Files" section in this chapter for more information.)

$VISUAL

(See "$CVSEDITOR.")

Chapter 10

Third-Party Tools That Work With CVS

What Are Third-Party Tools?

Many people have written programs to augment CVS. I call these "third-party tools" because they have their own maintainers, separate from the CVS development team. Most of these programs are not distributed with CVS, although some are. This chapter covers third-party tools that I have found useful, but that are not distributed with CVS.

Although there are some very popular and widely used non-command-line or non-Unix interfaces to CVS (download sites are listed in Chapter 4), this chapter does not discuss most of them. Their popularity makes it easy to find out more about them from mailing lists and newsgroups. One exception to this is the Emacs pcl-cvs interface, which is very useful, but sometimes tricky to install. We'll start there.

pcl-cvs: An Emacs Interface To CVS

Depends on: Emacs, Elib

URLs:

- ftp://rum.cs.yale.edu/pub/monnier/pcl-cvs/
- ftp://ftp.lysator.liu.se/pub/emacs/pcl-cvs-1.05.tar.gz
- ftp://ftp.red-bean.com/pub/kfogel/pcl-cvs-1.05.tar.gz

Authors: Per Cederqvist and Stefan Monnier (current maintainer)

pcl-cvs is one of two Emacs/CVS interfaces. The other is the native VC (Version Control) interface built into Emacs. I prefer pcl-cvs because it was written exclusively for CVS and, therefore, works smoothly with the CVS way of doing things. VC, on the other hand, was designed to work with several different back-end version control systems—RCS and SCCS, as well as CVS—and is not really "tuned" for CVS. For example, VC presents a file-based rather than a directory-based interface to revision control.

The advantages of pcl-cvs are strong enough that many people choose to download and install it rather than use VC. Unfortunately, pcl-cvs has two disadvantages: It can be a bit tricky to install (much of this section is devoted to overcoming possible installation hurdles), and its recent releases are a bit unstable.

The latter problem is likely to be temporary, but it does raise the question of which version to use. Stefan Monnier has just recently taken over the pcl-cvs maintainership; the latest release, 2.9.6 (available from the first URL in the preceding list), was a bit bumpy when I tried it. No doubt the problems will be smoothed out soon, but in the meantime, you might want to use an older version. Because I've been using Version 1.05 daily for a long time now and it's performed quite well, I'm going to document that version here. Fortunately, the installation procedures don't change much from version to version. If you decide to use pcl-cvs, I suggest that you check Monnier's download site for a version newer than 2.9.6; if there is one, try it out before regressing all the way to 1.05.

You'll notice that two URLs are given for Version 1.05. The first is Per Cederqvist's site, where he still makes available an old archive of pcl-cvs. However, since I'm not sure how much longer his archive will stay around, I'm also making the 1.05 distribution available from **ftp.red-bean.com**.

Although the rest of these instructions use examples from a Version 1.05 distribution, they should apply to later versions as well.

Installing pcl-cvs

If you don't normally deal with Emacs installation and site-maintenance issues, the pcl-cvs installation procedure may seem a bit daunting. A little background on how Emacs works may help.

Most higher-level Emacs features are written in a language called "Emacs Lisp" (Emacs itself is essentially an interpreter for this language). People add new features to Emacs by distributing files of Emacs Lisp code. pcl-cvs is written in this language, and it depends on a library of useful, generic Emacs Lisp functions called "Elib" (also written in part by Per Cederqvist, but distributed separately from pcl-cvs).

Elib is not included in the regular Emacs distribution (at least not FSF Emacs; I don't know about XEmacs), so you may have to download and install it yourself before you can use pcl-cvs. You can get it from **ftp://ftp.lysator.liu.se/pub/emacs/elib-1.0.tar.gz**. Installation instructions are contained within the package.

Once Elib is installed, you're ready to build and install pcl-cvs. These instructions applies both to Version 1.05 and the 2.x series (although you should check the NEWS and IN-STALL files in newer distributions to see what's changed).

First, unpack pcl-cvs (I'm using Version 1.05, but it could just as easily have been 2.9.6)

```
floss$ zcat pcl-cvs-1.05.tar.gz | tar xvf -
pcl-cvs-1.05/
pcl-cvs-1.05/README
pcl-cvs-1.05/NEWS
pcl-cvs-1.05/INSTALL
pcl-cvs-1.05/ChangeLog
pcl-cvs-1.05/pcl-cvs.el
pcl-cvs-1.05/pcl-cvs.texinfo
pcl-cvs-1.05/compile-all.el
pcl-cvs-1.05/pcl-cvs-lucid.el
pcl-cvs-1.05/pcl-cvs-startup.el
pcl-cvs-1.05/pcl-cvs.info
pcl-cvs-1.05/Makefile
pcl-cvs-1.05/texinfo.tex
```

and go into the source tree's top level:

```
floss$ cd pcl-cvs-1.05/
```

A Makefile is supplied there. According to the instructions in the INSTALL file, you're supposed to edit a few paths at the top of the Makefile and then run:

```
floss$ make install
```

If that works, great. However, this sometimes results in an error (the pcl-cvs code itself is very portable, but its installation procedures sometimes are not). Do this if you get an error:

```
floss$ make clean
floss$ make
```

If all goes well, these commands accomplish a significant part of the installation by byte-compiling all of the Emacs Lisp files. (Byte-compiling converts a file of human-readable Emacs Lisp code—an .el file—into a more compact and efficient representation—an .elc file. Emacs can load and run an .elc file with better performance than it can a plain .el file.)

I'll proceed as though the byte-compilation stage has succeeded. If the byte compilation does not appear to succeed, don't worry: The .elc files are a luxury, not a necessity. They improve performance slightly, but you can run pcl-cvs from the raw .el files with no problem.

If the **make install** failed, the next step is to get the Emacs Lisp (whether .el or .elc) into a directory where Emacs can load it automatically. Emacs has a designated directory on the system for locally installed Lisp. To find this directory—it will have a file named "default.el" in it—check the following locations, in this order:

1. /usr/share/emacs/site-lisp/
2. /usr/local/share/emacs/site-lisp/
3. /usr/lib/emacs/site-lisp/
4. /usr/local/lib/emacs/site-lisp/

Once you've found your site-lisp directory, copy all of the Lisp files to it (you may have to be root to do this):

```
floss# cp -f *.el *.elc /usr/share/emacs/site-lisp/
```

The last step is to tell Emacs about the entry points to pcl-cvs (the main one being the function **cvs-update**), so it will know to load the pcl-cvs code on demand. Because Emacs always reads the default.el file when it starts up, that's where you need to list the pcl-cvs entry points.

Fortunately, pcl-cvs provides the necessary content for default.el. Simply put the contents of pcl-cvs-startup.el into default.el (or perhaps into your .emacs, if you're just installing this for yourself) and restart your Emacs.

You may also want to copy the .info files into your info tree and add pcl-cvs to the table of contents in the dir file.

Using pcl-cvs

Once installed, pcl-cvs is very easy to use. You just run the function **cvs-update**, and pcl-cvs brings up a buffer showing what files in your working copy have been modified or updated. From there, you can commit, do diffs, and so on.

Because cvs-update is the main entry point, I suggest that you bind it to a convenient key sequence before going any further. I have it bound to Ctrl+c v in my .emacs:

```
(global-set-key "\C-cv" 'cvs-update)
```

Otherwise, you can run it by typing "M-x cvs-update" (also known as "Esc-x cvs-update").

When invoked, cvs-update runs **cvs update** as if in the directory of the file in the current buffer—just as if you typed **cvs update** on the command line in that directory. Here's an example of what you might see inside Emacs:

```
PCL-CVS release 1.05 from CVS release $Name:  $.
Copyright (C) 1992, 1993 Per Cederqvist
Pcl-cvs comes with absolutely no warranty; for details consult the manual.
This is free software, and you are welcome to redistribute it under certain
conditions; again, consult the TeXinfo manual for details.
  Modified ci README.txt
  Modified ci fish.c
---------- End ----
```

Two files have been locally modified (some versions of pcl-cvs show the subdirectories where the files are located). The next logical action is to commit one or both of the files, which is what the **ci** on each line means. To commit one of them, go to its line and type "c". You are brought to a log message buffer, where you can type a log message as long as you want (real log message editing is the major advantage of pcl-cvs over the command line). Type Ctrl+c Ctrl+c when done to complete the commit.

If you want to commit multiple files at once, sharing a log message, first use **m** to mark the files that you intend to commit. An asterisk appears next to each file as you mark it:

```
PCL-CVS release 1.05 from CVS release $Name:  $.
Copyright (C) 1992, 1993 Per Cederqvist
Pcl-cvs comes with absolutely no warranty; for details consult the manual.
This is free software, and you are welcome to redistribute it under certain
conditions; again, consult the TeXinfo manual for details.
* Modified ci README.txt
* Modified ci fish.c
---------- End ----
```

Now when you type **c** anywhere, it applies to all (and only) the marked files. Write the log message and commit them with Ctrl+c Ctrl+c as before.

You can also type "d" to run **cvs diff** on a file (or on marked files) and "f" to bring a file into Emacs for editing. Other commands are available; type Ctrl+h m in the update buffer to see what else you can do.

Error Handling In pcl-cvs

The pcl-cvs program has historically had an odd way of dealing with error and informational messages from CVS (although this may be corrected in the latest versions). When it encounters a message from CVS that it doesn't know about, it gets hysterical and throws you into a mail buffer, ready to send a pregenerated bug report to the author of pcl-cvs. Unfortunately, among the CVS messages that pcl-cvs may not know about are the ones associated with conflicting merges, which, although not common, certainly do occur from time to time.

If pcl-cvs suddenly dumps you into a mail buffer, don't panic. Read over the contents of the buffer carefully—the offending CVS output should be in there somewhere. If it looks like a merge, you can just get rid of the mail buffer and rerun **cvs-update**. It should now succeed, because CVS won't output any merge messages (because the merge has already taken place).

The Future Of pcl-cvs

Although I may be giving you the impression that pcl-cvs is barely maintained and a risky investment, the instability appears to be temporary. Stefan Monnier is a responsive maintainer (I contacted him several times during the writing of this chapter, and he always answered right away; he is already making headway on some of the bugs in Version 2.9.6). Very likely by the time this is published, you will be able to download Version 2.9.7 or later with confidence.

In fact, I just now got an encouraging email on this topic from Greg Woods, a former maintainer of pcl-cvs, reprinted here with his permission:

```
From: woods@most.weird.com (Greg A. Woods)
Subject: Re: pcl-cvs maintenance status, stability of recent "release"s?
To: kfogel@red-bean.com
Date: Sun, 29 Aug 1999 18:59:19 -0400 (EDT)

[...]
I've been using Stefan's releases for some time now, and indeed I have
abandoned my own branch of it.

He's done a lot of really good work on PCL-CVS and except for a few odd
quirks in the 2.9.6 version I'm using daily now it is quite usable (and
is approximately infinitely more usable with modern CVS than the one
that was in the CVS distribution! ;-).

I've added a pcl-cvs.README file to my FTP site to point out that the
files there are indeed quite old (at least in Internet time! ;-) and to
give a pointer to Stefan's FTP site too.

[...]
```

In a later email, Greg said that the FSF is considering including pcl-cvs in their next release of Emacs (20.5), which would render most of the preceding installation advice obsolete. Sigh. It's hard to keep up with free software, sometimes.

cvsutils: General Utilities For Use With CVS

Depends on: Perl

URLs:

- **http://www.typhoon.spb.ru/~proski/cvsu/**
- **ftp://ftp.red-bean.com/pub/kfogel/cvsu-0.1.4.tar.gz**

Authors: Tom Tromey (original author) and Pavel Roskin (current maintainer)

The suite of small programs called "cvsutils" generally (although not always) performs "offline" operations in the CVS working copy. Offline operations are those that can be done without contacting the repository, while still leaving the working copy in a consistent state for the next time the repository is contacted. Offline behavior can be extremely handy when your network connection to the repository is slow or unreliable.

The README file in Version 0.1.4 states:

```
The homepage of CVSU is
http://www.typhoon.spb.ru/~proski/cvsu/

This address will change by the end of the year 1999.
```

I have placed a copy of cvsutils on the **red-bean.com** FTP site listed at the beginning of this section. When a new home address for cvsutils is publicized, I'll include it there as well.

The cvsutils programs are listed below in approximate order of usefulness (according to my opinion), with the more useful ones coming first. Coincidentally, this also arranges them by safety. Safety is an issue because some of these utilities can, in their normal course of operation, cause you to lose local modifications or files from your working copy. Therefore, read the descriptions carefully before using these utilities.

Note

This documentation is accurate as of Version 0.1.4. Be sure to read the README file in any later versions for more up-to-date information.

cvsu

Danger level: None

Contacts repository: No

This does an offline **cvs update** by comparing the timestamps of files on disk with their timestamps recorded in CVS/Entries. You can thus tell which files have been locally modified and which files are not known to be under CVS control. Unlike **cvs update**, cvsu does not bring down changes from the repository.

Although it can take various options, cvsu is most commonly invoked without any options:

```
floss$ cvsu
? ./bar
? ./chapter-10.html
M ./chapter-10.sgml
D ./out
? ./safe.sh
D ./tools
```

The left-side codes are like the output of **cvs update**, except that "**D**" means directory. This example shows that chapter-10.sgml has been modified locally. What the example doesn't show is that cvsu ran instantly, whereas a normal **cvs update** would have required half a minute or so over my slow modem line.

Run

```
floss$ cvsu --help
```

to see a list of options.

cvsdo

Danger level: Low to none

Contacts repository: No

This can simulate the working copy effects of **cvs add** and **cvs remove**, but without contacting the repository. Of course, you'd still have to commit the changes to make them take effect in the repository, but at least the add and remove commands themselves can be sped up this way. Here's how to use it

```
floss$ cvsdo add <i>FILENAME</i>
```

or

```
floss$ cvsdo remove <i>FILENAME</i>
```

To see a list of further options, run:

```
floss$ cvsdo --help
```

cvschroot

Danger level: Low

Contacts repository: No

This deals with a repository move by tweaking the working copy to point to the new repository. This is useful when a repository is copied en masse to a new location. When that happens, none of the revisions are affected, but the CVS/Root (and possibly the CVS/Repository) file of every working copy must be updated to point to the new location. Using cvschroot is a lot faster than checking out a new copy. Another advantage is that it doesn't lose your local changes.

Usage:

```
floss$ cvschroot NEW_REPOS
```

For example:

```
floss$ cvschroot :pserver:newuser@newhost.wherever.com:/home/cvs/myproj
```

cvsrmadm

Danger level: Low to medium

Contacts repository: No

This removes all of the CVS/ administrative subdirectories in your working copy, leaving behind a tree similar to that created by **cvs export**.

Although you won't lose any local changes by using cvsrmadm, your working copy will no longer be a working copy.

Use with caution.

cvspurge

Danger level: Medium

Contacts repository: No

This removes all non-CVS-controlled files in your working copy. It does not undo any local changes to CVS-controlled files.

Use with caution.

cvsdiscard

Danger level: Medium to high

Contacts repository: Maybe

This is the complement of cvspurge. Instead of removing unknown files but keeping your local changes, cvsdiscard undoes any local changes (replacing those files with fresh copies from the repository), but keeps unknown files.

Use with extreme caution.

CVSCO

Danger level: High

Contacts repository: Maybe

This is the union of cvspurge and cvsdiscard. It undoes any local changes and removes unknown files from the working copy.

Use with truly paranoid caution.

cvsdate

This script is apparently incomplete and possibly may never be finished. (See the README file for details.)

cvs2cl.pl: Generate GNU-Style ChangeLogs From CVS Logs

Depends on: Perl

URL: **http://www.red-bean.com/~kfogel/cvs2cl.shtml**

cvs2cl.pl condenses and reformats the output of **cvs log** to create a GNU-style ChangeLog file for your project. ChangeLogs are chronologically organized documents showing the change history of a project, with a format designed specifically for human-readability (see the following examples).

The problem with the **cvs log** command is that it presents its output on a per-file basis, with no acknowledgement that the same log message, appearing at roughly the same time in different files, implies that those revisions were all part of a single commit. Thus, reading over log output to get an overview of project development is a hopeless task—you can really only see the history of one file at a time.

In the ChangeLog produced by cvs2cl.pl, identical log messages are unified, so that a single commit involving a group of files shows up as one entry. For example:

```
floss$ cvs2cl.pl -r
cvs log: Logging .
cvs log: Logging a-subdir
cvs log: Logging a-subdir/subsubdir
cvs log: Logging b-subdir
floss$ cat ChangeLog
...
1999-08-29 05:44  jrandom

    * README (1.6), hello.c (2.1), a-subdir/whatever.c (2.1),
    a-subdir/subsubdir/fish.c (2.1): Committing from pcl-cvs 2.9, just
    for kicks.

1999-08-23 22:48  jrandom

    * README (1.5): [no log message]

1999-08-22 19:34  jrandom

    * README (1.4): trivial change
...
floss$
```

The first entry shows that three files were committed at once, with the log message, "Committing from pcl-cvs 2.9, just for kicks." (The **-r** option was used to show the revision number of each file associated with that log message.)

Like CVS itself, cvs2cl.pl takes the current directory as an implied argument but acts on individual files if given file name arguments. Following are a few of the most commonly used options.

h, --help
Show usage (including a complete list of options).

-r, --revisions
Show revision numbers in output. If used in conjunction with **-b**, branches are shown as **BRANCHNAME.N**, where **N** is the revision on the branch.

-t, --tags
Show tags (symbolic names) for revisions that have them.

-b, --branches
Show the branch name for revisions on that branch. (See also **-r**.)

-g *OPTS*, --global-opts *OPTS*

Pass **OPTS** as global arguments to **cvs**. Internally, cvs2cl.pl invokes **cvs** to get the raw log data; thus, **OPTS** are passed right after the **cvs** in that invocation. For example, to achieve quiet behavior and compression, you can do this:

```
floss$ cvs2cl.pl -g "-Q -z3"
```

-l *OPTS*, --log-opts *OPTS*

Similar to **-g**, except that **OPTS** are passed as command options instead of global options. To generate a ChangeLog showing only commits that happened between July 26 and August 15, you can do this:

```
floss$ cvs2cl.pl -l "'-d1999-07-26<1999-08-15'"
```

Notice the double-layered quoting—this is necessary in Unix because the shell that invokes **cvs log** (inside cvs2cl.pl) interprets the "<" as a shell redirection symbol. Therefore, the quotes have to be passed as part of the argument, making it necessary to surround the whole thing with an additional set of quotes.

-d, --distributed

Put an individual ChangeLog in each subdirectory, covering only commits in that subdirectory (as opposed to building one ChangeLog that covers the directory where cvs2cl.pl was invoked and all subdirectories underneath it).

cvslock: Lock Repositories For Atomicity

Depends on: C compiler for installation; nothing for runtime

URL: **ftp://riemann.iam.uni-bonn.de/pub/users/roessler/cvslock/**

This program locks a CVS repository (either for reading or writing) in the same way that CVS does, so that CVS will honor the locks. This can be useful when, for example, you need to make a copy of the whole repository and want to avoid catching parts of commits or other people's lockfiles.

The cvslock distribution is packaged extremely well and can be installed according to the usual GNU procedures. Here's a transcript of an install session:

```
floss$ zcat cvslock-0.1.tar.gz | tar xvf -
cvslock-0.1/
cvslock-0.1/Makefile.in
cvslock-0.1/README
cvslock-0.1/COPYING
```

```
cvslock-0.1/Makefile.am
cvslock-0.1/acconfig.h
cvslock-0.1/aclocal.m4
cvslock-0.1/config.h.in
cvslock-0.1/configure
cvslock-0.1/configure.in
cvslock-0.1/install-sh
cvslock-0.1/missing
cvslock-0.1/mkinstalldirs
cvslock-0.1/stamp-h.in
cvslock-0.1/cvslock.c
cvslock-0.1/cvslock.1
cvslock-0.1/snprintf.c
cvslock-0.1/cvslssh
cvslock-0.1/VERSION
floss$ cd cvslock-0.1
floss$ ./configure
  ...
floss$ make
gcc -DHAVE_CONFIG_H -I. -I. -I.   -g -O2 -c cvslock.c
gcc -g -O2  -o cvslock  cvslock.o
floss$ make install
  ...
floss$
```

(Note that you may have to do the **make install** step as root).

Now, cvslock is installed as /usr/local/bin/cvslock. When you invoke it, you can specify the repository with **-d** or via the **$CVSROOT** environment variable, just as with CVS itself (the following examples use **-d**). Its only required argument is the name of the directory to lock, relative to the top of the repository. That directory and all of its subdirectories will be locked. In this example, there are no subdirectories, so only one lockfile is created:

```
floss$ ls /usr/local/newrepos/myproj/b-subdir/
random.c,v
floss$ cvslock -d /usr/local/newrepos  myproj/b-subdir
floss$ ls /usr/local/newrepos/myproj/b-subdir/
#cvs.rfl.cvslock.floss.27378  random.c,v
floss$ cvslock -u -p 27378 -d /usr/local/newrepos  myproj/b-subdir
floss$ ls /usr/local/newrepos/myproj/b-subdir/
random.c,v
floss$
```

Notice that when I cleared the lock (**-u** for "unlock"), I had to specify **-p 27378**. That's because cvslock uses Unix process IDs when creating lockfile names to ensure that its locks are unique. When you unlock, you have to tell cvslock which lock instance to remove, even if there's only one instance present. Thus, the **-p** flag tells cvslock which previous instance of itself it's cleaning up after (you can use **-p** with or without **-u**, though).

If you're going to be working in the repository for a while, doing various operations directly in the file system, you can use the **-s** option to have cvslock start up a new shell for you. It then consults the **$SHELL** environment variable in your current shell to determine which shell to use:

```
floss$ cvslock -s -d /usr/local/newrepos myproj
```

The locks remain present until you exit the shell, at which time they are automatically removed. You can also use the **-c** option to execute a command while the repository is locked. Just as with **-s**, the locks are put in place before the command starts and removed when it's finished. In the following example, we lock the repository just long enough to display a listing of all of the lockfiles:

```
floss$ cvslock -c 'find . -name "*cvslock*" ' -d /usr/local/newrepos myproj
cvslock: '/usr/local/newrepos/myproj' locked successfully.
cvslock: Starting 'find . -name "*cvslock*" -print'...
./a-subdir/subsubdir/#cvs.rfl.cvslock.floss.27452
./a-subdir/#cvs.rfl.cvslock.floss.27452
./b-subdir/#cvs.rfl.cvslock.floss.27452
./#cvs.rfl.cvslock.floss.27452
floss$ find /usr/local/newrepos/myproj -name "*cvslock*" -print
floss$
```

The command (the argument to the **-c** option) is run with the specified repository directory as its working directory.

By default, cvslock creates read-locks. You can tell it to use write-locks instead by passing the **-W** option. (You can pass **-R** to specify read-locks, but that's the default anyway.) Always remove any locks when you're finished, so that other users' CVS processes don't wait needlessly.

Note that cvslock must be run on the machine where the repository resides—you cannot specify a remote repository. (For more information, run **man cvslock**, which is a manual page installed when you ran **make install**.)

Other Packages

Many other third-party packages are available for CVS. Following are pointers to some of these.

CVSUp (Part Of The FreeBSD Project)

CVSUp is an efficient generic mirroring tool with special built-in support for mirroring CVS repositories. The FreeBSD operating system uses it to distribute changes from their master repository, so users can keep up to date conveniently.

For more information on CVSUp in general, check out **http://www.polstra.com/projects/ freeware/CVSup/**.

For its use in FreeBSD in particular, see **http://www.freebsd.org/handbook/synching. html#CVSUP**.

CVSWeb: A Web Interface To CVS Repositories

CVSWeb provides a Web interface to browsing CVS repositories. A more accurate name might be "RCSWeb," because what it actually does is allow you to browse revisions directly in a repository, viewing log messages and diffs. Although I've never found it to be a particularly compelling interface myself, I have to admit that it is intuitive enough and a lot of sites use it.

Although the software was originally written by Bill Fenner, the version most actively under development right now seems to be Henner Zeller's, at **http://linux.fh-heilbronn.de/ ~zeller/cgi/cvsweb.cgi/**.

You may also want to visit Fenner's original site at **http://www.freebsd.org/~fenner/cvsweb/** and possibly Cyclic Software's summary of the CVSWeb scene at **http://www.cyclic.com/ cyclic-pages/web-cvsweb.html**.

Finally, if you'd like to see CVSWeb in action, a good example can be browsed at **http:// sourceware.cygnus.com/cgi-bin/cvsweb.cgi/**.

The CVS contrib/ Directory

As mentioned in Chapter 4, a number of third-party tools are shipped with CVS and are collected in the contrib/ directory. Although I'm not aware of any formal rule for determining which tools are distributed with CVS, an effort may be in process to gather most of the widely used third-party tools and put them in contrib/ so people know where to find them. Until that happens, the best way to find such tools is to look in contrib/, look at various CVS Web sites, and ask on the mailing list.

Writing Your Own Tools

CVS can at times seem like a bewildering collection of improvised standards. There's RCS format, various output formats (history, annotate, log, update, and so on), several repository administrative file formats, working copy administrative file formats, the client/server protocol, the lockfile protocol.... (Are you numb yet? I could keep going, you know.)

Fortunately, these standards remain fairly consistent from release to release—so if you're trying to write a tool to work with CVS, you at least don't have to worry about hitting a moving target. For every internal standard, there are usually a few people on the **info-cvs@gnu.org** mailing list who know it extremely well (several of them helped me out during the writing of this book). There is also the documentation that comes with the CVS distribution (especially doc/cvs.texinfo, doc/cvsclient.texi, and doc/RCSFILES). Finally, there is the CVS source code itself, the last word on any question of implementation or behavior.

With all of this at your disposal, there's no reason to hesitate. If you can think of some utility that would make your life with CVS easier, go ahead and write it—chances are other people have been wanting it, too. Unlike a change to CVS itself, a small, standalone external utility can get wide distribution very quickly, resulting in quicker feedback for its author and faster bug fixes for all of the users.

Appendix A

CVS Maintenance And Development Today

The Cyclic-To-SourceGear Transition

During the writing of this book—somewhere around Chapter 7 or 8—the CVS maintainership changed hands. Cyclic Software's sole proprietor, Jim Kingdon, had been the keeper of the flame for several years and was ready for something new. He sold Cyclic Software to the SourceGear Corporation (**www.sourcegear.com**), who expressed their desire to become the lead maintainers of CVS. Although SourceGear had not previously been active in CVS development, they already had some credentials in the open source world as the authors of the free AbiWord word processor.

What happened next was a fascinating demonstration of free software dynamics in action. Jim Kingdon had never considered himself (publicly, at least) to be the maintainer of CVS, but simply one equal member of a development team. He also happened to be the administrator of the master repository and the development mailing list, but those were mere technical details. However, the other developers looked to him as the leader and generally took his decisions about the code as final. There was also some degree of public awareness that he was the maintainer—in fact, if not in name.

When Jim decided to sell Cyclic to SourceGear, he made it clear that he was withdrawing from the CVS scene. He openly advocated regarding SourceGear as the new lead maintainer—a position that SourceGear actively sought, although they also made it clear that all existing members of the development team would stay on.

Because SourceGear had made no previous contributions to CVS, and Jim Kingdon had always denied being the CVS maintainer anyway, some people (myself included, I must admit) publicly expressed skepticism about the wisdom and propriety of transferring the maintainership this way. SourceGear immediately sensed what was happening and posted some messages to the **info-cvs@gnu.org** list that expressed their commitment to serving the needs of the entire CVS user community, and reiterated that they were serious about becoming the maintainers.

At this point, the objectors (of whom I was probably the most active) had the same choice that every user of a free program has when they don't like the direction the maintainership seems to be going: We could start our own distribution, or wait and hope. SourceGear had made it clear that they would distribute a version of CVS no matter what; the only question was whether their version would be the only one. In other words, would CVS development fork?

A combination of factors decided the issue for the objectors. First of all, our main problem with SourceGear was that they had essentially bought the maintainership—an error of process, perhaps, but necessary from their point of view because they had already bought the Cyclic name and wanted to be the leaders in developing its software, too. As far as their technical ability, there was no reason to doubt that they could handle the job, and they had already announced their intention to devote salaried time to CVS work. Most importantly, a majority of the CVS development team indicated their willingness to give SourceGear a chance. Given all that, there seemed little point in forking the code (which could always be done later if SourceGear didn't seem to be working out).

So SourceGear took over and immediately made a much-needed bug fix release (1.10.7) of CVS. Since then, things have been largely quiescent. CVS development under Cyclic had been fairly conservative, with new features a rare occurrence. Many patches sent in by contributors were never incorporated into the source code, although Cyclic would usually post the patches somewhere on the **cyclic.com** Web site for others to try out. Following the 1.10.7 release, SourceGear announced that they would be organizing and evaluating all of those patches (quite numerous by now) and incorporating the ones that seemed worthwhile. This plan has met with widespread approval. Because it's a large task, it remains to be seen how successfully they will carry it off and how they'll do when they've settled into regular maintenance duties afterwards.

None of this should worry CVS users, of course. All signs are that SourceGear knows what they're doing and will be good maintainers. If they aren't, there are clearly many people willing to step up and take over (that is, fork the code and try to do a better job of maintaining it). The worst dilemma facing a user may be having to choose between various competing distributions, and even that's unlikely.

How To Get CVS Today

SourceGear has taken over the **cyclic.com** Internet domain and preserved all existing links, so the URLs given earlier in this book should remain valid for the foreseeable future. When in doubt, ask on **info-cvs@gnu.org**, or watch there for further announcements.

Appendix B
GNU General Public License

We have included the GNU General Public License (GPL) for your reference as it applies to the software this book was about. However, the GPL does not apply to the entire book, only to Chapters 2, 4, 6, 8, 9, and 10.

Version 2, June 1991
Copyright (C) 1989, 1991 Free Software Foundation, Inc.
59 Temple Place - Suite 330, Boston, MA 02111-1307, USA

Preamble

The licenses for most software are designed to take away your freedom to share and change it. By contrast, the GNU General Public License is intended to guarantee your freedom to share and change free software—to make sure the software is free for all its users. This General Public License applies to most of the Free Software Foundation's software and to any other program whose authors commit to using it. (Some other Free Software Foundation software is covered by the GNU Library General Public License instead.) You can apply it to your programs, too.

When we speak of free software, we are referring to freedom, not price. Our General Public Licenses are designed to make sure that you have the freedom to distribute copies of free software (and charge for this service if you wish), that you receive source code or can get it if you want it, that you can change the software or use pieces of it in new free programs; and that you know you can do these things.

To protect your rights, we need to make restrictions that forbid anyone to deny you these rights or to ask you to surrender the rights. These restrictions translate to certain responsibilities for you if you distribute copies of the software, or if you modify it.

For example, if you distribute copies of such a program, whether gratis or for a fee, you must give the recipients all the rights that you have. You must make sure that they, too, receive or can get the source code. And you must show them these terms so they know their rights.

We protect your rights with two steps: (1) copyright the software, and (2) offer you this license which gives you legal permission to copy, distribute and/or modify the software.

Also, for each author's protection and ours, we want to make certain that everyone understands that there is no warranty for this free software. If the software is modified by someone else and passed on, we want its recipients to know that what they have is not the original, so that any problems introduced by others will not reflect on the original authors' reputations.

Finally, any free program is threatened constantly by software patents. We wish to avoid the danger that redistributors of a free program will individually obtain patent licenses, in effect making the program proprietary. To prevent this, we have made it clear that any patent must be licensed for everyone's free use or not licensed at all.

The precise terms and conditions for copying, distribution and modification follow.

Terms And Conditions For Copying, Distribution, And Modification

This License applies to any program or other work which contains a notice placed by the copyright holder saying it may be distributed under the terms of this General Public License. The "Program", below, refers to any such program or work, and a "work based on the Program" means either the Program or any derivative work under copyright law: that is to say, a work containing the Program or a portion of it, either verbatim or with modifications and/or translated into another language. (Hereinafter, translation is included without limitation in the term "modification".) Each licensee is addressed as "you".

Activities other than copying, distribution and modification are not covered by this License; they are outside its scope. The act of running the Program is not restricted, and the output from the Program is covered only if its contents constitute a work based on the Program (independent of having been made by running the Program). Whether that is true depends on what the Program does.

1. You may copy and distribute verbatim copies of the Program's source code as you receive it, in any medium, provided that you conspicuously and appropriately publish on each copy an appropriate copyright notice and disclaimer of warranty; keep intact all the notices that refer to this License and to the absence of any warranty; and give any other recipients of the Program a copy of this License along with the Program.

You may charge a fee for the physical act of transferring a copy, and you may at your option offer warranty protection in exchange for a fee.

2. You may modify your copy or copies of the Program or any portion of it, thus forming a work based on the Program, and copy and distribute such modifications or work under the terms of Section 1 above, provided that you also meet all of these conditions:

   a) You must cause the modified files to carry prominent notices stating that you changed the files and the date of any change.

   b) You must cause any work that you distribute or publish, that in whole or in part contains or is derived from the Program or any part thereof, to be licensed as a whole at no charge to all third parties under the terms of this License.

   c) If the modified program normally reads commands interactively when run, you must cause it, when started running for such interactive use in the most ordinary way, to print or display an announcement including an appropriate copyright notice and a notice that there is no warranty (or else, saying that you provide a warranty) and that users may redistribute the program under these conditions, and telling the user how to view a copy of this License. (Exception: if the Program itself is interactive but does not normally print such an announcement, your work based on the Program is not required to print an announcement.)

These requirements apply to the modified work as a whole. If identifiable sections of that work are not derived from the Program, and can be reasonably considered independent and separate works in themselves, then this License, and its terms, do not apply to those sections when you distribute them as separate works. But when you distribute the same sections as part of a whole which is a work based on the Program, the distribution of the whole must be on the terms of this License, whose permissions for other licensees extend to the entire whole, and thus to each and every part regardless of who wrote it.

Thus, it is not the intent of this section to claim rights or contest your rights to work written entirely by you; rather, the intent is to exercise the right to control the distribution of derivative or collective works based on the Program.

In addition, mere aggregation of another work not based on the Program with the Program (or with a work based on the Program) on a volume of a storage or distribution medium does not bring the other work under the scope of this License.

3. You may copy and distribute the Program (or a work based on it, under Section 2) in object code or executable form under the terms of Sections 1 and 2 above provided that you also do one of the following:

   a) Accompany it with the complete corresponding machine-readable source code, which must be distributed under the terms of Sections 1 and 2 above on a medium customarily used for software interchange; or,

b) Accompany it with a written offer, valid for at least three years, to give any third party, for a charge no more than your cost of physically performing source distribution, a complete machine-readable copy of the corresponding source code, to be distributed under the terms of Sections 1 and 2 above on a medium customarily used for software interchange; or,

c) Accompany it with the information you received as to the offer to distribute corresponding source code. (This alternative is allowed only for noncommercial distribution and only if you received the program in object code or executable form with such an offer, in accord with Subsection b above.)

The source code for a work means the preferred form of the work for making modifications to it. For an executable work, complete source code means all the source code for all modules it contains, plus any associated interface definition files, plus the scripts used to control compilation and installation of the executable. However, as a special exception, the source code distributed need not include anything that is normally distributed (in either source or binary form) with the major components (compiler, kernel, and so on) of the operating system on which the executable runs, unless that component itself accompanies the executable.

If distribution of executable or object code is made by offering access to copy from a designated place, then offering equivalent access to copy the source code from the same place counts as distribution of the source code, even though third parties are not compelled to copy the source along with the object code.

4. You may not copy, modify, sublicense, or distribute the Program except as expressly provided under this License. Any attempt otherwise to copy, modify, sublicense or distribute the Program is void, and will automatically terminate your rights under this License. However, parties who have received copies, or rights, from you under this License will not have their licenses terminated so long as such parties remain in full compliance.

5. You are not required to accept this License, since you have not signed it. However, nothing else grants you permission to modify or distribute the Program or its derivative works. These actions are prohibited by law if you do not accept this License. Therefore, by modifying or distributing the Program (or any work based on the Program), you indicate your acceptance of this License to do so, and all its terms and conditions for copying, distributing or modifying the Program or works based on it.

6. Each time you redistribute the Program (or any work based on the Program), the recipient automatically receives a license from the original licensor to copy, distribute or modify the Program subject to these terms and conditions. You may not impose any further restrictions on the recipients' exercise of the rights granted herein. You are not responsible for enforcing compliance by third parties to this License.

7. If, as a consequence of a court judgment or allegation of patent infringement or for any other reason (not limited to patent issues), conditions are imposed on you (whether by court order, agreement or otherwise) that contradict the conditions of this License,

they do not excuse you from the conditions of this License. If you cannot distribute so as to satisfy simultaneously your obligations under this License and any other pertinent obligations, then as a consequence you may not distribute the Program at all. For example, if a patent license would not permit royalty-free redistribution of the Program by all those who receive copies directly or indirectly through you, then the only way you could satisfy both it and this License would be to refrain entirely from distribution of the Program.

If any portion of this section is held invalid or unenforceable under any particular circumstance, the balance of the section is intended to apply and the section as a whole is intended to apply in other circumstances.

It is not the purpose of this section to induce you to infringe any patents or other property right claims or to contest validity of any such claims; this section has the sole purpose of protecting the integrity of the free software distribution system, which is implemented by public license practices. Many people have made generous contributions to the wide range of software distributed through that system in reliance on consistent application of that system; it is up to the author/donor to decide if he or she is willing to distribute software through any other system and a licensee cannot impose that choice.

This section is intended to make thoroughly clear what is believed to be a consequence of the rest of this License.

8. If the distribution and/or use of the Program is restricted in certain countries either by patents or by copyrighted interfaces, the original copyright holder who places the Program under this License may add an explicit geographical distribution limitation excluding those countries, so that distribution is permitted only in or among countries not thus excluded. In such case, this License incorporates the limitation as if written in the body of this License.

9. The Free Software Foundation may publish revised and/or new versions of the General Public License from time to time. Such new versions will be similar in spirit to the present version, but may differ in detail to address new problems or concerns.

   Each version is given a distinguishing version number. If the Program specifies a version number of this License which applies to it and "any later version", you have the option of following the terms and conditions either of that version or of any later version published by the Free Software Foundation. If the Program does not specify a version number of this License, you may choose any version ever published by the Free Software Foundation.

10. If you wish to incorporate parts of the Program into other free programs whose distribution conditions are different, write to the author to ask for permission. For software which is copyrighted by the Free Software Foundation, write to the Free Software Foundation; we sometimes make exceptions for this. Our decision will be guided by the two goals of preserving the free status of all derivatives of our free software and of promoting the sharing and reuse of software generally.

No Warranty

11. BECAUSE THE PROGRAM IS LICENSED FREE OF CHARGE, THERE IS NO WARRANTY FOR THE PROGRAM, TO THE EXTENT PERMITTED BY APPLICABLE LAW. EXCEPT WHEN OTHERWISE STATED IN WRITING THE COPYRIGHT HOLDERS AND/OR OTHER PARTIES PROVIDE THE PROGRAM "AS IS" WITHOUT WARRANTY OF ANY KIND, EITHER EXPRESSED OR IMPLIED, INCLUDING, BUT NOT LIMITED TO, THE IMPLIED WARRANTIES OF MERCHANTABILITY AND FITNESS FOR A PARTICULAR PURPOSE. THE ENTIRE RISK AS TO THE QUALITY AND PERFORMANCE OF THE PROGRAM IS WITH YOU. SHOULD THE PROGRAM PROVE DEFECTIVE, YOU ASSUME THE COST OF ALL NECESSARY SERVICING, REPAIR OR CORRECTION.

12. IN NO EVENT UNLESS REQUIRED BY APPLICABLE LAW OR AGREED TO IN WRITING WILL ANY COPYRIGHT HOLDER, OR ANY OTHER PARTY WHO MAY MODIFY AND/OR REDISTRIBUTE THE PROGRAM AS PERMITTED ABOVE, BE LIABLE TO YOU FOR DAMAGES, INCLUDING ANY GENERAL, SPECIAL, INCIDENTAL OR CONSEQUENTIAL DAMAGES ARISING OUT OF THE USE OR INABILITY TO USE THE PROGRAM (INCLUDING BUT NOT LIMITED TO LOSS OF DATA OR DATA BEING RENDERED INACCURATE OR LOSSES SUSTAINED BY YOU OR THIRD PARTIES OR A FAILURE OF THE PROGRAM TO OPERATE WITH ANY OTHER PROGRAMS), EVEN IF SUCH HOLDER OR OTHER PARTY HAS BEEN ADVISED OF THE POSSIBILITY OF SUCH DAMAGES.

How To Apply These Terms To Your New Programs

If you develop a new program, and you want it to be of the greatest possible use to the public, the best way to achieve this is to make it free software which everyone can redistribute and change under these terms.

To do so, attach the following notices to the program. It is safest to attach them to the start of each source file to most effectively convey the exclusion of warranty; and each file should have at least the "copyright" line and a pointer to where the full notice is found.

```
one line to give the program's name and an idea of what it does.
Copyright (C) yyyy  name of author

This program is free software; you can redistribute it and/or
modify it under the terms of the GNU General Public License as
published by the Free Software Foundation; either version 2 of
the License, or (at your option) any later version.

This program is distributed in the hope that it will be useful,
but WITHOUT ANY WARRANTY; without even the implied warranty of
```

```
MERCHANTABILITY or FITNESS FOR A PARTICULAR PURPOSE.
See the GNU General Public License for more details.

You should have received a copy of the GNU General Public License
along with this program; if not, write to the Free Software
Foundation, Inc., 59 Temple Place - Suite 330, Boston, MA
02111-1307, USA.
```

Also add information on how to contact you by electronic and paper mail.

If the program is interactive, make it output a short notice like this when it starts in an interactive mode:

```
Gnomovision version 69, Copyright (C) yyyy name of author
Gnomovision comes with ABSOLUTELY NO WARRANTY;
for details type 'show w'.
This is free software, and you are welcome to redistribute it
under certain conditions; type 'show c' for details.
```

The hypothetical commands 'show w' and 'show c' should show the appropriate parts of the General Public License. Of course, the commands you use may be called something other than 'show w' and 'show c'; they could even be mouse-clicks or menu items—whatever suits your program.

You should also get your employer (if you work as a programmer) or your school, if any, to sign a "copyright disclaimer" for the program, if necessary. Here is a sample; alter the names:

```
Yoyodyne, Inc., hereby disclaims all copyright interest
in the program 'Gnomovision' (which makes passes at compilers)
written by James Hacker.

signature of Ty Coon, 1 April 1989
Ty Coon, President of Vice
```

This General Public License does not permit incorporating your program into proprietary programs. If your program is a subroutine library, you may consider it more useful to permit linking proprietary applications with the library. If this is what you want to do, use the GNU Library General Public License instead of this License.

Index

@ signs as full delimiter in RCS files, 123–125

A

Acceptable date formats, 59–60
add command, 51, 228, 241–242
admin command, 170–171, 242–24
-a flag, 160–161, 237
– –allow-root option, 236–237
Alpha release, 213
annotate command, 175–180, 246
Annotations and branches, 178–180
Apache Group, 95
Apache WWW server, 9, 95
Ask Slashdot archives, 82
Atomicity, lock repositories for, 296–298
autoconf, 210–211
Autoconfiscation, 151
Automated testing, 207–208

B

Behlendorf, Brian, 10
Benevolence, 90
Berliner, Brian, 7
Beta release, 213
Binary files, 52, 229
Blandy, Jim, 66
-b option, 237
Borderlessness as distinguishing characteristic
   of free software, 146
Bourne shell, 210
-branch, 184
Branches, 66–78
   and annotations, 178–180
   creating, without working copy, 77–78
   development versus stable, 205–206
   and keyword expansion, 193–194
   working with, 182–199
Branch tags, 73, 184
BUGS file, 106
Byte-compiling, 287

C

Cederqvist, Per, 17, 285, 286
Cederqvist manual, 17–18, 78, 108–110
Certainties, dividing, from uncertainties, 143–144
ChangeLog, 294, 296
Check out, 16
checkout, 26, 64, 69, 171, 174, 247–248
checkoutlist, 273
chmod command, 166
clog.in file, 231
Code, dividing
   into files and directories, 144–145
   into modules, 145–147
Code design, 143
   dividing certainties from uncertainties, 143–144
Code freeze, 204
Collaboration, 13, 14
Commands, 235–236. *See also* specific commands.
   general patterns in, 236
   list of, 241–269
   options, 18
Commit, 16
commit command, 26, 35–43, 51–53, 156, 214,
   248–249
Commit emails, 169–171
commitinfo, 131–133, 273–274
Communication device, CVS as, 153–172
Comprehensibility in software design, 139, 140, 148
Concurrent Versions System (CVS), 7–8
   basics, 13–17
   checking out working copy, 24–26
   as a communications device, 153–172
   contrib/ directory in, 299
   controlling actions, 160–162
   day with, 17–18
   distribution
      information files, 106–107
      removing files, 125–127
      sources of information, 110
      subdirectories, 107–108
   ending editing session, 160
   getting and installing, 101–106